Introduction to
Software
Project
Management

Introduction to
Software
Project
Management

Adolfo Villafiorita

CRC Press
Taylor & Francis Group
Boca Raton London New York

CRC Press is an imprint of the
Taylor & Francis Group, an **informa** business
AN AUERBACH BOOK

CRC Press
Taylor & Francis Group
6000 Broken Sound Parkway NW, Suite 300
Boca Raton, FL 33487-2742

Printed on acid-free paper
Version Date: 20140108

International Standard Book Number-13: 978-1-4665-5953-0 (Hardback)

Library of Congress Cataloging-in-Publication Data

Villafiorita, Adolfo.
    Introduction to software project management / author, Adolfo Villafiorita.
        pages cm
    Includes bibliographical references and index.
    ISBN 978-1-4665-5953-0 (hardback)
    1. Software engineering--Management. 2. Project management . I. Title.

QA76.758.V528 2014
005.1068--dc23   2013048948

Visit the Taylor & Francis Web site at
http://www.taylorandfrancis.com

and the CRC Press Web site at
http://www.crcpress.com

To Barbara

Contents

Preface

Software development is considered among the most complex activities carried out by man. The steady growth of software systems' size, the increasing role software is playing in safety critical applications, and the speed at which technology and software change are some of the causes frequently mentioned to support the above claim. Although techniques and tools to build software have improved considerably in the last 60 years, a proper development process and a sound project management are and will remain the top reasons software projects fail or succeed.

Software project managers share many of the goals of project managers in other domains, namely, ensuring an appropriate quality of the end product, while, at the same time, keeping under control all the other project variables, like time and costs. Different from other domains, however, software has specific characteristics, such as invisibility, complexity, and flexibility (in its application and production means), that call for specific management techniques.

This book is an introduction to the area of software project management. After a presentation of the main definitions and concepts, the book is organized in two main parts.

The first part overviews the technical activities for developing software (Chapter 2) and techniques for managing projects (Chapters 3 through 6). The goal is providing the basic building blocks and the techniques to mitigate the complexity of software development and control the uncertainty of projects.

The second part of the book organizes the technical activities in a coherent process and shows how this process is customized in practice to fit common software-development scenarios (Chapter 7). An analysis of existing development and management frameworks (Chapter 8) and a discussion about how to setup a tool infrastructure to manage projects (Chapter 9) close the book.

In recent years, I have found myself mixing traditional and agile techniques more often, using traditional techniques for planning and developing some of the software components with agile methodologies and iterative processes. This book, thus, presents both techniques. It tries to do so in a manner to favor some freedom and creativity in assembling the process which best fits one's needs.

Accompanying this text is a web site (http://www.spmbook.com) that provides teaching material for instructors and additional reference material for students.

I hope you enjoy the textbook and web site!

Acknowledgments

Writing a book requires many resources, and this book would have not been possible without the support, help, and encouragement of family, friends, and colleagues.

A special thank you goes to Ali Al-Shammari, Aaron Ciaghi, Andrea Nodari, and Pietro Molini and the other colleagues of the ICT4G group for the comments they gave me on preliminary versions of this book. If you enjoy reading this book, that is because of the feedback they gave me on earlier versions. My sincere gratitude also goes to my editor John Wyzalek, who believed in this project and to all the team who made the book possible, among which Kate Gallo, Robert Sims, and Karthick Parthasarathy.

I wish also to thank my family and friends. A first big thank you goes to my wife Barbara, for her patience and support. Another goes to my nephew Marco, who told me once I have a sweet tooth and thus gave me the inspiration for the millefoglie example. My dad Enzo, Andrea, Ombretta, and Rienzo also provided a lot encouragement.

Least but not last, I wish to thank the friends of the Argentario Squash club, Max, Rudy, Maurizio, Paolo, Michele, Piero and all the others who made sure I would not get too fat while writing this book!

Author

Adolfo Villafiorita, PhD, is a senior researcher at Fondazione Bruno Kessler where he leads the ICT4G unit, whose mission is the use of ICT to foster social and economic development.

With long experience in the area of formal verification, he has led various technology transfer and development projects in the national and international context.

He is a contract professor at the University of Trento, where he teaches software project management.

Chapter 1

Introduction

1.1 What is a Project

1.1.1 Projects and Operational Work

Project Management Institute (2004) defines a **project** as *a temporary endeavor undertaken to create a unique product or service*. The definition entails five important characteristics of a project, some explicitly mentioned and some following as a consequence. These characteristics also define some of the requirements of a good project manager, as we will see later.

The first characteristic is that a project is **temporary**, that is, it has a beginning and an end. In many cases, determining the start and the end is easy. Consider the following examples: a contract sign-off, a formal authorization to proceed from senior management, a system going in production. In practice, however, many projects begin by slowly building up resources and interest, while the official start happens sometime after the resources and work have been invested. Others have residual work and activities going on after the official end, for instance to follow up on defects and problems found in project outputs. In all cases, however, projects have a start and a conclusion.

The fact that a project is temporary has a natural consequence. Every project will, in fact, have

1. An **initiating** phase, during which the project infrastructure and the project's goals are drafted.
2. A **planning** phase, during which project goals are refined, activities identified and scheduled, and many other support activities are properly planned.

3. An **executing** phase, during which the actual work takes place. Running in parallel, a **monitoring** phase measures the progress and raises flags when plans and reality disagree.
4. A final **closing** phase, where the project outputs are handed out and the project is closed.

The amount and intensity of work in a project change according to the project phase. The initiating and planning phases will require a relatively small amount of work. Work will accumulate fast during the execution phase, as the project activities, many of which are running in parallel, unfold. As the project gets near to its conclusion, work will reduce and stop, of course, when the project delivers its outputs. If we plot the cumulative work produced in a project, we get an s-shaped curve. Both the phases of a project and the typical trend of cumulative work are shown in Figure 1.1.

As a side remark, Figure 1.1 also introduces the notation we will use for process diagrams, which was inspired by the activity diagram notation of the Unified Modeling Language (UML). In particular, rounded rectangles represent activities, a black dot represents the initial state, and a bull's eye represents the final state. The arrow shows the order in which activities run. Although not shown here, we will also use rectangles to denote artifacts and diamond for choices.

The second characteristic is that a project **delivers an output** in the form of a product, a service, or a capability. The outputs are tangible, and often their properties are also measurable. Thus, a project can be set up and organized, starting from the description and the characteristics of the outputs it delivers. Such description, in fact, entails the work that has to be done to build the outputs. The description of the project outputs also defines the project completion criteria: the project

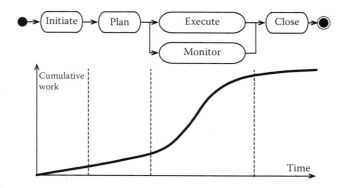

Figure 1.1   Project phases and cumulative work.

ends when the outputs are delivered as specified. Things are not always so simple, however. Many projects have a clear output, but the way in which this is achieved might not be clear. Consider, for instance, a situation in which we want to improve the performances of a software system. The goal is clear, but the means to achieve it might not. In other situations, the outputs might not be completely clear or well spelled out. This is quite common in software development, where coming out with a complete and unambiguous description of a system is not always easy.

The third characteristic is that projects are **resource constrained**. A limited time is available to build the project outputs. Also limited will be other project resources, such as the budget and the team. An important consequence is that the project manager and the team have to find an achievable solution, while respecting all project constraints. Thus, the output of a project is seldom the best possible solution but rather the best solution *given the constraints*.

The fourth characteristic is that a project requires a **progressive elaboration** to build the project outputs. At the beginning, different ways are possible to achieve the project goals. As we move along, many project activities require to take choices, which reduce the degrees of freedom, till we get to the end of the project with the only possible implementation of the project goals. Thus, the cost of changes increases as a project progresses, since the amount of rework necessary to implement a change increases as we reduce our degrees of freedom.

The fifth and final characteristic is that a project delivers a **unique** output. Thus, what a project delivers has some novelty, one way or the other. This allows us to introduce the last important characteristic, namely, that a project always has some **risk** coming in the form of menaces or opportunities. Risks come from the unique characteristics of the project outputs, which sometimes are not fully understood or not clear when a project starts. Other risks derive from additional constraints that are set in a project; consider, for instance a situation in which a customer pushes for a schedule that is too tight or for quality requirements that are set too high.

Having seen the main qualities of a project, we need to mention that not all work is a project. Work that is not a project is called **operational**, even though one might still call it a project. The techniques for managing a project, however, can also be useful for operational work.

1.1.2 Programs, Subprojects, and Portfolios

Projects come in different sizes. Small projects might require the work of a few people for a few weeks or a few months. Larger projects might involve the work of thousands of people for years. Consider, for instance, the development of the F22 fighter aircraft. The development started in 1986 with a first phase to build two prototypes, which lasted 50 months. After the demonstration of the prototypes and the selection of the best model, the actual development started in 1991, with the first production aircraft delivered in 2003. The total costs of the project are estimated at 67.3 USD billion, in then-year dollars, that is, without any adjustment for inflation (Gertler, 2012).

Although in principle the development of the F22 could be organized as a single project, a more practical approach organizes its construction at different levels of abstraction and granularity. Projects are thus often organized and combined to achieve objectives larger than those of any single initiative. A common classification distinguishes among **portfolios**, **subprojects**, and **programs**.

1.1.2.1 Programs

A **program** is a set of related projects managed in a coordinated way. The underlying motivation is that coordination allows one to achieve additional benefits.

The most famous program is probably the U.S. manned space program, which culminated with men landing on the moon.

Program management uses many project management techniques, but it has a different focus and goal. The higher abstraction level at which program management takes place, in fact, requires a manager to reason in terms of vision, rather than goals, and roadmaps, rather than detailed plans.

1.1.2.2 Subprojects

Complex projects for which program management is an overkill can be organized and broken down into **subprojects**.

A subproject is thus the way in which one can organize the implementation of some specific objectives of a larger project. We will see in Chapter 3 how the organization of project activities can naturally lead one to identify a set of subprojects, with the definition of the contract work breakdown structure.

The distinction between a subproject and a project is often just a matter of terminology, since the approach and techniques are identical. A similar consideration applies to the boundaries between a project organized in subprojects and a program with different projects.

1.1.2.3 Portfolios

Organizations often use projects to develop similar systems. The term *portfolio* management thus identifies a situation in which a set of independent projects are coordinated to achieve better results.

A common situation is one in which a portfolio includes projects with similar functional aspects or technical challenges. Different groupings are possible. For instance, Project Management Institute (2004) highlights that a portfolio could include projects with the same class of risks, since they might benefit from the application of similar techniques.

1.2 What is a Software Project

When we think about software projects, probably the first thing that comes to mind is developing applications. While this is true in many cases, software-related projects take different forms. Even when the main goal is developing a system, coding is just one of the required activities, as we will see in Chapter 2.

In this section, we look at the main types of software-related projects.

1.2.1 Application Development

Application development might not be the only type of software-related project, but it is probably one that is great fun. The goal in this kind of project is building an application and providing the additional services and outputs to support it.

From the project management point of view, we can distinguish the following types of applications:

- **One-offs** or **bespoke systems** that are software systems specifically created for a customer. A bespoke system often implements a specific need of a customer, although in some cases the customer base of the final product could be large. Some examples of bespoke systems include a luggage tracking software, a compiler for a specific hardware platform, and a system to monitor a fleet of trucks. For bespoke systems, the specification of the application to develop (more in general of the project goals) will be driven and have to be agreed with the customer. The ownership and the source code of the final product might also be handed over to the customer. This kind of projects offers an opportunity for the supplier to enter a new market or establish a long-term relationship with a new customer. Consider, for instance, activities related to the long-term maintenance of a complex software system. The uniqueness and novelty of the product also constitute the main risk both for the customer and the supplier.
- **Off-the-shelf applications** are software systems implementing a function which is useful to many different users. It is the software we buy from marketplaces or stores and it is the equivalent of the Ford Model-T: one size fits all.* The goals and functions of the applications, in this case, come from the company developing the system, which sometimes conducts user surveys, to better understand needs and features that are most useful. Larger organizations might involve different departments in the specification of the software, making the activity similar to the previous case. A marketing department might play the role of the customer, defining the requirements, while an engineering department plays the role of the supplier and delivers the solution. The main characteristic is that the system is the same for each user and that the

---

* This is not completely true as many applications come in different versions, for instance, a base and a pro, or with a plugin system that allows some customization.

company developing the system sets the roadmap, choosing when to upgrade, what functions to add, and when to do maintenance.

■ Finally, a **customized off-the-shelf application** sits somewhere between the two other types of applications. They are systems that are developed similar to off-the-shelf applications. However, they need to (or can) be customized to fit the customer needs. An example of a customized off-the-shelf application is an **enterprise resource planning** (ERP) system. An ERP system helps plan the resources of an organization and automate information management. While the engine of many ERPs is generic (and developed as an off-the-shelf application), many other characteristics (modules to use, what data has to be stored, how information flows) need to be customized for each client.

1.2.2 Process and Systems Reengineering Services

Process and Systems Reengineering Services are projects related to improving the efficiency of an organization, by changing the way in which they conduct their operational work. These projects often accompany the introduction of one or more systems. In many cases, the system being introduced is an ERP. According to the project goals and size of the client, these projects might be significant and complex.

Consider the example of a multinational company revising its customer help-desk to improve quality and responsiveness. This project requires to understand how the organization currently works, what are the bottlenecks, and thus the possible interventions. These could include modifications to the current practices, training, and perhaps the introduction of a customer relationship management system to support the new processes.

See also Section 2.2 for a discussion on the topic.

1.2.3 System Integration Services

System integration services are projects and services related to automating the information flow among the different and independent systems used by an organization. The goals are to improve the efficiency of work and to reduce data duplication and errors. The approach is chosen when migrating to a new system is impractical or too costly.

Two types of integration are possible, **vertical** or **horizontal**. The first refers to the integration of different systems performing similar functions (e.g., putting together data about customers kept by different departments of a multinational company). The latter refers to automating or improving business functions (e.g., automating the flow of orders from marketing to production).

System integration services are more common in large organizations, which have a long history of system automation, or organizations in which departments have large autonomy. In these cases, in fact, different departments might automate similar functions without paying too much attention to data integration. Over time, the portfolio of applications grows and data coherence problems start to pop up. For instance, the IT systems of a company might still grant access to its premises to a person whose contract has expired, if the contracts and accesses are managed by two independent systems and someone forgot to manually update the data.

According to the project scope, these kinds of projects might be large, like in the case of reengineering services, or very focused, like it could be the case of a project to interface two systems. In the first case, the project requires an analysis of the business procedures and of the IT infrastructure. Compare the previous section and Section 2.2. In the second case, they are organized similar to an application development project.

1.2.4 Other Types of Projects

Consulting services might be asked to gain know-how, which is outside a company's core competence. An example of consulting services is the evaluation of the reliability of a software system conducted using very specific techniques, which could not be part of the core business of a company. Another very common request is the assessment of the state of the art in a particular sector.

Installation and training services are services related to the installation of specific software systems (also in the open source domain) and/or training in the use of specific technologies or systems.

1.3 Managing Projects

1.3.1 The Project Manager and the Project Stakeholder

In my career, I have met project managers with different characters, qualities, and capacities, and I believe there is no such thing as the ideal project manager. Similar to a sport, talent, studying the techniques, practicing a lot, and learning from experience determine the kind of manager one becomes.

We have hinted above, however, that the characteristics of a project determine some of the features of a good project manager. Let us elaborate a bit on the concept.

As we have seen, projects are characterized by constraints and uncertainty. A bit of inventiveness and some predisposition to risk and flexibility can thus be of help in integrating the techniques we will present in the rest of this book. Notice that project management is about taming and mitigating risks, rather than passively accepting them. However, even when one tries and plans for the unexpected, unplanned unknowns will happen and a good project manager deals with them.

Another important distinctive feature is that projects are time limited. Thus, a sense of *urgency* can help set up a project fast and deliver according to the time constraints. The project manager, however, is also responsible for setting a sustainable pace in a project, so that the right rhythm is set and the team can work more effectively.

Some projects are also characterized by enormous complexity and require difficult choices to be taken. Cox and Murray (2004), a very nice reading about the Apollo program, describes many situations in which the project team had to take difficult decisions. One example that I found particularly striking is when George Low, manager of the Apollo program, faced with the possibility of the program slipping after the deadline set by President Kennedy, decided to change the schedule of flights, reducing the number of unmanned test flights, since these would not have provided any significant information to the program. History and system engineering proved him right.

I have not yet mentioned technical proficiency, namely, mastering the tools and techniques, which will be used in a project. I did it on purpose. Technical competence is certainly an important asset for a project manager, since it simplifies various tasks, such as forming a vision on the product, choosing a sound approach to project development, and identifying the main project criticalities and risks. Management is also about delegation, and technical proficiency can backfire, if, for instance, it comes with stubbornness or an incapacity to listen or second the choices of experienced teams.

People are a key contributor to the success or failure of projects. It is the work of people that makes the project outputs possible, mitigating the impact of technologies that do not work as expected and finding creative solutions when the unexpected occurs. They can also contribute to the failure of a project, with their sloppiness or disinterest. A good project manager thus deals with and manages people effectively. This is so important that Project Management Institute (2004) dedicates to these activities three of the 10 areas it defines to manage a project: stakeholder management, human resource management, and communications management.

1.3.2 Project Stakeholders

Project Management Institute (2004) defines a **project stakeholder** as *any individual or an organization that is actively involved in a project, or whose interest might be affected as a result of project execution or completion.*

Some stakeholders are simple to identify. Since the definition includes all people working in a project, the **project manager** and the **project team**, namely, the people responsible for carrying out the work in a project, are stakeholders.

Other stakeholders are those who benefit from the project execution or the project outputs. Among these are the **client**, the **performing organization**, and the **project sponsor**. The first, in fact, benefits from the project outputs, the second from the know-how and the revenues made in the project, and the third because of the peculiar interest he or she has in the project.

The remaining stakeholders might be directly or indirectly affected by the project. For instance, a company producing a software system might be negatively affected by a project of another organization developing a competing product.

Understanding who are the project stakeholders and effectively managing them is an important activity of a project manager. We will see in Chapter 3 some techniques to identify and manage stakeholders. Here, it is sufficient to mention that stakeholders have different interests and influence. Some might be interested to see the project that fails, while others might support it strongly. The influence a stakeholder can exert is usually a combination of how close the stakeholder is to a project and how much power he or she has.

1.3.3 Code of Conducts and Ethical Aspects

I do not want to go here into a philosophical discussion about what is good and evil and why one should behave good rather than bad. So I will take a rather practical approach and say that sticking to a code of conduct and behaving ethically is often also the most efficient and best choice both for the manager and for the project.

In an informal survey conducted among the members of the Project Management Institute (PMI®), about 80% of the managers interviewed faced ethical dilemmas (Cabanis, 1996). This is not surprising as many decisions taken by project managers are in the *gray area*, in which distinguishing what is good from what is wrong can be difficult. Consider, for instance, a situation in which a "buy in" bid is made to get a contract.* Surely it does not sound right. Consider the same situation, however, when getting the contract makes the difference to some employees of a company, who will get fired if the contract is not awarded. The situation becomes a bit more blurry.†

Organizations provide different codes of conduct. We will stick to that promoted by the PMI®, one of the reference organizations for project management, which we will briefly present here.

The code of conduct of the PMI® has been written by practitioners and is organized in four areas:

1. **Responsibility:** the duty of taking ownership of decisions made or failed to make and their consequences
2. **Respect:** the duty of treating with respect the resources assigned to us, such as people, money, reputation, environment, and so on
3. **Fairness:** the duty of taking decisions impartially and objectively
4. **Honesty:** the duty of acting in a truthful manner.

---

* A "buy in bid" underestimates project costs to make it more appealing. The costs are then raised as the project develops to match the actual expenditure.
† It is still wrong should you have had any doubt.

For each area, two types of requirements are listed. **Mandatory** requirements have to be met in any situation. **Aspirational** requirements are nice to have (Project Management Institute, 2013).

Thus, for instance, while a mandatory requirement is that of getting informed and sticking to regulations and laws governing one's work (Requirement 2.3.1), listening to and understanding other people's point of view is an aspirational requirement (Requirement 3.2.2). (As a side remark, the fact that the requirement of listening to and understanding other people's point of view is only aspirational tells a lot about how daunting the task is and how patient project managers are.)

Other codes of conducts are available and applicable to the profession of project managers. For instance, the IEEE Board of Directors (2006), the code of ethics of the Association of Electrical and Electronics Engineers, similar to another famous code of conduct, lists in 10 items the rules one should stick to.

Although one's values are often sufficient to take sound and ethical decisions, reading one or more codes of conduct is a good idea to help individuate those situations that might pose ethical choices in the profession and give project managers and professionals a reference framework when needed.

1.4 Software Project Management

Software project management is the integration of management techniques into software development. The need for such integration has its root in the 1960s, in the days of the "software crisis," when practitioners recognized the increasing complexity of delivering software products meeting the specifications. A number of works started then to improve the software development practices, detailing and structuring technical activities more rationally.

In parallel with this, some big engineering projects started by the U.S. Government in the 1960s contributed to the consolidation and introduction of important project management techniques. The two areas, however, were too young or growing too fast to look at each other, and for a while they grew independent of each other.

Similar to system engineering, software engineering shares many concerns that can be dealt with by sound management practices. As software engineering matured as a discipline, more interest grew in the systematic integration of management activities in the software production process. Software development and project management thus started to be integrated more tightly. This is exactly what we start doing in this section.

People in operating systems often compare the architecture of an operating system to that of an onion. Similar to an onion, operating system architectures define different layers of functions, each layer building on top of the lower level ones. Taking inspiration from this analogy, we try and build our own tastier comparison between software project management and the millefoglie pastry, which is made up of layers of pastry and custard cream.* It requires quite a bit of fantasy, and maybe it does not work as well as the onion analogy, but it is certainly tastier!

Similar to the pastry, in fact, we organize software project management activities in two groups. The *pastry* gives structure and helps deliver. The *custard* binds the pastry together and ensures a harmonious result.

Our millefoglie is composed of four layers of pastry. The bottom layer includes all the activities that are essential to develop software. The other layers are made of management flour and butter. The second layer is **scope management**, which includes all the activities to ensure that a project delivers according to the goals it sets. The third layer is **time management**, which defines a schedule for a project and delivers according to the schedule. The fourth layer is **cost management**, which defines a budget and controls spending during a project.

With four layers of pastry, we need three layers of custard. These come in the form of technical and managerial activities to help ensure a coherent development of a project and of its results. Their common characteristics are that they run along the whole process and interact with the other activities, guaranteeing order and coherence.

The first layer of the custard is composed of **change** and **configuration management**, which help manage changes in a project, while maintaining a coherent view on its outputs. These processes interact with all software development activities and also influence goals, schedules, and costs.

The second layer of the custard is **risk management**, the set of activities to effectively manage menaces and opportunities. Similar to the previous case, risk management runs throughout a project, reducing the influence of unexpected events.

Finally, the third layer of the custard is made of **quality management**, the set of activities to ensure that a project defines quality goals and delivers accordingly the goals.

Finally, **human resource management** and **stakeholder management** are the powdered sugar sprinkled at the top. Try it without it, and it does not taste as good.

To continue the analogy, we can split our millefoglie into four slices, corresponding to the four phases we have introduced in Section 1.1.1. Each slice will still have all the layers. As a matter of fact, all the management concerns we have introduced in our analogy have an initiating, a planning, a monitoring, and a closing phase. (Software development is a bit of an exception, since it is mainly concentrated in the execution phase.)

This is shown in Figure 1.2, where we present our millefoglie. The horizontal axis represents the various project phases, while the vertical axis presents the pastry

---

* Good food seems to be particularly relevant for people working in the area. A report about the meeting where the "software crisis" term was coined includes the following quote: "The conference had been held outside Rome in a rather charmless American-style hotel whose facilities and cuisine I'm sure did little to engender a harmonious atmosphere" (Randell, 1996).

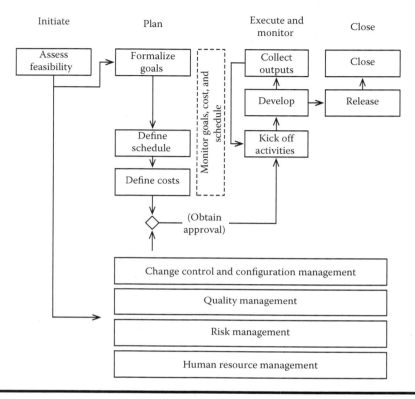

Figure 1.2 The software project management millefoglie.

and custard, one per row. In Figure 1.2, we have deconstructed the millefoglie a bit, so that we can present more elementary activities and suggest one ordering in which the activities can be executed.

The first row contains the management of the project goals. The process spans all the four phases, including an assessment of the feasibility, the formalization of the project goals, the collection of the outputs, and closing the project.

The second row shows the software development activities, in which we have highlighted only two of the phases, namely, development and release.

The third row contains time management. We distinguish three activities, namely, the definition of a schedule, kickoff of activities and, in the dotted box, monitoring and control.

The fourth row contains cost control, including the definition of the budget and its monitoring (dotted box).

The remaining four layers contain the activities to manage changes, control software configurations, assess quality, tame risks, and manage human resources.

The arrows show a possible ordering of the activities. As we will see, it is one of different possible ways to organize work.

Notice that not all layers are always necessary to have a good project. Practitioners distinguish between **traditional** and **agile management**. The first favors structure, while the second prefers more lightweight approaches. Thus, some projects are better managed by reducing the fat and the infrastructure, while others can succeed only if you have the full deal. This also holds true for the millefoglie: more is not always better.

To conclude, I hope that you enjoyed the analogy with gusto. In the next chapters, we will have a look at the techniques in each area.

1.5 Goals and Organization of the Book

This book is organized in two parts. The first part introduces the building blocks and techniques to develop and manage software projects, while the second puts them together in an organized process.

To go back to Figure 1.2, the first part describes the boxes, while the second part shows how these boxes can be organized in different ways. The goal of this approach is to achieve flexibility and to allow readers to be creative by selecting and mixing the techniques they find more effective for their projects. For this reason, traditional and agile techniques are presented side by side.

The first part of the book develops in the next four chapters. In more detail, Chapter 2, introduces the main activities characterizing software development projects. It covers the execution phase of a project and also helps understand why a sound management structure is also necessary for software development.

Chapter 3 covers the essentials, namely, how to manage goals, time, and costs. Starting from project selection, which describes some of the factors to consider before starting a project, the chapter develops by introducing techniques to define project goals, making them into a specification and a schedule of the work to be performed. A discussion on algorithmic techniques helps us understand how we can come out with reliable estimations and, consequently, with a budget for the project. The chapter covers the different project phases, including monitoring and control. Thus, it introduces the basic management techniques from end to end.

Chapter 4 introduces the variability and uncertainty that characterize any project and describes the techniques that can be used to ensure that these do not affect a project and its outputs. We will look, in particular, at techniques to deal with change requests and changes and demonstrate why a sound configuration management is essential. We will continue by analyzing the main techniques to deal with risks. A discussion on quality and on the techniques to ensure that quality goals are met concludes the chapter. Some might argue that quality management is an essential process deserving to be presented alongside goals, time, and costs management. I understand the point of view. Quality and quality management, however, not only set the baseline characteristics of the project outputs but also ensure that they are met in spite of the unexpected. I prefer to emphasize this second aspect.

Chapters 5 and 6 close the first part of the book. Chapter 5 introduces some theories about what motivates people and the techniques to manage team and stakeholders, establishing appropriate project structures and communication channels. Chapter 6 introduces some concepts related to software pricing and procurement activities.

The second part of the books puts the techniques together in a coherent process. Over the years, the way in which software projects are organized has changed considerably. Chapter 7 thus describes how to organize software development projects, introducing traditional and agile processes. Thus, the technical and managerial activities presented in the first part of the book are put together in different ways to try and tame the complexity of software development.

Chapter 8 concludes the description of processes by presenting standards and frameworks for software project management.

Automation has always been important to present and track information in a project. Today, it has become an essential infrastructure to also organize and allocate work. Chapter 9 thus closes this book by presenting some open source tools to support planning, management, and the organization of work.

The simplest way to read the book is, of course, from end to end. Each chapter, however, should be sufficiently self-contained to be readable and understandable by itself. The chapters in the second part of the book (Chapters 7 through 9) make more sense after reading the first part of the book.

1.6 Further References

The literature on project management, software engineering, and software project management is huge. There are some references that I have found myself resorting to over and over again during my career as a teacher and as a professional. So, while you will find specific references in the chapters, if you are building your software project management bookshelf or if you want to complement this book with some additional readings in the area, the following references are some starting points.

Project management books:

■ Burke (2006) is a very well-written introduction to project management. With its many diagrams and techniques, it clearly explain many topics of project management. I have found particularly interesting the discussion on project selection and budgeting techniques. All in all, the book is clear and fun to read.

■ Wysocki (2011) is another very readable book on project management. With its 734 pages, it is also a considerable challenge to reading, but worth the effort or worth consulting, if you prefer to pick topics here and there. I found the description of traditional, agile, and extreme project types particularly interesting. Critical chain management and project closing are two other topics to look at.

■ Maylor (2010) provides many insights from case studies while presenting techniques to manage projects. The presentation is based on the 4-D model: define it, design it, do it, and develop it.

■ Project Management Institute (2004) is the definitive reference guide on project management. Sponsored by the PMI®, it illustrates the techniques that are most appropriate at each phase of project development. Given the breadth, the book only hints at the techniques and is a starting point to look for further references. The organization in process groups and knowledge areas, which we will see in Section 8.2, is very effective.

There are also various books explicitly focused on software project management. Among them

■ Brooks (1995) is a seminal book on the topic, covering and introducing various important concepts that distinguish software project management from other management areas. Worth reading.

■ Henry (2003) is the first book on software project management that I came across. It also raised my interest to the function points estimation techniques, which are clearly introduced there. We will cover function points estimation in Section 3.4.5.1.

■ Hughes and Cotterell (2009) is a nice introduction to the topic. With a nice discussion on software quality and procurement, it introduces many of the concepts related to software project management.

A huge number of books cover **software development** and the management of software projects. I will mention only a few:

■ McConnell (1996) presents critical aspects of software development, suggesting how becoming more agile can help tame wild software schedules. Rich in examples, the description of how stakeholders can make the project goals impossible to achieve is very interesting.

■ Rothman (2007) provides a very practical approach to managing a project, with many insights and techniques to cope with the difficulties of software development projects.

■ Ruby et al. (2013) provides the clearest and most readable example of agile development that I came across recently. So, while the book presents Ruby on Rails, a web development framework, its presentation is organized as a Scrum sprint. We will cover Scrum in Section 7.3.3.

Finally, I need to mention the many reports and books on the topic made available by NASA. While only partially overlapping with project management, NASA (2007) is very interesting to read. So are various other reports, including NASA (1990).

1.7 Questions and Topics for Discussion

1. Recap the main characteristics of a project.
2. Try and see which of the activities you commonly do could be organized as projects and which are operational work. Consider the following examples: writing an essay; studying at the university; preparing a meal; preparing dinner every evening; painting a house; exercising; training for the Olympic games.
3. Consider the construction of a web application that allows people to donate food. Who could be the stakeholders of the project?
4. Many software development processes are iterative. Each iteration delivers a software system that gets refined as development progresses. Go back to Figure 1.2 and think about how you could modify the process to make it iterative. How many possible loops can you envisage?

References

Brooks, F. P. J., 1995. *The Mythical Man Month* (Anniversary ed.). Addison-Wesley, Boston, MA, USA.

Burke, R., 2006. *Project Management, Planning and Control Techniques* (4th ed.). John Wiley & Sons, New York, NY, USA.

Cabanis, J., 1996, December. A question of ethics: The issues project manager face and how they resolve them. *PM Network*, 19–24.

Cox, C. B. and C. Murray, 2004, September. *Apollo*. South Mountain Books, Burkittsville, MD.

Gertler, J., 2012, October. Air force. Technical Report RL31673, Congressional Research Service. Last retrieved July 11, 2013. Available at http://www.fas.org/sgp/crs/weapons/RL31673.pdf

Henry, J., 2003. *Software Project Management: A Real-World Guide To Success*. Pearson Education, Addison-Wesley, Boston, MA, USA.

Hughes, B. and M. Cotterell, 2009. *Software Project Management*. McGraw-Hill Higher Education.

IEEE Board of Directors, 2006, February. IEEE code of ethics. Available at http://dusk.geo.orst.edu/ethics/codes/IEEE_code.pdf. Last retrieved May 31, 2013.

Maylor, H., 2010. *Project Management* (4th ed.). Pearson, Harlow, England.

McConnell, S., 1996. *Rapid Development—Taming Wild Software Schedules*. O'Reilly, Sebastopol, CA, USA.

NASA, 1990. Manager's handbook for software development. Software Engineering Laboratory Series SEL-84-101, NASA Goddard Flight Center.

NASA, 2007, December. Systems engineering handbook. Technical Report NASA/SP-2007-6105 Rev1, NASA.

Project Management Institute, 2004. *A Guide to the Project Management Body of Knowledge (PMBOK Guides)* (4th ed.). Project Management Institute, Newtown Square, Pennsylvania 19073-3299 USA.

Project Management Institute, 2013. Project Management Institute—code of ethics and professional conduct. Available at http://www.pmi.org/en/About-Us/Ethics/~/media/PDF/Ethics/ap_pmicodeofethics.ashx. Last retrieved May 31, 2013.

Randell, B., 1996. The 1968/69 NATO software engineering reports. Last retrieved July 11, 2013.

Rothman, J., 2007. *Manage IT! Your Guide to Pragmatic Project Management.* The Pragmatic Bookshelf, Raleigh, NC.

Ruby, S., D. Thomas, and D. H. Hansson, 2013. *Agile Web Development with Rails.* The Pragmatic Bookshelf, Raleigh, NC.

Wysocki, R. K., 2011, October. *Effective Project Management: Traditional, Agile, Extreme* (6, illustrated ed.). John Wiley & Sons, New York, NY, USA.

Chapter 2

The Basics: Software Development Activities and Their Organization

Software development projects range from the very small to the very large and encompass a wide range of complexity, starting from software developed by a small team in their spare time and ending with projects lasting several years and involving the work of many people.

Similarly, the concept of what it means for a software development project to *succeed* also varies according to the context. For the small team developing an open source solution, it could be the intellectual challenge of solving a complex problem or the satisfaction of contributing to a community. Time is not critical, nor are costs: having fun in the process probably is.

For people developing safety-critical systems, the challenge is different. They need to ensure that the system will perform as expected in a wide array of operational conditions, including those in which there are malfunctions. Quality and a controlled process are paramount in this context.

Finally, for people developing a web application or another desktop system, the most important aspect could be the the price that can be set for the product or making sure that the product is released before the competition. In this context, time and costs might be the main drivers.

Thus, the activities that are required or beneficial to develop successful software vary from project to project. Some projects might allow a more informal approach, while others are better served by a very structured and controlled process. Going back to the *millefoglie* example, the goal of this chapter is to present the "pastry," that is, the activities that are needed to develop software. These are the technical building blocks for constructing software, that is, what we do in the "execute" phase of a software development project. These building blocks will be selected, composed, and organized in different ways, according to the project size and formality, the process adopted, and other management choices in Chapter 4.

2.1 Software Requirements Definition

The first step of any nontrivial software development project is to form an idea about the system that has to be developed.

Software requirements definition includes the methods to identify and describe the features of the system to be built. The main output of this activity is one or more artifacts describing the **(software) requirements** of a system, namely, the functions it has to implement and the other properties it has to have.

Software requirements are strongly related to the **scope document**, which defines the goals of a project and which we will see in Chapter 3.

There are two main output formats for these artifacts, textual or diagrammatic.

When the textual format is used, the requirements are written in English, in some cases using a restricted set of language or predefined linguistic patterns. For instance, special words, such as "shall," might be required to indicate an essential requirement—see, for example, Brader (1997).

Concerning the structure, the requirements are often presented as lists of items, one per requirement. Another very common representation writes requirements in the form of **user stories**, using the following pattern:

As a [user] I want to do [this] because of [that].

The advantage of this approach is that each requirement clearly identifies the user, the function that has to be performed, and the motivation for the function to be implemented, something that helps identify the priority or importance of a requirement.

The diagrammatic notation describes requirements with a mix of diagrams and textual descriptions. Diagrams depict the interaction between the user and the system and the textual description explains the interaction using a sequence of steps. The most common graphical notation is that of the **use case diagrams** of UML and the corresponding textual descriptions are called **use cases** (Booch et al., 1999; Fowler and Scott, 2000).

The **requirement engineering** discipline includes the activities necessary to define and maintain requirements over time. Simplifying a bit, requirements engineering entails a cyclical refinement process in which the following steps are repeated at increasing levels of detail till a satisfactory level of know-how about a system is achieved.

In more detail, the process is composed of four steps:

1. Requirements elicitation
2. Requirements structuring
3. User experience design
4. Requirements validation.

2.1.1 Requirements Elicitation

Requirements elicitation is the activity during which the list of features of a system are elicited from the customer. This activity can be performed with interviews, workshops, or the analysis of existing documents.

2.1.2 Requirements Structuring

Requirements structuring is the phase during which the requirements are annotated to make their management and maintenance simpler.

During the process, requirements are

- **Isolated and made identifiable.** Each requirement is clearly isolated and distinguished from the others and is also assigned a unique identifier. This allows one to reason and manipulate each requirement more easily. Concerning identification, a commonly used practice is that of assigning each requirement a number or a combination of some characters (describing the type of requirements) and a number.
- **Organized and classified.** A simple classification distinguishes between **functional** and **nonfunctional** requirements. The former are requirements describing what the system has to do. The latter are requirements describing what other properties the system should exhibit (e.g., "the system will have to run on Windows devices"). Functional requirements are usually organized in *functional areas*. Each functional area groups requirements describing a homogeneous set of functions. For instance, a requirement document might have an "accounting functions" section describing all requirements pertaining to accounting functions. Nonfunctional requirements are often organized in four groups: **usability**, **reliability**, **performance**, and **supportability**.
- **Annotated.** Requirements are annotated to simplify their management and to support planning activities, like, for instance, which requirements should be implemented first. It is a good practice to assign each requirement at least two properties, namely, the **importance for the customer** and the **difficulty to develop**, for instance, using values from 1 to 5. We will see other types of classifications in Section 3.2.1.

Requirements evolve over time and a sound approach to requirement management also necessitates defining a proper strategy to control the evolution of

```
Description
    [ID] As a [user] I want to do [this] because of [that]

Attributes
    Importance:    [IMPORTANCE]
    Priority:      [PRIORITY]
    Traceability:  [THIS REQUIREMENT RELATES TO ...]

Revision History
    - [DATE] [AUTHOR] [DESCRIPTION]
```

Figure 2.1   A template for a requirement.

requirements. We will see some of the issues in Section 4.1. Here, it is sufficient to mention that requirements are often annotated with

- **Traceability** information, which has the goal of highlighting where a requirement originates from. Traceability shows the relationships among requirements and the relationships among requirements and other artifacts of software development. This allows one to understand the impact of changes. See Gotel and Finkelstein (1994) for a formal definition and more details.
- **History log**, which records the changes each requirement has undergone. The history log traces how requirements have changed over time.

Figure 2.1 shows an example of a template of an annotated requirement.

2.1.3 User Experience Design

User experience design has the goal of providing a coherent and satisfying experience on the different artifacts that constitute a software system, including its design, interface, interaction, and manuals. It is defined in International Organization for Standardization (2010) as *the extent to which a product can be used by specified users to achieve specified goals with effectiveness, efficiency, and satisfaction in a specified context of use.*

The typical user experience design activities include

- **User-centered analysis**, which has the goal of understanding how users will interact with the system. It runs in parallel with the requirements definition and requires the organization of workshops and other activities (e.g., surveys) to profile the users, analyze which tasks they will perform, and define which style guides will be followed in designing the system.
- **User-centered design**, which has the goal of specifying how users will actually interact with the system. It runs in parallel with the requirements definition and system design (see the next section). The outputs include **storyboards**

describing the interaction, **mock-ups**, and **prototypes**. (A mock-up is a full-size model of something that has not yet been built, showing how it will look or operate (Cambridge University Press, 2013).)

2.1.4 Requirements Validation

Requirements validation is the phase during which the requirements are analyzed to find

- **Inconsistencies**, for example, two requirements require a system to behave in contradictory ways. In a common situation, a requirement document includes two requirements, the first prescribing a general behavior (e.g., "the system should always abort in case of error") and the other suggesting the opposite one in a specific situation comprised also in the general requirement (e.g., "the system should recover from a sensor-reading error").
- **Incompleteness**, when no information is given about a specific situation.
- **Duplicates**, when one requirement describes a function already described by another requirement.

Different techniques can be used to validate requirements. We mention inspections and formal analyses. Document inspections are based on the work of a team that analyzes the content of documents and highlights any issue. The technique relies on the ability and experience of the team. Formal analyses use mathematical notations (such as first-order logic) to represent requirements and automated tools (such as theorem provers and model checkers) to prove properties about the requirements. Several notations and approaches are available; see, for instance, Clarke et al. (2000), Bozzano and Villafiorita (2010), and Spivey (1989) for more details.

Notice that the goals of this phase overlap with those of quality management. We will see more about verification and validation techniques in Section 4.3.

2.2 Business Modeling

In the 1990s, the university where I teach—a complex organization in which different offices have considerable organizational autonomy—kept personnel records in different databases: one for contracts, another for teaching assignments, another for granting entrance to laboratories, to name some. The database was not connected; any change had to be propagated manually to all databases, causing inconsistencies, omissions, and a lot of extra work to try and keep data in sync.

Enterprise resource systems (ERP) are systems that can automate and simplify the processes of an organization, integrating the data and the procedures of different business units. These systems are usually composed of standardized components, which implement the main procedures of an organization in a particular business sector (e.g., government, logistics, services). Their introduction in an organization typically requires them to act not only on the system, personalizing data, procedures, and functions, but also on the organization, by changing the existing procedures to take full advantage of the system being introduced.

In this kind of project, understanding how work is carried out in an organization is often more relevant than eliciting the requirements of the system to be built, since an important part of the project work will focus on mapping the current procedures and changing them to accommodate those that supported by the ERP.

The activity to understand how an organization is structured and works is called **business process modeling** or **business modeling** in short. Those to modify the current procedures go under the name of **business process re-engineering**.

Business modeling and **business re-engineering** are usually organized in two main steps. An initial "**as is**" analysis describes the organization before the introduction of a new system. The "as is" analysis helps one understand the current infrastructure and needs. A complete analysis will include

- A description of the organizational structure, highlighting the chain of responsibility and accountability.
- A description of the business processes, describing how the organization carries out the different procedures.
- A map of the existing IT infrastructure, highlighting hardware, systems, and databases.
- A list of the business entities, highlighting the data produced and processed by the organization.

Following the "is" analysis, a "**to be**" phase defines how the organization will change with the introduction of the new system. The "to be" analysis produces the same set of information required by the "as is" analysis, but it describes the processes, the systems, and the business data that will be introduced to make operations more efficient.

Let us see in more detail the information produced with the "as is" and the "to be" analyses.

2.2.1 Mapping the Organizational Structure

Mapping the organizational structure has the goal of understanding how an organization is structured.

The information to collect includes the list of the different business units and the lines of responsibility. More detailed analyses also include the roles or the staff employed by each business unit and the functions assigned to each role or person.

The output is a text document or an **organizational chart** describing the units and their functions. It is used to identify the changes that will have to be implemented in the organization to support the new processes.

2.2.2 Modeling the Business Processes

Modeling the business processes has the goal of documenting how an organization carries out its procedures.

These are typically represented with **flow diagrams** sketched, for instance, using the **business process modeling notation**—BPMN (OMG, 2011). Business processes highlight, for each process, which steps need to be performed, by whom, and what outputs are produced and consumed. The specification should model both nominal and exceptional situations. For instance, if the target of the analysis is a paper-based procedure to authorize a trip, a good process description will document what happens when everything flows as expected and how the organization recovers if some error occurs—for example, a paper form is lost in the middle of a procedure.

A difficult aspect of this analysis is capturing not only the formal procedures but also the **current practices**, namely, how people actually carry out the procedures. The **ethnography software engineering** field focuses on methods to simplify this activity. See, for instance, Rönkköa (2010) for an introduction on the matter.

The output is a document containing the processes, possibly organized by area or by business unit. It is the basis to specify the new business processes or the requirements of the systems that will have to implement them.

2.2.3 Mapping the Existing IT Infrastructure

Mapping the IT infrastructure has the goal of understanding what IT systems are currently used in an organization, with what purpose, which data they store, and what lines of communications exist, if any.

Various notations can be used; the most formal ones are based on UML and could include **component** and **deployment** diagrams. Textual descriptions often complement the diagrams.

The output is a document. It is the basis to plan data migration and data integration activities. The former occurs when an existing system will be dismissed and the data it manages have to be migrated to a new system. The latter occurs when the system will remain in use and will have to communicate with the new system being introduced.

2.2.4 Mapping Business Entities

Mapping the business entities has the goal of documenting which data are processed by an organization, by whom, and with what purpose.

During this activity, analysts typically produce **data models** and **CRUD matrices**. The former list the data processed by the business processes. They are presented with **class diagrams** or **textual descriptions**.

The latter define the access rights to the data. It is presented as a matrix, whose rows list the data and whose columns list the business units. Each cell contains any combination of the CRUD letters to indicate which unit creates ("C") specific data, which unit reads ("R") it, which unit can update ("U") the data, and which units delete ("D") the data.

2.3 Design and Implementation

The goals of **design** (also **system design** or **architectural design** in the rest of the book) and **implementation** are, respectively, to draw the blueprint of the system to be implemented and actually implement it.

2.3.1 System Design

System design defines the structure of the software to build or **system architecture**. The output of this activity is one or more documents which describe, with diagrams and text, the structure of the system to build, namely: what software components constitute the system, which function each component implements, and how the components are interconnected. The activity is particularly relevant for technical and managerial reasons.

In fact, design allows one to break the complexity of building a system by *separating concerns*, that is, by allocating functions to components, and by specifying functions in terms of more elementary and simpler to implement components.

The system architecture can also be used as an input to plan development. In fact, given the list and structure of components that have to be developed, there is a natural organization of work that follows the structure of the system. We will see this in more detail in Section 3.3.

The definition of a system architecture can be based on a pattern or predefined blueprints. Many different architectural blueprints have been proposed in the literature. Among these, some of the most commonly used include:

- **Pipe and filter**, that is, a paradigm according to which the application is structured as a chain of processing elements. Each element of the pipe takes an input from the previous element, processes it, and passes it onto the next element. In a pipe and filter architecture, once the boundaries among the elements of the pipe are clearly defined, the development of each element can proceed in parallel with that of the others. In this architecture, the input/output specification is a critical piece of information to ensure that all components integrate as expected. See the discussion about integration testing in Section 2.4 for more details.
- **Layered/hierarchical**, by contrast, is an architectural style in which the different elements of a system are organized hierarchically. Lower levels of the architecture perform simpler functions, while higher levels are responsible for

the implementation of more complex functions. Lower layers pass information about the environment or their status to the higher levels, which in turn send commands to the lower levels. An example of layered architecture is that of an embedded system in which we can distinguish two levels. At the lower level, sensors are responsible for reading data from the environment and processing inputs. At the higher level, a controller takes the input of the sensors and decides the action to perform, sending appropriate commands to the actuators. These, in turn, are responsible for interacting with the environment executing the commands of the controller.

■ **Data-centric** is an architecture used when data storage and elaboration are central. Many data-centric architectures rely on a database to store data and are often based on the **model view controller** (MVC) pattern, according to which, for each data to be processed by the application:

  – The **model** defines how data are to be stored and manipulated.
  – The **view** defines how data are to be presented to the user or other systems interacting with the one we are developing. Multiple views can be associated with a single model or, vice versa, some views can display the data of different models.
  – The **controller** defines the logic of the operations, that is, what sequences of transformations make sense of the data and what actions the users can perform.

Many web applications and many desktop applications use the data-centric architectural style.

■ **Client-server** is an architecture in which the functions of a system are split between a **server**, which performs the main functions, and various **clients**, which interact with the server, requesting services.

Figure 2.2 provides a pictorial representation of the different architectural styles we have just presented. Notice how the data-centric architecture is composed of two MVCs.

A popular way of presenting the architecture of a software system is the one proposed in Kruchten (1995), which is based on the UML, and according to which the architecture of a software system is described by "**4+1**" diagrams.

Four diagrams describe the structure of the system. In particular

1. The **logical view** identifies the main elements and data structures of the system to build. It is best described with class and sequence diagrams.
2. The **component view** provides a programmer-oriented view of the system. It is mainly concerned with the components to be developed and is best described in UML with class and component and package diagrams.
3. The **process view** provides a specification of the behavior of the system: interactions among components and the sequence of actions that are required to implement the user functions. It is best described with sequence and communication diagrams.

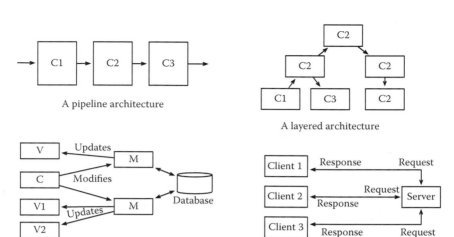

Figure 2.2 Some examples of architectural styles.

4. The **physical view** provides a specification of the physical deployment of a system, that is, on what computer or process each element of the architecture will run. It is best described by a deployment diagram.

The last view is the use case diagram view, which we have briefly described in Section 2.1.

2.3.2 Implementation

The goal of the **implementation** phase is writing the code implementing the components individuated in the architecture.

Some of the aspects of this activity that are more closely related to project management include

■ Collection of **productivity** and **size** metrics, which allow one to measure the speed at which code is delivered and the amount of work that has been performed. This is covered in more detail in Section 3.4.5, where we introduce estimation techniques based on software size, and in Section 3.9, where we present monitoring techniques.

■ Collection of **quality metrics**, which allow one to measure the quality of the system to be developed and trends in the development process. This is covered in more detail in Section 4.3.

■ The use of **coding standards**, which are guidelines describing best practices and the preferred styles to write code. Coding standards are adopted to ensure that the work of different programmers is similarly structured. Different standards are available. One which is adopted by the open source community is described in (Free Software Foundation, 2013). See Section 4.3 for more details.

2.4 Verification and Validation

Verification is the set of activities performed on a system to ensure that the system implements the requirements correctly. The definition is taken from SAE (1996) and distinguishes verification from **validation**, which is instead performed to ensure that the requirements describe the intended system. Thus, validation ensures that we are *building the right system*, while verification ensures that we *built the system right*.

Verification and validation are collectively known by the acronym **V&V**. The main way of performing V&V of software systems is testing. However, also see Sections 2.1.4 and 4.3 for a more complete discussion.

2.4.1 Testing

Testing is one way of performing verification and validation. Other methodologies include simulation, formal validation, and inspections.

Testing activities can be classified according to their scope. In this case, we distinguish between the following:

- **Unit testing**, when the goal is to verify the behavior of a piece of code, such as a class. Unit testing verifies that the code under investigation behaves as specified by the system architecture. The execution of unit tests can be easily automated, since they can be written as pieces of code. Some development paradigms, in fact, suggest writing unit tests before the code, as a way to encourage testing and to define executable and unambiguous specifications of the expected behavior of a piece of code.
- **Integration testing**, when the goal of the testing activity is to ensure that the components of a system behave as expected when they are assembled. Integration testing looks for inconsistencies in the way data are exchanged between components. These errors are relatively simple to introduce and their effect can be catastrophic. Consider a situation in which one component returns an array of characters, while the one connected to it expects a string.
- **System testing**, when the goal of the testing activity is to ensure that the system behaves as expected and correctly implements all the requirements. System testing uses the requirements document as input and defines a set of **test cases** that verify whether a system implements the requirements. See Section 2.4.2.1 for more details.

■ **Usability testing**, running in parallel with the other testing activities, has the goal of verifying whether the user experience and interaction are intuitive, effective, and satisfying. Usability testing is particularly relevant in designing user interfaces for safety-critical systems to reduce the probability of human errors.

2.4.2 Organizing Testing Activities

While unit tests are written and executed by the developer writing the code being tested, integration and system test are typically performed by an independent team and are organized in the following two steps:

1. Test plan definition
2. Test execution and reporting.

Many software engineering books also include a **test planning** activity, which has the goal of identifying the resources, the schedule, and the order in which the tests will be executed. This emphasizes the fact that testing can be organized as a subproject and have its own plans and schedule.

2.4.2.1 Test Plan Definition

Starting from the requirements of a system, the goal of the **test plan definition** is to write the tests that will be performed on the system.

The output of this activity is a document listing a set of **test cases**, each of which describes how to perform a test on the system. Test cases are structured natural language descriptions that specify all the information needed to carry out a test, such as the initial state of the system, the inputs to be provided, the steps to be performed, the expected outputs, and the expected final state of the system.

Different test cases need to be defined for each requirement. Each test case, in fact, verifies either a particular condition specified by the requirement or the implementation of the requirement in different operational conditions.

Traceability information, which links a test case to the requirement it tests, helps manage changes and the overall maintenance process.

2.4.2.2 Test Execution and Reporting

Starting from the test plan definition, **test execution and reporting** is the activity during which the team or automated procedures execute tests and report on the outputs, that is, which tests succeeded and which failed.

Manual test execution is time consuming and demands motivation and commitment from the people performing it. There are various reasons for this.

The first is that it is repetitive: some operations have to be repeated over and over again to put the system in a known state before starting a test. Attention, however, has to remain high to ensure that all glitches are properly recognized and reported.

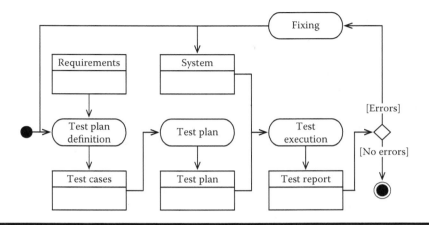

Figure 2.3 The testing workflow.

The second is that testing is the last activity before releasing a system. It requires quite some commitment to work hard at this stage of development to demonstrate that a system does not work and needs one to go back to the design room.

The third is that when an error is found, the process stops till a fix is found. When the fix is ready, it is necessary to start the testing activities all over again, possibly including the definition of new test cases, to verify that the bug has actually been fixed. This is to ensure that there are no **regressions**, that is, working functions have not been unintentionally broken by the fix. The corresponding workflow is shown in Figure 2.3.

Different strategies have been proposed to write effective test cases. It has to be remarked, however, that testing is rarely complete and it can only demonstrate that a system does not work, rather than proving that a system is correct.

2.5 Deployment

The final step of the development process is releasing and installing a system so that it can be used by the customer and operations start. The transition to operations can be very simple for the project team. Consider, for instance, a case in which a software is handed to the client as a self-installing application in a CD, or made available on a website for customers to download.

In other situations, deployment needs to be carefully planned. This happens when a new software system replaces an obsolete system performing business- or mission-critical functions. In this situation, the goal is to move to the new technology without interrupting the service.

Consider a case in which a system controlling the routing of luggage in an airport needs to be upgraded. The development and installation of the new version of the system has to be organized so that no interruptions occur and no luggage is mismanaged.

A standard practice for projects of this kind makes sure that any change or software evolution does not interfere with production. To achieve this goal, the project team sets up three exact and independent replicas of the same operating environment, as shown in Figure 2.4. In particular, we distinguish between the following:

- A **development environment**, where the actual development of the software takes place. The development environment is completely isolated from production, and therefore there is no concern of blocking any critical activity. If data are needed to verify the behavior of the software being developed, a replica of the data in production is used. If there are privacy concerns, like in the case of medical or banking systems, the data on which developers operate are fake or an anonymized version of the data in production.
- A **testing environment**, where the team tests a system that is ready for deployment. The testing environment is isolated from the development and the production environment, so that, on the one hand, no changes made by developers interfere with testing and, on the other, that testing activities can proceed without any risk of interrupting production. Similar to the production environment, testing activities use replicas of the production data or fake versions.
- A **production environment**, where the system is actually used. Any change to the production environment interferes (positively or negatively) with the operations for which a system is used.

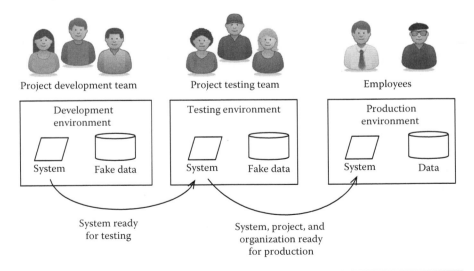

Figure 2.4 Development environments.

Even if we separate development and testing from production, alas, it is still necessary to ensure a smooth transition of operations when the new system is ready. In general, three factors need to be taken into account when deploying a new system. They are

1. The **human factor**: are the people ready to use the system?
2. The **data factor**: are all the data that are needed for the system to run available to the new software?
3. The **hardware factor**: are all interfaces ready and functional?

The deployment process thus typically requires to perform an **assessment of readiness and evaluation of the gaps**, which has the goals of understanding the main criticalities and risks. An analysis of documents and interviews with project stakeholders highlights all the critical issues related to the deployment of the new technology.

This is followed by the selection of a **migration strategy**, which defines an approach to the introduction of the new system. According to Wysocki (2011), the following approaches are possible:

- **Cut-over**, when the old system is replaced by the new one.
- **Parallel approach**, when the old and the new systems operate simultaneously for a period. This allows the new system to be tested and evaluated before the actual switch takes place.
- **Piloting**, when the system is installed for a limited number of users or for a specific business unit. This approach reduces the burden to users (who do not have to live with two systems), but it maintains the complexity of having two environments—the old and the new systems—both alive.
- **Phased approach**, when functions are rolled out incrementally.

Notice that, in all the approaches mentioned above, with the exclusion of the **cut-over** approach, appropriate measures have to be taken to maintain or transfer data from the old system to the new system. For instance, in the piloting approach, adequate procedural or technical interfaces need to be defined, so that the data produced by the business unit operating the new system can be used by the units using the old system.

When the strategy is agreed upon, the final step is the implementation of the release process, which in turn consists of the following steps:

1. **Deliver training**, to ensure that the users acquire the necessary skills to use the new system.
2. **Perform data migration**, which includes updating the data used in the production environment so that it can be used by the new system. This is a delicate step, which requires a thorough testing of the migration scripts and a backup of the existing data structures.

3. **Install the new system**, which puts the new system in production.
4. **Set up the support infrastructure**, namely, set up an infrastructure to support operations. More on this in the next section.

Notice that data migration and the installation of the new system need to be performed contextually. They are typically performed in a period and time where a service can be interrupted and system can be taken off-line to reduce pressure on the team and risks, should something not go as expected.

2.6 Operations and Maintenance

Operations and **maintenance** include the activities to ensure that a product remains functional after its release.

2.6.1 Supporting and Monitoring Operations

In general, operations are outside the scope of a project. However, many one-off development projects plan a support activity after a system is released to ensure that the project outputs meet the quality goals and the transition to operations is as smooth as possible.

The goals of this activity typically include

- **Providing technical support**. The support is meant to help users get acquainted with the system and it can be organized as a help-desk collecting tickets from users. Some of these tickets are requests for clarifications on the use of the system. Others will signal malfunctions, glitches, and requests for improvement, triggering maintenance activities. See the next section for more details.
- **System monitoring**. A set of metrics might be collected on the system after its initial release to monitor performances, issues, and other system features.

2.6.2 Maintenance

Maintenance occurs throughout the lifecycle of a system, before it is retired. It can be framed either as a project or operational work and, as such, it often poses a dilemma to the project manager.

ISO/IEC (2006) identifies four categories of maintenance for software:

1. **Corrective**, if relative to fixing an issue discovered after the release of the system.
2. **Preventive**, if relative to fixing an issue that was discovered but has not occurred (or at least signaled by users).

3. **Adaptive**, if relative to adapting a system to changed external conditions. Adaptive maintenance includes, for instance, activities related to updating a software to work with a new release of an operating system.
4. **Perfective**, if relative to improving some characteristics of a system, like, for instance, performances.

Of these, perfective and corrective maintenance are triggered by suggestions and **bug reports** sent by users. Suggestions and bug reports are also called **issues** or **tickets**.

When maintenance is the last activity of a project, two points have to be considered. The first is how much work has to be allocated, since we do not know in advance how many defects will be signaled. A general strategy is considering the complexity of the system, looking at the outputs of the testing phase, and allocating a percentage of the overall development effort. The second point is distinguishing between tickets that are in the scope of the project (called "nonconformance reports") and tickets that are outside the scope of a project (called "concessions"). In fact, as users start using the system, they might come out with new ideas and proposals. However, the implementation of these new features is often better framed within the scope of a new project.

When the planned maintenance period ends, tickets might still arrive. In these situations, organizations and managers are faced with the dilemma of whether the activities should be framed in the context of a new project or not. In some cases, in fact, the amount of work required for the fixes does not justify setting up the machinery of a project. The choice, of course, can boomerang if a continuous stream of small change requests keeps coming in or if the fixes turn out to be more complex than initially envisaged. While there is no silver bullet to decide on the matter, one good practice is to have the team always monitor the time they spend on maintenance activities.

Agile methodologies, by contrast, blur the distinction between development and maintenance by organizing the development of a system in iterations. Each iteration includes the development of new planned features and selected tickets identified since the last release. This will be explained in more detail in Chapter 7.

2.6.3 *Organizing Support and Maintenance Activities*

One important aspect of support and maintenance activities is keeping formal track of the tickets.

This is usually achieved by

■ **Defining a workflow for tickets**, which describes how bug reports are formally tracked and managed. Workflows can be very simple or more articulated, if a formal quality control or configuration management process is in place.

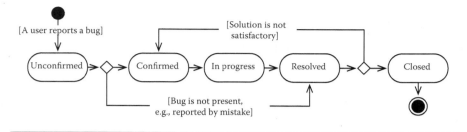

Figure 2.5   The lifecycle of a bug.

■ **Automating the collection and management of tickets**. This is usually achieved by introducing a bug tracking system. A **bug tracking system** allows one to maintain a list of tickets and trace their workflow states. Many of these tools also allow one to produce reports and statistics, which can be used by managers to infer information about a system's quality and about the efficacy of testing activities.

Figure 2.5 shows an example workflow, adapted from the Bugzilla Development Team (2013). A bug starts in the state **unconfirmed** after it is reported by a user. If the quality assurance team confirms its presence, the bug goes in the state **confirmed**, where it can be taken in charge by a developer. The state of the bug thus moves to the state **in progress**. When the developers consider the fix to be adequate, he or she sets the state to **resolved**. V&V by the quality assurance team, finally, determines whether the solution is satisfactory, in which case the bug is **closed**. Alas, if V&V determines the fix is not adequate, the bug returns in the state **confirmed** and another solution has to be found.

2.7 Questions and Topics for Discussion

1. We have seen many artifacts and document produced by the software development activities. A **documentation plan** is a specification of the documents that will be produced in a project. Define a documentation plan for the technical documents of a one-off development project.

2. Software development is a progressive refinement and many of the documents defined in the early stages are used to guide the development of subsequent activities. This generates a series of dependencies among the artifacts. For instance, the design document depends on the requirement document, since any change to the requirement document might cause a change to the design document. Highlight the dependencies among the documents produced in a business re-engineering project.

3. On which technical documents does the "test plan definition document" depend? (Refer to the previous question for the definition of dependency.)

4. Define a template for a test case. Many templates are available on the Internet. Try and see how your template differs from the ones you can find on the Internet.

5. Suppose a company is about to switch to a new system for managing the reimbursements of travel expenses. Discuss the merits and risks of the different approaches we have presented, namely, cut-over, parallel approach, piloting, and phased approach for the case at hand.

6. On many occasions, the implementation of tickets is a planned activity. Define a workflow for tickets that involves an authorization from the project manager and an acceptance of the fix from the customer.

References

Booch, G., J. Rumbaugh, and I. Jacobson, 1999. *The Unified Modeling Language*. Addison-Wesley, Boston, MA, USA.

Bozzano, M. and A. Villafiorita, 2010. *Design and Safety Assessment of Critical Systems*. Boston, MA: CRC Press (Taylor & Francis), an Auerbach Book.

Brader, S., 1997. Key words for use in rfcs to indicate requirement levels. Request for Comments 2119, Network Working Group. Available at http://www.ietf.org/rfc/rfc2119.txt. Last accessed May 1, 2013.

Bugzilla Development Team, 2013, March. *The Bugzilla Guide—4.2.5 Release*. Bugzilla. http://www.bugzilla.org/docs/4.2/en/html/index.html. Last retrieved November 15, 2013.

Cambridge University Press, 2013. *Cambridge Advanced Learner's Dictionary & Thesaurus*. Cambridge University Press, Cambridge, England. Available at http://dictionary.cambridge.org/dictionary. Last retrieved May 1, 2013.

Clarke, E. M., O. Grumberg, and D. A. Peled, 2000. *Model Checking*. MIT Press, Cambridge, MA, USA.

Fowler, M. and K. Scott, 2000. *UML Distilled (2nd Ed.): A Brief Guide to the Standard Object Modeling Language*. Boston, MA: Addison-Wesley.

Free Software Foundation, 2013, April. Gnu coding standards. Available at http://www.gnu.org/prep/standards/. Last retrieved May 1, 2013.

Gotel, O. C. and A. C. W. Finkelstein, 1994. An analysis of the requirements traceability problem. In *Proceedings of ICRE94, 1st International Conference on Requirements Engineering*, Colorado Springs, CO: IEEE CS Press.

International Organization for Standardization, 2010. Ergonomics of human-system interaction. Technical Report 9241-210:2010, ISO.

ISO/IEC, 2006, September. Software engineering—software life cycle processes—maintenance. Technical Report IEEE Std 14764-2006, ISO/IEC.

Kruchten, P., 1995. Architectural blueprints—The "4+1" view model of software architecture. *IEEE Software 12*(6), 44–50.

OMG, 2011, January. Business process model and notation (bpmn). Technical Report formal/2011-01-03, OMG. Available at http://www.omg.org/spec/BPMN/2.0/. Last retrieved June 10, 2013.

Rönkköa, K., 2010, November. Ethnography. *Encyclopedia of Software Engineering*.

SAE, 1996. Certification considerations for highly-integrated or complex aircraft systems. Technical Report ARP4754, Society of Automotive Engineers.

Spivey, J. M., 1989. *The Z Notation: A Reference Manual.* Upper Saddle River, NJ: Prentice-Hall, Inc.

Wysocki, R. K., 2011, October. *Effective Project Management: Traditional, Agile, Extreme* (6, illustrated ed.). John Wiley & Sons, New York, NY, USA.

Chapter 3

Making IT Right: Managing Goals, Time, and Costs

3.1 Before You Start: Assessing Value and Risks

Projects create new products, new services, or new capabilities. The first step of a sound management process is to understand whether the new products, services, or capabilities are worth our effort. The relevance of a project depends, in general, upon two main factors:

1. The **value** generated by the project
2. The **risks** associated with the project.

The meaning of *value* and *risk*, however, is not absolute and depends on the circumstances and on the project environment. For instance, a project developed for humanitarian reasons measures value in a different way from a project to launch a commercial product. Similar is the concept of risk. As mentioned by Maylor (2010), the first projects related to the Apollo mission, although they were considerably high risk, were critical to gain the know-how necessary to send a man to the moon. A typical scenario in the software industry is represented by a **make or buy** decision, namely, choosing between developing a new system or acquiring an existing one with features similar to those needed.

In the rest of this section, we look at factors and techniques to assess the value of a project. These can be used with different purposes:

1. To decide whether a project is worth pursuing
2. To select which project to start out of a portfolio of possible proposals
3. To choose the best project plan, given a project with different plans.

3.1.1 Project Value: Aspects to Consider

Three main factors determine the value generated by a project:

1. **Direct and indirect value**. As mentioned earlier, the value of a project does not refer necessarily and only to the revenues it generates directly and through its outputs. Considerations relative to the social and environmental impact, image and publicity, entering a new market, and know-how acquired are some of the considerations that could add or subtract value from a project.
2. **Sustainability**. Many IT projects start without an idea or a strategy to sustain their outputs. Thus, the outputs of a project might not live long after a project and its resources end. Taking into account the operational costs of a project's outputs and the way in which the project outputs will survive after a project ends is an important consideration to understand whether a project is worth doing.
3. **Alignment with the strategic objectives of the organization**. Ensuring that the project aligns with the goals of an organization is an essential point to consider before a project is worth starting. Alignment with the strategic objectives can determine the **priority** of a project. As pointed out in Maylor (2010), Toyota is a leader in defining priorities: projects are started only if they directly contribute to one of the strategic objectives of the company, namely, *quality, cost*, or *delivery performance*.

3.1.2 Project Risks: Aspects to Consider

Various factors determine the risk profile of a project. Among them are

- **Resource availability**. Projects require the availability of resources—human, financial, and technical—in specific time frames. Although it might be difficult to preempt the required resources in advance, a check on the project's needs is a good sanity check to verify whether a project is worth pursuing.
- **Timing**. Many projects have specific time windows for the delivery of their outputs. Deliver too early or too late and the outputs of the project might be useless. Consider, for instance, a project to build a rocket to reach another planet. The actual launch can occur only on a specific time frame, to take advantage of the relative position of planets. Deliver the rocket too early, and docking and maintenance might become an issue. Deliver too late and you might lose the opportunity to launch.
- **Technical difficulty or uncertainty**. The success of many projects relies on the actual capability of solving various technical challenges. Pointing out what

these challenges are, understanding the level of risk associated with such challenges, and possible corrective or alternative courses of action are important in determining the values and risks of a project.

■ **Project environment and constraints.** Projects are influenced by various constraints, both internal and external. Various internal and external stakeholders will have an interest in positively or negatively influencing a project. Regulations and standards can severely limit what can be done on a project.

3.1.3 Techniques to Assess Value and Risks

Different techniques are available to assess the value and risk generated by a project. Some are based on financial considerations, while others are more qualitative. In the following, we present some of the most used techniques.

3.1.3.1 Financial Methods

3.1.3.1.1 Payback

The simplest financial evaluation is the **payback** method, which measures how long it will take to return a project's investment. When using the payback method, an estimation of the project expenses and incomes determines the profits and losses at the end of each project year. The payback is the year at which the project covers all expenses and starts earning. The shorter the payback, the better.

The payback favors projects that minimize financial exposure. One of the issues with payback is that it does not take into account total profit. This second issue is that it does not measure the *efficiency* with which the money invested in the project is paid back.

3.1.3.1.2 Return of Investment

To overcome some of the limitations of the payback method, another technique that is often employed is the **return of investment** (ROI), which measures how much we get back for each dollar invested. ROI is calculated from the **annual profit**, defined as the *average profit per year* and computed by dividing the profit by the duration of a project:

$$\text{Annual profit} = \frac{\text{incomes} - \text{expenses}}{\text{project duration}} \tag{3.1}$$

The ROI is then computed by dividing the *annual profit* by the total project expenses:

$$\text{ROI} = \frac{\text{annual profit}}{\text{expenses}} \tag{3.2}$$

3.1.3.1.3 Net Present Value and Internal Rate of Return

Payback and ROI do not take into account the effects of inflation, namely, the fact that an amount of money in the future has a lower value than the same amount available now. (In a sense, "better an egg today than a hen tomorrow"). Thus, for longer projects, payback and ROI tend to overestimate profits, which are usually gotten toward the end of a project.

The **net present value** technique (or NPR for short) overcomes this issue by taking into account the inflation rate. Thus, if a reliable estimation of the inflation rate can be provided, the value of future expenses and incomes for a project can be recomputed in terms of their actual value.

In particular, when using NPR, profit and losses are computed using the following formula:

$$\text{Value} = \frac{1}{(1 + r)^i} * \text{amount} \tag{3.3}$$

where r is the inflation rate, *amount* is the net profit at year i, and *value* is the current value of *amount*. Note that the first project year is year 0.

An even more complex method is the **internal rate of return** (IRR for short), which determines the inflation rate which zeroes profits. The interested reader can consult Burke (2006), which contains a nice discussion about financial methods.

3.1.3.1.4 Applying Financial Methods: An Example

Consider two projects, called "Project A" and "Project B," for which we have estimated expenses and incomes as described in Table 3.1. In particular, the table shows that project A is not profitable in the first 2 years and then starts earning. Project B has a similar behavior, but both expenses and incomes are higher.

Suppose we have the resources to start only one of the two projects and we use a financial method to choose which project to activate.

If we use the payback method, we select Project A, since it has a shorter payback period. In fact, year 0 is forecast to end with losses, for Project A. So will year 1. At the end of year 2, however, the financial statement will show earnings of €10, 000.

Table 3.1 Assessing Two Projects Using Financial Methods

	Project A	Project A
Year 0	−€20,000.00	−€30,000.00
Year 1	−€10,000.00	−€30,000.00
Year 2	€40,000.00	€50,000.00
Year 3	.	€100,000.00

Project B's payback is 4 years. Years 0 and 1 end with losses. In year 2, project B earns profits of €50,000, but these are not yet sufficient to cover the expenses of the first 2 years. In year 3, however, the project pays back the initial investment.

If we use the ROI method, we select Project B, since it has the highest ROI. Project A, in fact, has an ROI of 11%, computed as follows:

$$\text{Annual profit} = \frac{€40,000 - (€20,000 + €10,000)}{3} = €3333 \quad (3.4)$$

$$\text{ROI} = \frac{€3333}{€300,000} = 11\% \quad (3.5)$$

The ROI of Project B, whose calculation we leave to the reader, is 38%.

3.1.3.2 Score Matrices

Financial methods help determine the financial viability of a project, but tell nothing about the project characteristics that are not measurable with profits and losses. Therefore, other methods have been proposed to assess a project. One of the simplest is the **score matrix**, which allows one to measure a project along several dimensions and assign it a value.

A **score matrix** is a list of project criteria, each of which is assigned a weight, which measures the importance the criteria have for us or for the organization we work for. The criteria highlight the desirable and undesirable aspects of a project; the weights of desirable features are positive numbers (e.g., from 1 to 5) and the weights of undesirable features are negative numbers (e.g., from −1 to −5).

When we evaluate a project using a score matrix, we measure how well the project satisfies each criterion we have identified, for instance, by assigning a number from 1 (very low) to 5 (very high). We then multiply the scores with the weights and sum all values. Projects scoring a higher value are more desirable than projects with a lower score. Projects can also be compared side by side; hence, the use of the term "matrix" in the name of the technique.

> **EXAMPLE 3.1**
> Table 3.2 shows an example of a score matrix used to evaluate three different projects.
> The starting point is a list of criteria and weights, which we imagine have been selected by an evaluation committee. Note that the last criterion is negative and it has been assigned a high relevance. Thus, the selection process will tend to favor projects in which stakeholders are not difficult to manage.
> The second step is the evaluation of how well each criterion is met by a project. Table 3.2, for instance, shows the value assigned to each project.
> The third and final step is computing the scores, which are shown in the last row of the table. According to the data, "Project 1," the one with the highest score, is preferred over the others.

Table 3.2   A Score Matrix Example

Factor	Description	Weight	Project 1		Project 2		Project 3	
			Value	Total	Value	Total	Value	Total
Profit >30%	The project will yield a profit >30% if no exceptional events occur	3	4	12	4	12	4	12
Low-risk profile	The project does not present particular risks. That is, there is no risk with a very high impact	2	2	4	3	6	3	6
Schedule is not tight	Project delivery does not require activities to be performed in a very tight schedule	3	3	9	2	6	2	6
Manageable complexity	The complexity is manageable	2	1	2	1	2	1	2
Consistent with current business	The project is mainstream with the activities of the organization	1	1	1	1	1	1	1
Stakeholders	Stakeholders are difficult to manage	−4	2	−8	4	−16	3	−12

3.1.3.3 SWOT Analysis

The **strengths, weaknesses, opportunities, and threats** analysis technique is credited to Albert Humphrey, who used it to determine the competitive advantages of the Fortune 500 companies in the 1970s (Friesner, 2013). The technique can also be used to evaluate the feasibility of a project.

The SWOT analysis is usually performed on a two-by-two matrix, like that shown in Figure 3.1. The analysis proceeds by identifying the strengths, weaknesses, opportunities, and threats related to the project under analysis, and by listing them in the matrix shown in Figure 3.1. (Other formats, of course, are possible.) Once the elements of the SWOT analysis are identified, decision makers use the information to evaluate whether the opportunities are worth the effort and how strengths can overcome weaknesses and threats.

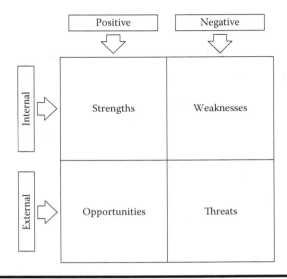

Figure 3.1 A SWOT matrix.

3.1.3.4 Stakeholder Analysis

Stakeholders can exert quite a lot of influence on a project and determine the success or failure of a project. Understanding how stakeholders can influence, positively or negatively, a project is good practice to assess the project's chances of success and to define a **stakeholder management policy**.

The stakeholder identification process is informal as it usually proceeds with a mental swipe of the project environment and the actors who might be directly or indirectly involved or affected by the project and its outputs. Once the stakeholders have been identified, the next step consists in understanding what kind of influence each stakeholder can exert in a project. This allows one to *cluster* the stakeholders and define specific policies for each cluster.

Various ways have been proposed to classify stakeholders. In Maylor (2010), stakeholders are classified in two dimensions:

1. The **power** they can exert in the project
2. The **interest** they have in the project.

This classification allows one to define different policies according to the positioning of the stakeholders in this two-dimensional space.

The extreme case is the one with high-influence and high-power stakeholders. In this case, careful analysis and specific treatment are necessary.

Other situations can use more generic strategies. For instance, it is good practice to keep high-influence and low-power stakeholders informed, while it is safer to keep low-influence and high-power stakeholders satisfied.

Finally, low-influence and low-power stakeholders require minimum effort.

For more complex stakeholder analyses, Yu et al. (2011) propose the **i*** model, which was developed for requirements engineering. The model is based on two concepts, **actors** and **goals**, and models dependencies between these entities. Using the notation, it is thus possible to identify, for each project goal, the stakeholders who have the most influence, whether this influence is positive or negative, and their motivations. The information can then be used to define adequate management strategies.

3.1.3.5 Assessing Sustainability

Evaluating the operational cost of the project outputs helps assess the long-term benefits of a project and what additional actions a project should include to ensure that its results will live after the project ends. This analysis is relevant in several high-risk or highly constrained projects, such as projects to start new companies, research projects, and projects to foster economic development. Often, in fact, these projects deliver benefits as long as steady financing is available; little or nothing survives when the project ends.

For products and services, the two important pieces of information that constitute the basis for a sustainability analysis are (1) the definition of the **business model**, a specification of how the operating costs will be paid for, and (2) when applicable, how profit will be generated. At a minimum, a good business model includes a **value proposition**, which clearly identifies the offering, that is, the product or service being offered and its value for the customers. Additionally, an analysis of the key partners, the key activities, and the key resources allows one to understand which resources are needed. Finally, a financial analysis of costs and revenues helps understand the profitability. This is composed of an analysis of the **cost structure**, which identifies costs and the most costly resources, and of a **revenue stream** analysis, which lists the sources of incomes, highlighting the most important sources.

The financial analysis might also include a **break-even** analysis, which identifies the break-even point, that is, the point at which a product generates neither losses nor gains. If the break-even point is not reached, a product will cause losses; any number of items sold above the break-even point will yield a gain.

The break-even point is computed by looking at three pieces information: the operational costs, the price of each item, and the number of items. The first determines the minimum profit that has to be reached. The second determines the profit in terms of items sold. The break-even point is the number of items in which profit equals the operational costs.

See The Business Model Generation (2013) for a freely available and very compact template, which also includes the identification of **distribution channels** and **customer segments**.

3.1.3.6 A Recap of Project Selection Techniques

Table 3.3 recaps the project selection techniques presented so far, highlighting the type of support each technique offers to evaluate the value and risk generating factors of a project.

Table 3.3   Recap of Project Selection Techniques

	Payback	ROI	NPR	Goal Analysis	Score Matrix	SWOT	Stakeholder Analysis
Direct value	Fully	Fully	Fully	Partially	Partially	Partially	
Indirect value	Partially	Partially	Partially		Partially		
Sustainability	Partially	Partially	Partially		Partially		
Alignment with strategic objectives				Fully	Partially	Fully	
Resource availability					Partially	Fully	
Timing					Partially	Fully	
Technical difficulty or uncertainty					Partially	Fully	
Environment and constraints				Fully	Partially	Fully	Partially

Some techniques provide better coverage than others to specific characteristics. This is qualitatively captured in the table using the terms "Fully," "Partially," or leaving a cell blank, when the technique does not offer support. Thus, for instance, the stakeholder analysis helps one to get a better understanding of the project environment. The technique, however, is very specific and does not offer support to measure other criteria.

3.1.4 The Project Feasibility Document

The **project feasibility document** closes the assessment phase by describing the main characteristics of a project and by analyzing, using the techniques presented above, the value and risks of a project. The document can be used to formally authorize the start of a project.

Thus, a feasibility document contains at least the following information:

- A **statement of work**, which describes what the project will accomplish
- The **business objectives** of the project and its outputs (value) and information about the **business model**, if relevant
- A summary of the **project budget**, which forecasts expenses and incomes
- A summary of the project **milestones**, which is a rough schedule of the project identifying the most important events
- An **analysis of the stakeholders**
- The project **risks**

■ Possible **alternatives** to the project, such as a **make-or-buy** decision
■ An **evaluation** of the project and alternatives, using the techniques described above.

3.2 Formalizing the Project Goals

If the analyses performed with the feasibility study are convincing enough, one of the first activities is fixing and having stakeholders agree on the project scope. This, in fact, constitutes the basis for any further management activity, namely, the definition of the work to be performed, schedule and budget, and the skills required by the team that will perform the work. Project goals, together with the schedule and the budget, are also the basis for contractual agreements with the clients.

Defining project scope is one of the most delicate activities in setting up a project, since

1. It ensures that the project includes all and only the work necessary to achieve the project goals.
2. It establishes a baseline of the work to be performed.
3. It defines a reference document for project acceptance.

The first point is obvious. Adding unnecessary work, in fact, would cause a burden that needs to be sustained either by the project team, which will work on features that are not really necessary, or by the client, who pays for unnecessary work, which, in any case, would negatively affect the project, adding risks and increasing costs.

Ensuring that a project will not include any useless work, however, can be more difficult than it looks. Among the reasons, we mention uncertainties about the product to be built. A customer, for instance, might be uncertain about whether a particular feature is needed or not and, in doubt, add it among the ones to be developed, just to play on the safe side.

In a more difficult scenario, an ambiguous description of the project goals causes the stakeholders to form slightly different opinions about the objectives to achieve. This lack of **integrity** in a project's vision will most likely cause additional work, glitches, and anomalies.

A clear project scope mitigates the risks illustrated above by ensuring that all project stakeholders form a clear view of the project.

The second and third items on the list should also be quite clear. The specification of the project goals determines the characteristics of the products to build. These, in turn, define the work to build the project outputs and the criteria to verify whether the goals have been met.

An additional consideration is that sometimes tight timing constraints tend to compress this activity, shortening the time the manager has to precisely define the goals. The assumption is that the goals are clear and agreed among the stakeholders, even if there is no document describing them in details. Therefore, the limited time available in the project is better used in more productive activities. The risks of this approach, however, typically become clear too late.

The project scope is fixed in a **project scope document**. In particular, it is a good idea to include at least the following information in a project scope document:

- **Project goals and requirements**, which describe what we intend to achieve with the project and the main characteristics of the project and its outputs
- **Assumptions and constraints**, which describe the conditions which have to be met for the project to succeed
- **Project outputs and control points**, which describe the *outputs* of the project and, in some cases, a rough timing of their delivery
- **Project Roster**, which describes the *who*.

The first two items should be written in a way that also defines the **project acceptance criteria**, namely, the minimum conditions for the client to accept a project. Although my experience (together with that of many other project managers) is that client and stakeholders satisfaction is more important than the syntactic compliance with the acceptance criteria, making these explicit beforehand can contribute significantly to establishing a good relationship with the stakeholders and simplify project closing.

Another important piece of information that might be included in a scope document is the procedure to manage changes, namely, how request for changes will be dealt with. This is described in more detail in Chapter 4.

In the rest of the section, we look in more detail at the main content of the scope document.

3.2.1 Project Goals and Requirements

The **project goals and requirements** define what is inside and what is outside the scope of a project and the characteristics of the project outputs.

To elaborate a bit, two good practices help make the goals **SMART** and assign them priorities using the **MoSCoW** classification.

SMART stands for **simple, measurable, agreed upon, realistic**, and **time bound**. A goal is SMART when it has the qualities specified by the acronym. Thus, a SMART goal is simple in its formulation, so that there are no ambiguities in its interpretation; it has measurable criteria to understand whether it has been achieved or not; it is agreed to by all the stakeholders; it can be reached with the resources available in the project; and finally, it has a date by which it has to be reached.

MoSCoW allows the project manager to assign a priority to the goals. The acronym stands for **must have** (features that are essential), **should have** (features that are important but not essential), **could have** (features that would be nice to have), and **won't have** (features that will not be included in the product).

Note that a classification with MoSCoW allows the manager to distinguish between **base scope**, which is the scope required to meet the business requirement and **value-added scope**, which is discretionary but improves the economics of the overall project. This is similar to what Cameron (2005) and Tomczyk (2005) suggest with the identification of the critical success factors.

In many cases, it is also worthwhile to point out goals and work products that will **not** be delivered by the project, because they fall **outside the scope of the work**. The list, of course, should focus on elements typically included in similar projects or items some stakeholders might *assume* as included in the project scope. The goal is to reduce ambiguities and false expectations.

Consider, for instance, a project related to the development of a one-off software for a specific client. Although not explicitly mentioned in the project scope, some stakeholders might take for granted that user documentation and training will be part of the deal. The work necessary for such items, however, might be beyond the resources available to the team. Making clear that such items will not be included can be a way to better align expectations with actual delivery.

Note that, in general, project requirements differ in two ways from the software requirements we have introduced in Chapter 2. The first is that the project requirements are a superset of the software requirements. Many software development projects, in fact, will include activities that are indirectly related to the software being built, such as, for instance, training of resources, production of user manuals, hardware procurement, setup of an infrastructure to provide user support, and setup of the infrastructure to distribute the system. The second is that project requirements are often at a higher level of abstraction than the software requirements.

A final test that should be performed on the requirements is double checking that the **project goals are under the power and control of the project team**. If they are not under the control of the project team, in fact, they are, in the best scenario, under the control of some other project stakeholder or, in the worst scenario, completely out of the control of the project. In the first case, it is better to list the constraints and assumptions that make the goals achievable (see Section 3.2.2). In the second case, their achievement will depend on the good luck of the manager.

Once again, things are not so simple. Consider, for instance, a project related to the experimentation of a new technology. One could set the following measurable criteria as a project goal: "the system will be used by 20,000 people during the experimentation." However, unless people are coerced to use the system, there is no way for the project manager to **ensure** that the system **will** be used by 20,000 users. A more realistic wording could highlight that the "experimentation will be set so that at least 20,000 people will be offered the chance to try the system."

3.2.2 Project Assumptions and Constraints

Project **assumptions** and **constraints** define important hypotheses on which the manager bases the achievement of the project goals.

Assumptions are those conditions that are considered to be true, but might not in fact be. Assumptions are not under the control of the project manager, but they might be under the control of some project stakeholders. When this is the case, assumptions can be used to define the duties and obligations of project stakeholders. Consider a case in which the installation of a new system requires the client to stop operating his or her business for a given period. Stopping operations is clearly not in the power of the project manager, who will list this operation as an essential assumption for project success.

Whether they are under the control of project stakeholders or not, assumptions should be properly addressed in the risk management plan, finding appropriate management strategies in case they cannot be satisfied or turn out to be false (see Section 4.2).

Constraints, by contrast, are known limitations, which shape and define the work we can do. They are used to explain why we set some goals and not others and why we structure the work in some way rather than another.

3.2.3 Project Outputs and Control Points

A **deliverable** is defined in Project Management Institute (2004) as **a unique, measurable, and verifiable work product**. Deliverables are the result of work performed in the project and, in many cases, they are also the prerequisites of project activities. For software development projects, examples of deliverables include a software system, a requirements document, and a user manual.

A very common classification distinguishes between **internal** and **external** deliverables. The former are functional to the implementation of the plan and are used only by the project team. As such, they can maintain a level of informality, which often simplifies their production and management. The latter are delivered to the customers. They often require additional work to ensure proper quality and formal procedures and, in some cases, a bit of ceremony, like, for example, delivery in hard copy through courier.

Deliverables might contain sensitive information. It is thus good practice to define the **dissemination level** of each deliverable. In common scenarios, circulation can be public, limited to selected stakeholders, to the project team, or only to selected project members. Such classification is an integral part of the project communication plan and is described in further detail in Section 5.3.

Milestones are defined by the Project Management Institute (2004) as **a significant event in the project**. Milestones are identified, at a minimum, by a label and a date, and they are typically used to highlight, significant control points, in the plan. Examples of milestones include a *mid-term project review*, or *phase transition milestones*, to identify the transition from one project phase to the next.

Deliverables and milestones can be presented as textual lists (like we do in the example below). They are also very often inserted in the graphical representation of plans (e.g., AON or Gantt chart), with the advantage of showing which activity or activities are responsible for the production of any specific deliverable.

According to the formality of the project development process that is being adopted, milestones can be used in different ways:

- To form (and present) a **high-level roadmap** of the project: milestones represent how the project unfolds in a series of significant events.
- As a **verification point** in the project: milestones identify control points in the project, which serve as a general "orientation" mechanism to steer the project in one direction or another.
- As a **gate** in the project: milestones clearly separate different phases of the project; if the goals of the milestone are not achieved, the transition to the next phase is blocked.

There is no mechanical technique to identify the milestones and deliverables of a project. They depend on the project type and their identification can be supported by adopting a development standard, by personal experience, or by discussing and negotiating them with the project stakeholders.

EXAMPLE 3.2

Table 3.4 shows the standards the European Union enforces for the specification of deliverables produced by the research projects it sponsors. In particular, the following information is associated with each deliverable:

- A unique identifier, typically an integer number
- The name of the deliverable
- The nature of the deliverable, which can be one of the following: a report (R), a prototype (P), a demonstrator (D), or other (O)
- The dissemination level, which, simplifying a bit on the EU rules, can be public (PU), restricted to the project team (RE), or restricted to the project stakeholders (CO)
- The delivery date, expressed in the number of months after the start of the project
- The partner (team member) responsible for the delivery of the project.

Similarly, Table 3.5 shows (a subset of) the milestones of a European Research project. Milestones have the following information:

Table 3.4   An Example of Deliverables

Del. ID	Deliverable Name	Nature	Dissemination Level	Delivery Date (Project Month)	Responsible Parter
1	Requirements	R	CO	0	FBK
2	Architecture UML diagram	R	CO	1	FBK
3	Software	P	PU	6	FBK
4	User manual	R	PU	12	FBK

Table 3.5 An Example of Milestones

Milestone Number	Milestone Name	Date (Month from Start)	Means of Verification
M0.1	Kick-off	1	Kick-off meeting done, meeting minutes available, project collaboration tools available.
M0.2	Experimental sites 1&2 up and running	12	Experimental sites 1 & 2 up and running.
M0.3	Midterm review	18	At least 80% of activities starting before M18 have started; at least 80% of activities ending before M18 have ended.
M0.4	Experimental sites 2&4 up and running	24	Experimental sites 3 & 4 up and running.

- A unique identifier
- A name
- A date, for instance, expressed in months from the start of the project
- A description of the purpose of the milestone
- Means of verification, which specify how it is possible to verify the achievement of the work associated with the milestone.

3.2.4 *Project Roster*

The **project roster** is the list of people participating in the project, together with their role and other information, such as the contact point. The project roster is a simple practice that allows the project manager to identify the project stakeholders and, in the process, simplify the definition of a project communication plan and favor team interaction.

3.3 Deciding the Work

Now that we have properly described the main goals and the boundaries of our project; we can start identifying the activities that we need to carry out in the project. This is very often accomplished with a **work breakdown structure** or WBS from now on. The notation, developed in the 1960s alongside the program evaluation and review technique (PERT), is defined in Project Management Institute (2004) as "a (deliverable-oriented) hierarchical decomposition of the work to be executed by the project team to accomplish projects objectives and create the required deliverable."

Today, the technique is widely adopted and many project management and process standards make its use compulsory. For instance, NASA (1994) and NASA

(2007) require a WBS to be built for each major program or project and suggest its use in any project, big or small, when it can be practically done so.

A WBS establishes the basis for

- Defining the work to be performed in a project
- Showing how various activities are related to the project objectives
- Establishing a framework for defining, assigning, and monitoring work and costs
- Identifying the organizational elements responsible for accomplishing the work.

See PERT Coordinating Group (1963) for a more detailed description.

In the rest of this section, we are going to describe the main construction techniques for WBSs and some rules of thumb to build and evaluate their quality and soundness.

3.3.1 Building a WBS

A WBS is a tree in which the root node represents a project or its main output. Each level of decomposition shows how a node of the tree can be structured and organized in more elementary work components.

WBSs come in two different notations. The first is graphical: the WBS is shown as a tree unfolding from top to bottom. The second is textual and similar to the table of contents of a book. The nodes of a WBS can be labeled according to their position in the tree: the top level is numbered "1," its children "1.1," . . ., "1.n," and so on for all the nodes.

> **EXAMPLE 3.3**
>
> Figure 3.2 shows a graphical representation of a WBS for the development of a software application for mobile phones.
>
> The WBS is structured in four levels.
>
> The first level of decomposition contains the main activities, including the procurement of tools we need for development (1.5) and writing the user manual (1.6). Tests (1.3.4) are organized in three different types of activities: unit tests (1.3.4.1), system tests (1.3.4.2), and integration tests (1.3.4.3).

From the example above, we can infer various important characteristics of a WBS:

1. The WBS does not specify the order in which the activities have to be executed, nor does it specify any dependency among activities. For instance, the procurement of development tools has to be completed before coding can start; the WBS, however, does not show this dependency.
2. The decomposition follows the **100%** and the **mutual exclusion rules**. That is, each level of decomposition includes all and only the items that are nec-

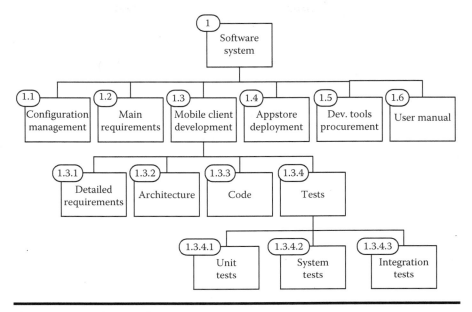

Figure 3.2   WBS example.

essary to develop the parent node. Moreover, there are no overlaps between nodes. Each node specifies work different from that of any other node. In this way, the WBS becomes a powerful tool to define what is in the scope of the project and to allocate responsibility for the development of each activity.

3. The WBS tree does not need to be balanced. In the diagram, for instance, some activities stop after the first level of decomposition, while others are refined up to the fourth level.

4. The WBS can contain support activities, such as "management" and "development tools procurement."

The level of decomposition and detail of a WBS depends upon its use. For instance, if the WBS is used as the basis for planning, its refinement process stops when we reach a level for which we can reliably estimate duration and effort.

According to NASA (1994), the leaves of the WBS must be such that the "completion of an element is both measurable and verifiable by persons (i.e., quality assurance persons) who are independent of those responsible for the element's completion." Thus, the advantage is that the WBS provides a solid basis for planning and monitoring and "no other structure (e.g., code of account, functional organization, budget and reporting, cost element) satisfactorily provides an equally solid basis for incremental project performance assessment."

3.3.2 WBS Decomposition Styles

Different decomposition styles allow one to build a WBS.

In a **product-oriented** WBS, the decomposition proceeds by identifying the items that must be developed to build deliverables. A product WBS thus establishes a one-to-one correspondence between project activities and project (sub)products. This simplifies accountability, since the responsibility for a group of activities in a project will correspond to the responsibility of delivering a specific system component. When using a product-oriented WBS, a good rule is to ensure that tightly connected components are not separated in the WBS, since such a decomposition style does not allow one to allocate responsibility for integration.

In a **process-oriented** WBS, the decomposition proceeds by taking into account the activities that are necessary to carry out the project. One advantage of the process-oriented decomposition is that it can include activities, such as management, which are not directly related to the development of a product, but which are still necessary in a project. Another advantage is that it is simpler to build a WBS by analogy, using a similar project as a reference. This can also be considered a weakness, since the WBS could result in being too generic and uninformative.

To get the best of both worlds, one can use a **hybrid** WBS. A hybrid WBS contains both process- and product-oriented nodes. This approach is the one suggested, for instance, by NASA (2007), where a part of the WBS is a specification of the components of a product and the remaining parts are the activities necessary to manage the project, integrate the components, and perform quality control.

Other types of WBS highlight the **organizational** or **geographical** aspects of work. For these WBSs, the first level of decomposition contains, respectively, the **organizational structure** or the **geographically distributed teams** responsible for the development of a group of activities. Starting with the second level, the WBS contains the work to be performed. These decomposition styles can be effective for highly cross-functional projects or for projects in which geographical distribution is significant.

As a specific case of organizational WBS, we mention that defined in NASA (1994) and the Department of Defense (2011), which distinguish between **Project Work Breakdown Structure** (PWBs) and **Contract Work Breakdown Structures** (CWBs). In this case, the top levels of the WBS contain a logical structuring of the project or program, while the lower levels represent the WBSs of the contractors responsible for the development of the project. Thus, for instance, NASA (1994) and the Department of Defense (2011) suggest defining PWBs organized at three levels:

1. Level 1 is the entire project or program.
2. Level 2 includes the projects or major elements to develop the project.
3. Level 3 includes the components necessary to develop the major elements.

Level 3 items constitute the statement of work for contractors and the first level of decomposition of the CWBs, whose development proceeds according to the standards of the different contractors, as shown in Figure 3.3.

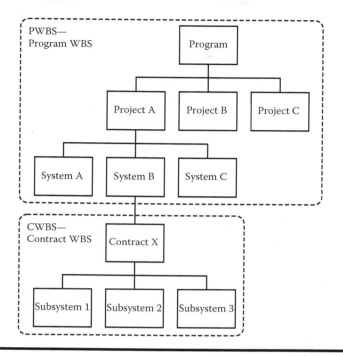

Figure 3.3   Example of PWBS and CWBS.

Remark

When defining the work to be performed, the term **work package** is often used. There are different usages and slightly different definitions of the term, so it might be worthwhile to have a look at them.

According to the Project Management Institute (2004), a work package is an element of the WBS at which **estimation for time and costs can be reliably provided**. In bigger projects, this can correspond to the leaves of the WBS, rather than the higher level of the WBS. Note, however, that the leaves of a WBS could be the top level element of finer-grained work breakdown structures, like we have seen for a contract WBS.

NASA (1994) adopts a different definition. A work package is the **unit of work required to complete a specific job**, such as a report, a test, a drawing, a piece of hardware, or a service, which is within the responsibility of one operating unit within an organization.

Finally, in common practice, the term *work package* is often used to denote the **first level of decomposition of a WBS**. This is, for instance, the notation used for research projects sponsored by the European Union and other funding agencies.

3.3.3 WBS Dictionary

A **WBS dictionary** helps to annotate each element of the WBS with more detailed and structured information, such as

- Title and item number, to connect the description to an element of the WBS
- Detailed description of the element, including, for instance, quantities, relevant associated work, and contractual items, where applicable.

Additional information can help manage a WBS dictionary over time. Some WBS dictionary templates thus require one to provide **references and links to other elements of the project**, such as references to the scope document, budget and reporting, contract reference, and **information about the history of the element**, such as, for instance, revision number, author, and authorization.

See CDC (2013) for a template of a WBS dictionary and Space Division—North American Rockwell (1971) for a good example of a WBS and a WBS dictionary.

3.3.4 WBS Construction Methodologies

WBSs can be built top-down, bottom-up, or by analogy.

In the **top-down** approach, the construction of the WBS proceeds from the top level down to the leaves. It is usually best suited for projects that are well known or whose structure is clear. One risk is overlooking activities (e.g., achieving a "90% decomposition").

In the **bottom-up** approach, the process proceeds in the opposite way. First, the leaves of the WBS are identified and then these are grouped in homogeneous items, thus giving structure to the WBS. It is best suited for projects that are new for a company or for the team responsible for their development and they work better with brainstorming sessions in which the whole team is involved. One technique that can be used for building the WBS elements is the so-called **post-it on a wall**. As each element of the WBS is identified, it is written on a post-it and posted on a wall. The post-it can then be physically grouped together to form the WBS structure. The main risks with bottom-up constructions are building WBSs that are too detailed and violate the mutual exclusion rule.

The third option, construction by **analogy**, starts from an existing WBS, which is adapted and customized for the project at hand. It can be very effective when an organization standardizes the structure of its projects.

3.4 Estimating

Yogi Berra is reported to have said that "it is difficult to make predictions, especially about the future." The sentence could not be more appropriate for estimations of the work to be performed in a project. When we consider software projects, some of the characteristics of software, such as intangibility, flexibility, and complexity, make the estimation process even more complex.

In this section, we will look at some of the most common estimation techniques. The starting point is a discussion about what characterizes a project task. We then discuss the nature of estimations and continue with the presentation of the main techniques to estimate.

3.4.1 Effort, Duration, and Resources

Estimation is the process that determines the requirements to carry out an activity. These are expressed in terms of

- Duration, namely, how long an activity will last
- Effort, namely, the amount of work necessary to complete an activity
- Resources, necessary to complete an activity.

Duration is the amount of time an activity lasts. It is measured in calendar units, such as days, weeks, months, and years. Sometimes the string "calendar-" is prefixed to unambiguously specify the nature of the measure.

Effort is the amount of work required to perform a task, and is measured using man-hours, man-days, man-months, or man-years meaning, respectively, the amount of work expressed by one worker in an hour, a day, a month, or a year. Thus, for instance, an activity requiring 40 man-hours can be completed by a person working for 40 h.

The main **resource** needed for software development projects is **manpower**, which is expressed in terms of **units of work**, that is, the effort that can be produced per calendar period.

Manpower is further qualified by identifying the **type of resource** required to carry out the work, namely, by identifying which kind of competences and what kind of personnel is needed. For instance, the development of a simulator for a rocket system might require the work of an expert in aerodynamics.

Finally, **manpower** is determined by the **work calendar** and the **percentage of availability**.

The first determines the maximum number of units of work that can be expressed during a calendar unit. For the service industry, typical values for one resource (one person) are 8 man-hours per calendar-day and 40 man-hours per calendar-week, considering 2 days of rest per week. Other calendars are used. For instance, industries working in shifts have a one-to-one relationship between units of work and calendar time; this is achieved by having three people working 8 h each throughout the day.

The percentage of availability reduces the maximum presence of a resource and it is used when a resource is not available full-time. For instance, if a resource is working part-time for an organization or for a project, the percentage of availability might be 50%.

For many tasks, a simple relationship links effort, duration, and manpower:

$$D = \frac{E}{M} \tag{3.6}$$

where D is the duration of an activity, E is the effort required by the activity, and M is the manpower required to carry out an activity. Of the three variables, one is usually estimated, another chosen, and the third computed.

The equation holds for *reasonable* values of D, E, and M. In fact, as M increases, so does the burden of coordinating the work and exchanging information (Brooks, 1995). So, please, never plan to use 1000 people so that you can finish in half a day an activity that requires an effort of 500 man-days, like a famous Dilbert cartoon suggested.

Most activities are estimated either in duration or in effort, according to the nature of the work. For instance, the activity "writing a document" is best estimated by looking at the effort. In this case, for instance, we can estimate the effort, choose the manpower to allocate to the task, and use the equation above to compute the duration of the task.

The equation does not hold for any type of task, though. For instance, the activity "waiting for the foundations of a home to solidify" requires a fixed duration and is independent of manpower and effort.

Finally, note that some activities might also require one to specify other types of resources, namely, materials and equipment:

■ **Material** is necessary for certain activities and is consumed while work progresses. The measurement unit for material depends on the kind of material used. For instance, in building a house, a given amount of concrete will be used to carry out the construction activities.

■ **Equipment** includes the tools required for carrying out work. In an oil exploration project, for instance, certain activities will require drilling equipment. Equipment is measured by the number of units that are necessary to carry out a given activity. Equipment is not consumed by the execution of the activity; that is, after the activity has been completed, the equipment can be used for another purpose. The availability of equipment introduces constraints in a plan. Thus, the equipment typically specified in a plan includes tools that are available in limited quantities or that are costly to use (and might impact the project's budget). Consider, for instance, the development of a software system to control a robotic surgeon. Certain project activities might require access to a robotic arm. If this requirement is made explicit in the plan, it becomes possible to schedule activities so that no overlaps or conflicts arise in the usage of this limited resource.

3.4.2 The "Quick" Approach to Estimation

The simplest and probably most commonly used approaches to estimation are **expert judgment** and **analogy**. The project manager, possibly in collaboration with the team or other experts, provides estimations using his/her experience or by looking at similar projects. The approach has the advantage of being very fast and simple. See the next section, however, for a discussion about some of the limitations.

These estimations can either proceed bottom-up or top-down.

In the bottom-up approach, the manager provides an estimation for each leaf of the WBS. If the estimations are effort-based, these can be easily propagated upward, thus determining the effort required for each node of the WBS. For instance, the effort required by a node A of the WBS whose children are $A_1, \ldots, A_n$ is the sum of the efforts of its children, namely, $effort(A_1) + \cdots + effort(A_n)$.

In the top-down approach, the process is reversed. The manager provides an estimation for the overall project. If the estimations are effort-driven, the effort of each activity of the WBS is then determined by distributing it to the lower levels. The propagation to the lower levels, however, is constrained by a relationship that is weaker than the one we defined above. If a node A of the WBS, for which we have estimated an effort of E_a, has children $A_1, \ldots, A_n$, then we can only say that $effort(A_1) + \cdots + effort(A_n) = E_A$, but we cannot tell exactly how much effort has to be allocated to each of $A_1, \ldots, A_n$, using the structure of the WBS only. Rules of thumb are often used: for instance, the total effort of a project is split into different activities in percentages that are similar to those measured in previous projects.

Whether a top-down or bottom-up approach is more appropriate depends on the project at hand. The rule of thumb is that top-down estimations will tend to underestimate the duration or effort (since they might abstract away details), while bottom-up estimations tend to overestimate the effort or the duration, because too much importance is given to details. In my experience, bottom-up estimations are simpler to come out with. It is, however, a subjective matter and your experience might be different.

If more than a person is involved in the estimation process, various techniques can be used to elicit information. We mention the Delphi method, which is presented in more detail in Section 5.3.3.3.

3.4.3 The Uncertainty of Estimations

(Software) project managers make many implicit and explicit assumptions when estimating the resources necessary for an activity and many estimations are based on a number of "ifs."

For instance, consider the problem of estimating how long it will take to complete a "requirement definition" activity, which produces a software requirements document. The reasoning could proceed as follows: *if* the final requirement document will be *about* 100 pages and *if* analysts can produce *about* 2.5 pages per hour, then the work will require *about* 40 man-hours. If one person will be able to dedicate *about* 80% of her time, then the actual duration will be *about* 50 h. The final estimation depends upon all these assumptions. For instance, if the estimation on the number of pages to write is increased by 10% and the productivity is reduced to 2 pages per hour, the duration of the tasks increases to 68.75 h.

On top of the "random" guess of the project manager, work has some implicit variability, which depends on many factors. Weather, for instance, might interfere with the construction of a house. The productivity of workers changes the speed at which progress is achieved.

We can look at estimations as random variables characterized by a mean and a variance. Thus, precise scheduling techniques should or could be based on the rules of probabilistic reasoning. This is what certain techniques, like PERT and critical chain management, do. However, the requirement of coming out with *precise* numbers (e.g., "When does the project end? How much does it cost?") and the need to keep plans simple (e.g., "The requirements document will be delivered on April 1, 2013" and not "between April 1 and April 13, with a probability of 68%") favors an approach in which we choose a value and use it like it was a certain measure.

Thus, when we provide an estimation, we give our best guess of a task duration. An important implication, however, comes from considering the error between our estimation and the mean value of the actual duration (work) of a task. In fact, estimations (and estimators) can be **optimistic** if they are below the mean value or **pessimistic**, if they are above the mean value. In the first case, the actual plan is more likely to run late; in the second case, the plan will more likely over allocate resources (e.g., time and manpower). This is shown in Figure 3.4, where the area

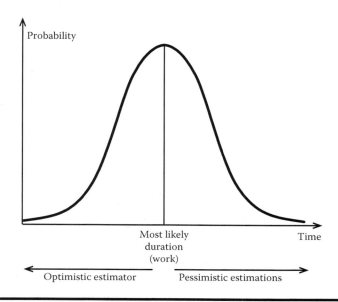

Figure 3.4 Estimations as random variables.

left of the mean corresponds to an optimistic estimation, while the area right of the mean includes the pessimistic estimations.

We tend to be optimistic in our estimations. For this reason, it is often the case that estimators *pad* their estimations to make sure they end above the most likely duration. If worst comes to worst, the reasoning goes, we will end earlier. Some rules of thumb go up to doubling the value of the estimation. Thus, in the example above, given our initial estimation of 40 h, we would schedule a plan in which the task takes twice as much time, namely, 80 h. This would easily accommodate the variations we mentioned above, but the consequence, in general, is that of building plans that are equally unrealistic.

There is also a subtler risk. As we acknowledge our implicit or explicit padding, we might be tempted to use estimations as a negotiation factor. If our estimations do not satisfy upper management (which is responsible for allocating resources) or our client, we might be tempted to just change the numbers so that they end up as the ones our stakeholders expect. Consider the example above: if 40 h of writing requirements are too long, why not reduce them to 30? After all, it is still relatively close to what we believe to be the most likely duration. The risks of such an attitude are clear, both in the short term and in the long term. In the short term, our plan becomes unreliable, since it is based on numbers chosen to please stakeholders, rather than to measure the work that has to be done. In the long term, it becomes difficult not only to make sense of our past plans, but also to use past experience and know-how to become more reliable in our estimations.

Various techniques have been proposed to tackle or mitigate the problems described above. **PERT** considers the random nature of estimations. **Algorithmic techniques** support the estimation process of the software system by relying on mathematical models that take stock of data collected over the years. **Agile methodologies**, by contrast, take a more radical approach by iterating the estimation process many times till convergence is reached or the project ends.

3.4.4 PERT

PERT was developed in the 1960s as a methodology to define and monitor projects (PERT Coordinating Group, 1963; Hamilton, 1964). The goal of the technique is to assess the probability of a plan to finish on a certain date, given the probabilistic estimations of the activities of composing the plan.

To use PERT, three values have to be assigned to each activity: an **optimistic value**, a **most likely value**, and a **pessimistic value**. (The values can be elicited using the techniques described above.) The most likely duration of an activity is then computed assuming a beta distribution. According to the distribution, the median duration of an activity is

$$t = \frac{(a + 4m + b)}{6} \tag{3.7}$$

where a is the optimistic value, b the pessimistic value, and m the most likely value. The variance of t is given by the formula

$$\sigma^2 = \frac{(b-a)^2}{6} \tag{3.8}$$

Standard statistical methods can then be used to sum all the activities of a plan and determine, in such a way, the duration of the overall plan, together with the confidence of the data.

3.4.5 Algorithmic Techniques

Algorithmic techniques determine the effort or the duration required for developing a software system, given some of its characteristics. In other words, given a set of measurable features of a system $x_1, \ldots, x_n$, an algorithmic technique defines a function $f(x_1, \ldots, x_n)$, such that

$$f(\overline{x_1}, \ldots, \overline{x_n}) \tag{3.9}$$

returns the *effort*, *duration*, and *team size* required to develop a system described by $\langle \overline{x_1}, \ldots, \overline{x_n} \rangle$. The function f is typically defined by analyzing and interpolating data of sample projects for which both the input values (the measurable characteristics) and the output characteristics (effort, duration, and manpower) are available.

The advantages of the algorithmic techniques are evident, since they potentially provide a reliable, repeatable, and objective way to estimate fundamental parameters of a software development plan. Delivery dates, project budget, and so on can be derived from the measures computed by these algorithms.

Algorithmic techniques also have some limitations. The first is given by the models themselves, since they are derived from a limited (although growing) number of sample projects.

The second is given by the inputs to the models, namely, the values characterizing the system to build. These are not always easy to assess and might require significant analysis work, often performed by people with specific training and certifications.

It must be pointed out, however, that the analysis process required to come out with estimations has a value in itself, if not in the values it produces. In fact, the application of the algorithmic technique helps one to get a better understanding of the system to build.

Two big families of algorithmic techniques exist:

1. **Function-based** estimations measure a system in terms of its functions. The most well-known technique in this family is probably the **function point** (FP) technique. A more recent addition includes the **object point** technique, to mention one.

2. **Size-based** estimations measure a system in terms of its physical size, as well as measures in lines of code. The most well-known technique is probably the **constructive cost modeling** (COCOMO) family of models.

Finally, some techniques mix both function- and size-based approaches. This is the case, for instance, of **web-objects**, a technique to estimate web applications.

Several studies have been published on software estimations. One famous historical reference is Boehm (1981). An analysis of the existing literature, based on 304 papers and pointing to many resources, can be found in Jørgensen and Shepperd (2007).

3.4.5.1 Function Points

The FP technique was proposed by Albrecht in the 1970s (see, e.g., Albrecht (1979)). It finds its original application in business systems, but it has since evolved to embrace a wide range of systems and applications. Today, it has a large user base and an organization, the **International Function Points User Group**, to support its diffusion, application, and evolution (International function point user group, 2013c).

FP estimations are based on 19 different characteristics of a system, five of which refer to the functional characteristics of a system and 14 of which refer to nonfunctional aspects. These characteristics can typically be provided once the requirements of a system have been defined. The technique can, thus, be applied only after a part of the development process has started.

The five functional measures are

1. **User inputs:** the number of user inputs, or elements in the system which require an input from the user.
2. **User outputs:** the number of user outputs, or elements in the system which produce an output.
3. **User inquiries:** the number of user inputs that generate a software response, such as word count, search result, or software status.
4. **Internal logical files:** the number of files created and used dynamically by the system.
5. **External interfaces:** the number of external files that connect with the software to an external system. For instance, if the software communicates with a device, it is counted as one external interface.

The data above are collected and classified according to a three-step complexity scale, which distinguishes among simple, average, and complex elements. Thus, for each of the five characteristics described above, we need to produce a three-dimensional vector: number of **simple** elements, number of **average** elements, and number of **complex** elements.

The technique defines a matrix of weights to take into account the impact that different elements have in determining the complexity of a project. Each pair *functional characteristic, complexity* has a weight. Thus, for instance, simple user inputs have a weight of 3, average user inputs a weight of 4, and complex user inputs a weight of 5.

The functional size of a system S, called by the method **unadjusted function points** (*UFP*), is the weighted sum of the characteristics of the system.

It is computed as follows:

$$\text{UFP} = \sum_{i=1}^{5} \begin{bmatrix} k_i^S & k_i^A & k_i^C \end{bmatrix} \cdot \begin{bmatrix} n_i^S \\ n_i^A \\ n_i^C \end{bmatrix} \qquad (3.10)$$

where the index i runs over the five characteristics (user inputs, user outputs, ...); the vector $[n_i^S, n_i^A, n_i^C]$ is the number of simple (^{S}), average (^{A}), and complex (^{C}) elements of type i that we forecast in S. Finally, $[k_i^S, k_i^A, k_i^C]$ is the weight assigned by the method to simple (^{S}), average (^{A}), and complex (^{C}) elements of type i.

UFP provides an estimation of the functional size of the system. Systems with a higher *UFP* are more complex to develop than systems with a lower *UFP*. However, *UFP* does not take into account the complexity deriving from nonfunctional characteristics of a system. For instance, high reliability systems are difficult to implement, requiring more effort. The method therefore introduces 14 questions that list various nonfunctional features of a system, which can positively or negatively affect a project. The questions are summarized in Table 3.6.

Similar to the functional evaluation, managers answer the 14 questions by providing, for each question, a qualitative answer ranging from 0 (irrelevant) to 5 (very influential).

The answers are summed together and added to the magic number 65, thus yielding a value in the range 65–135, where 135 is obtained when the answer to all the questions is 5, since $65 + 5 * 14 = 135$. The value, divided by 100, is called the **value adjustment factor**, or VAF, and measures the additional (or reduced) effort that is necessary to take care of the implementation of nonfunctional requirements.

Formally,

$$\text{VAF} = \frac{65 + \sum_{i=1}^{14} C_i}{100} \qquad (3.11)$$

VAF is then multiplied by *UFP* to yield the function points (*FP*):

$$\text{FP} = \text{VAF} * \text{UFP} \qquad (3.12)$$

FP measures the complexity of the system to be developed.

Table 3.6 Nonfunctional Characteristics of a System (FP Method)

1. Does the system require reliable backup and recovery?
2. Are data communications required?
3. Are there distributed processing functions?
4. Is performance critical?
5. Will the system run in an existing, heavily utilized operational environment?
6. Does the system require online data entry?
7. Does the online data entry require the input transaction to be built over multiple screens or operations?
8. Are the master files updated online?
9. Are the inputs, outputs, files, or inquiries complex?
10. Is the internal processing complex?
11. Is the code to be designed reusable?
12. Are conversion and installation included in the design?
13. Is the system designed for multiple installations in different organizations?
14. Is the application designed to facilitate change and ease of use by the user?

Once we have the estimation in function points, we can use it to estimate the effort required for the implementation of the system. There are two main approaches to map function points into effort. The first transforms the function points into a size measure (for which effort estimations can then be provided).

The second, which is preferred by the people advocating the use of function points, uses productivity metrics, such as **man-months per function point**, to estimate the effort required to develop a system. The actual values of productivity metrics depend on many factors, among which are team experience, organization maturity, and application fields.

Some example values can be found in Longstreet (2008), where work increases exponentially with a system's size. It starts at 1.3 h/FP for a system of 50 FP, continuing with 12.1 h/FP for a system of about 7000 FP, and ending with 133.6 h/FP for a system of about 15,000 FPs. See Longstreet (2008) for the complete set of data.

Organizations willing to use the technique, however, should establish their own measurement programs to determine their productivity metrics.

3.4.5.2 COCOMO

Constructive cost model (COCOMO) is a family of estimation techniques first introduced by Barry Boehm in the 1980s and steadily improved over the years. The method was defined in the context of a broader analysis of software economics, which focused on improving the capacity of reasoning about software development costs and benefits, value delivered, and quality (Boehm, 1984; Boehm and Sullivan, 2000). The techniques are very detailed and make assumptions about the development process that is used to build a system. Moreover, different models are used during the development process to increase the accuracy of the estimations.

In this book, we will present the basic model, called COCOMO81, abstracting away many details and just hint about the more recent formulation of the model, called COCOMO II and introduced in 2000.

The COCOMO models use a size measure as the starting point for estimations and define a simple relationship between size and effort and duration of a project, which is captured by the following formula:

$$\text{OUTPUT} = A \cdot (\text{SIZE})^B \cdot M \tag{3.13}$$

that is, the *OUTPUT* of the estimation (effort and duration) depends on a system's *SIZE* and three other elements *A*, *M*, and *B*. In general, *A* and *B* are organizational-dependent constants, while *M* depends on the project at hand. Note that *A* and *M* have a multiplicative effect, while *B* has an exponential effect over the *size*. Reference values for *A* and *B* are given by the model.

3.4.5.2.1 COCOMO81

COCOMO81 is the first COCOMO model. It was defined by Barry Boehm and his group using a carefully screened sample of 63 projects developed between 1964 and 1979 (Boehm, 1981). The model applies to the software development practices in use by then, among which the use of the waterfall development process is probably the most relevant assumption.

The method defines three different variants, which can be applied at different stages of the development process as the information about a project increases. The **basic model** can be used when little information is available; the **intermediate model** can be used when the requirements are defined, and the **advanced model** can be used when the architecture is sketched.

In more detail, COCOMO81 computes effort and development time as follows:

$$\text{PM} = A_{\text{PM}} \cdot (\text{KSLOC})^{B_{\text{PM}}} \cdot M \tag{3.14}$$

$$\text{TDEV} = A_{\text{TDEV}} \cdot (\text{PM})^{B_{\text{TDEV}}} \tag{3.15}$$

$$\text{TEAM} = \text{PM}/\text{TDEV} \tag{3.16}$$

where *PM* is the total effort, *TDEV* is the ideal duration of the project, *TEAM* is the team size, and *KSLOC* is the estimated number of thousands of lines code. In all three variants, *A* and *B* are constants, while *M* (which is not required in the basic model) is computed by looking at various project and product characteristics.

The actual values of *A* and *B* depend on the overall complexity of the project. COCOMO81, in particular, distinguishes between three types of projects, **organic**, **semidetached**, and **embedded**, according to the project characteristics listed in Table 3.7. For each type of project, the model provides values for A_{PM}, A_{TDEV}, B_{PM}, and B_{TDEV}, as shown in Table 3.8.

Table 3.7   COCOMO Development Modes

Project Type	Main Characteristics
Organic	Simple projects with clear requirements and about which the performing organizations have a thorough understanding and experience. No or few technical and development risks.
Semidetac head	More complex projects. The performing organization has considerable know-how in the application field and with tools to be used for development. Some technical or development risks.
Embedded	Complex system with high variability in requirements. The organization has moderate know-how in the area. Various technical and development risks.

Table 3.8   COCOMO Base Model

	APM	BPM	ATDEV	BTDEV
Organic	2.40	1.05	2.50	0.38
Semidetached	3.00	1.12	2.50	0.35
Embedded	3.60	1.20	2.50	0.32

Finally, note that the formula to determine the team size is the same as in Equation 3.6.

The intermediate model takes into account various project- and product-related characteristics, which can contribute positively or negatively to the overall effort and to the project schedule. This is reflected by computing M as the product of 15 different parameters obtained by answering 15 different questions with a value from 1 (very low impact) to 6 (extremely high impact). Different from the FP method, each evaluation corresponds to a numerical constant, with values ranging from a minimum of 0.75 to a maximum of 1.56.

Tables 3.9 and 3.10, for instance, show the values assigned to the parameter RELY (required software reliability) and the corresponding assignment criteria. If RELY is evaluated as very low, for instance, the corresponding value to be used for the computation of M is 0.75, yielding a reduction in the effort of 25%.

The parameters considered for the M factor can be organized in four different classes. Two of them describe the characteristics of the project outputs. They are

1. **Product attributes**, which model aspects related to the software to be developed and include aspects such as expected reliability, database size, and overall product complexity

Table 3.9   COCOMO RELY Parameter

	Very Low	Low	Nominal	High	Very High	Extremely High
Required Software Reliability (RELY)	0.75	0.88	1	1.15	1.4	–

Table 3.10 Explanation of the COCOMO RELY Parameter

Very low	The effect of a software failure is simply the inconvenience incumbent on the developers to fix the fault.
Low	The effect of a software failure is a low level, easily recoverable loss to users.
Nominal	The effect of a software failure is a moderate loss to users, but a situation for which one can recover without extreme penalty.
High	The effect of a software failure can be a major financial loss or a massive human inconvenience.
Very high	The effect of a software failure can be the loss of human life.
Extremely high	No rating—defaults to very high.

2. **Computer attributes**, which take into account aspects related to the platform that will be used to run the software and include aspects such as constraints related to performance and stability.

The remaining two classes describe project attributes. They are

1. **Personnel attributes**, which model the influence of the personnel involved in the project and include five parameters related to the capability and experience of the personnel
2. **Project attributes**, which model some aspects related to the project organization and include three parameters describing tool support and automation and schedule constraints.

3.4.5.2.2 COCOMO II

COCOMO II significantly revises and enhances COCOMO81 to take into account several new factors that intervened after the first definition of the model. Among them are new development processes, new development paradigms (e.g., object orientation), and new development techniques (e.g., code reuse). The model also takes advantage of an enlarged set of project data, which is based on 161 projects in place of the 63 used in the definition of COCOMO81 and an improved definition of the term "source lines of code." Finally, COCOMO II uses the spiral development process as its reference process.

COCOMO II introduces three main changes:

1. UFPs are used at an early stage of the development process to determine a system's size. The UFP are then transformed into lines of code using translation tables that map UFP into SLOCs. Some example values can be found in Center for Software Engineering (2000) and Quantitative Software Management (2013). This helps solve the "chicken–egg" problem with the original definition of the model. In fact, the accuracy of the model depends on the accuracy of the estimation of the system size, which however is known only when development ends.

2. The computation of lines of code is adjusted to take into account reused code and requirements volatility. The first is computed using a nonlinear model derived by analyzing about 3000 projects from NASA. The latter simply increases the count of SLOC by a percentage that represents the number of requirements that will change. This allows one to use the method with more modern programming practices.

3. The parameters are refined or updated. In detail, more the exponent is computed as the sum of five scale factors. The scale factor includes aspects related to the development process. They are assessed similar to the effort adjustment factors; the result is always between 0.91 and 1.226. Finally, the other parameters are updated to match analyses conducted on a larger set of data.

The Center for Software Engineering (2000) and Merlo-Schett et al. (2002) give more information about the application, while the University of Southern California (2013) and NPS (2013) make available an online calculator.

We conclude the section on COCOMO by mentioning that various extensions have been proposed to the model, among which are COQUALMO, to estimate software defects, COCOTS, to estimate integration of COTS component, and COSYSMO for system engineering.

3.4.5.3 Web Objects

Web object is a technique that mixes FP analysis and COCOMO models to estimate the effort and schedule of web application development. The main motivations for the definition of (yet another) estimation technique are some fundamental differences between desktop and web applications development.

In fact, the development of web applications tends to be driven by time, rather, that costs; it prefers more informal (and speedy) processes; it uses smaller teams (3–6 people), often composed by younger and less experienced personnel. According to Reifer, who defined and proposed the model, these motivations make the application of other techniques less effective (see, e.g., Reifer (2000), Ruhe et al. (2003)).

The method is organized in two phases, **Web objects** and **web modeling**. The first, similar to the FP estimation, is used to estimate a web application size. The application of the technique requires one to measure nine different characteristics of a system, classifying them as simple, average, or complex. Five of these nine characteristics are those we already saw in the FP estimation. Four new elements are specific to the web application domain and they include **multimedia files**, **scripts**, **links**, and **web building blocks**. Using a weighted count of the characteristics yields the number of **web objects**, that is, a measure of a system's size.

The second part of the method, **web modeling**, is structured similarly to the COCOMO method and it transforms the number of web objects into effort and schedule. The relationship between web objects and effort is given by the following formulas:

$$\text{Effort} = A \cdot \prod_{i=1}^{9} cd_i (\text{Size})^{P_1} \tag{3.17}$$

$$\text{Duration} = B \cdot (\text{Effort})^{P_2} \tag{3.18}$$

where A, B, P_1, and P_2 are constants (similar to COCOMO81), *Size* is the size in web objects, and cd_i are nine cost drivers similar to those defined by the COCOMO model.

3.4.5.4 Effort and Project Phases

FPs and COCOMO provide top-down estimations. As we have seen, to distribute the total effort and duration to lower elements of the WBS, we need to select an appropriate approach. COCOMO provides reference tables that break down effort and schedule for different software development processes. The breakdown is given in terms of percentages and ranges of percentages and can be found in Boehm (1981).

Thus, for instance, for a small project, the effort computed using the COCOMO81 model can be distributed as follows: 21% to *plan and requirements and product design*; 26% to *detailed design*; 42% to *coding* and *unit testing*; 16% to *integration* and *testing*.*

See Boehm et al. (2000) and Boehm (1984) for more information and Yang et al. (2008) for a critical study related to phase distribution in various projects.

3.5 Scheduling a Plan

WBS identifies the work that it is necessary to carry out, but it does not show any constraints between activities, nor does it specify anything about scheduling, that is, when each activity should start and how long it should last. This is exactly what we are going to do in this section.

Scheduling the plan is composed of the following steps:

1. **Identify dependencies among activities.** During this step, we highlight the dependencies in our project to understand the degrees of freedom we have in scheduling our project. Some activities will have no dependencies and we will be able to schedule them more freely. Others will depend on tasks to finish (or to start) before they can be started; for these, we will clearly have less options.

---

* Note that the sum of percentages is 106%; this is because the planning phase is outside of the scope of the COCOMO81 computation; analysis of effort and schedule distribution, however, allowed the planning phase to be estimated as an additional 6% on top of the values provided by the model.

2. **Identify the critical path of the plan.** The goal of this activity is to identify the most critical activities in the plan. These are the activities that, if delayed, will delay the plan.
3. **Allocate resources to tasks and level resources.** The goal of this activity is to allocate actual resources to the different activities. During this step, various additional constraints emerge, due to the availability of resources and the maximum amount of work that can be allocated to each resource. The process of dealing with such constraints is called **resource leveling**. The output is a plan that introduces additional constraints, called *soft constraints*, which ensure that the limitations related to resource availability are actually met.

Note that the order in which we listed the activities above is merely for presentation purposes. In practice, there is a lot of freedom in the way in which these steps are executed. In many cases, schedules are constructed by looking at the different concerns in parallel, trying different scenarios. In the current practice, the use of a modern Gantt charting tool integrates the steps above, promoting a process in which the schedule is built by looking at all these concerns in parallel.

3.5.1 Identify Dependencies among Activities

No one will start building a house from the roof. Thus, the first step to scheduling our plan is to identify the order in which the activities can be executed. This is done by identifying the dependencies among activities. In general, a **dependency** between two activities A and B defines some kind of constraint in the executability of A and B and imposes a partial ordering on the execution of the activities.

The dependencies can be characterized according to different dimensions, as illustrated in the following paragraphs.

3.5.1.1 Type of Dependencies

Four types of dependencies can be set between two activities, according to whether the constraints involve the start or the end of the two activities.

Two types of constraints are relatively common. These are

1. **Finish to start** (FS). An FS constraint between A and B expresses the fact that B can start only after A is finished. This is probably the most common constraint between activities. For instance, the activity "baking a cake" can start only when all the ingredients have been poured into the baking pot.
2. **Start to start** (SS). An SS constraint between A and B expresses the fact that B can start only when A starts. For instance, a "monitoring" activity can start only when the activity that is being monitored starts.

Two types of constraints are used and found less often. These are

1. **Finish to finish** (FF). An FF constraint between A and B describes a situation in which B can finish only when A finishes.
2. **Start to finish** (SF). An SF constraint between A and B describes a situation in which B can finish only when A starts.

Another classification distinguishes between hard and soft constraints. A **hard constraint** between two activities A and B models a dependency that is in the nature of the work to be performed. A hard constraint cannot be broken without violating the logic of the project. An exception is fast tracking, which optimizes a plan by breaking hard constraints, at the cost of a riskier project execution—see Section 3.6 for more details.

Vice versa, a **soft constraint** between two activities A and B can be set as a convenience to simplify project execution or to reduce risks in the project execution. A soft constraint can be broken without violating the logic of the project.

An example can be of help. In the preparation of a meal, a hard constraint exists between the preparation of the ingredients and cooking them. Cooking, in fact, cannot start if the ingredients have not been prepared. The constraint is in the logic of the activities and there is no way to break it, unless you decide to be extremely creative in your cooking.

In the same scenario, we could decide to impose a soft constraint between preparing the dessert and preparing the main course, that is, arbitrarily decide that we will start preparing the dessert and then move on to prepare the main course. No dependency between the two activities exists. In principle, we could even prepare both dishes in parallel, if we wanted to. Soft constraints can be broken, if required, by changing the hypotheses for which the links were introduced in the first place.

Remark

When people start using Gantt charting tools, sometimes they introduce dependencies between activities to schedule them in a specific order, even if there is no hard constraint between the activities.

The introduction of these soft constraints in a plan is a questionable practice, since it reduces the degrees of freedom one has in scheduling. Moreover, it can make rescheduling and evaluating alternatives a lot more complex when it becomes difficult to distinguish between the hard and the soft constraints.

The use of task priorities, resource leveling, and scheduling constraints are more effective means to achieve the same goal. See Section 3.5.3 for more details.

3.5.1.2 Lead and Lag Time

When defining dependencies between two activities, sometimes it is convenient to specify a time interval, positive or negative, that occurs between the activities. We speak of **lag time** if the time interval is positive. We use the term **lead time** if the interval is negative. Thus, for instance, if *A* and *B* are connected by an FS dependency with a lag time of 3 days, it means that *B* can start three days after *A* has finished. In the example above, if the FS dependency had a lead time of 3 days, *B* could start 3 days before *A* ends.

A typical usage of lag time is with SS constraints, when some progress in the first activity is necessary to start the second one. For instance, in a roadwork project, an SS constraint with a lead time of one or two weeks could be set between *digging* and *laying pipes*. The lag time, in fact, is to allow the *digging* to progress sufficiently to actually make the *laying pipes* activity doable.

Similar to the identification of constraints, it is good practice to introduce lead and lag times between activities only if strictly imposed by the logic of the plan. Introducing arbitrary constraints reduces the degrees of freedom and it could make scheduling a lot more complex than needed.

3.5.1.3 Network Graphs

The dependencies among activities in a project can be represented using a table. Each row contains an activity, identified by a unique number. The dependencies are shown as a list of identifiers, possibly followed by the type of dependency, if different from FS, and the lead and lag times, if present.

Table 3.11 shows an example in which activity C depends on activity A with an FS dependency; C also depends on activity B with an SS dependency. Similarly, activity E depends on activity C with an FS dependency and on activity D with an FS dependency with a lag of three days (+3d).

A far more intuitive notation uses a graph, called **network diagram**, in which all the constraints between activities can be shown visually. Two kinds of network diagrams exist. Network diagrams that represent activities on the nodes are called **activity on node** (AON) diagrams. Network diagrams with activities on the edges are called **activity on arrow** (AOA) diagrams. Both notations were introduced in the 1950s. Of the two, the AON notation usually yields a more natural representation

Table 3.11   A Plan Specification

ID	Activity	Dependency
1	A	
2	B	
3	C	1, 2SS
4	D	
5	E	3FS + 3d, 4

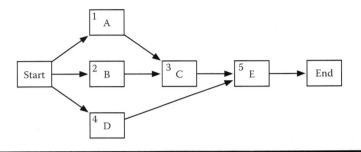

Figure 3.5 AON representation of the plan of Table 3.11.

of a plan, while the AOA notation, initially developed for PERT, is less used, now. Project Management Institute (2004) uses the term **precedence diagram** for AON and **arrow diagram** for AOA.

Figure 3.5 shows the AON representation of the plan presented in Table 3.11. Each activity is represented by a rectangle and arrows represent dependencies among activities. Two special activities Start and End represent, respectively, the start and the end of the project. A popular extension of the AON notation enriches the description of the nodes with duration, start date, and end date, as shown in Figure 3.6. The notation will be used for the computation of the critical path of a plan.

Figure 3.7 shows the AOA representation of the same plan. As can be seen from the figure, activities are shown on arrows and circles are used to represent dependencies. AOA diagrams might require the introduction of dummy activities to represent the dependencies correctly. Consider, for instance a plan with four activities, P, Q, R, and S, in which Q depends upon P and S depends upon R and P. The dependency between S and P requires the insertion of a dummy activity, represented with a dotted line in Figure 3.8.

3.5.2 Identify the Critical Path

In complex plans, the start or the end date of certain activities can be chosen or moved without affecting the overall schedule of the plan, that is, without affecting

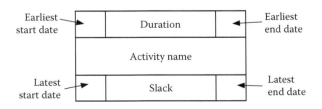

Figure 3.6 Adding information to a node.

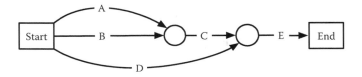

Figure 3.7 AOA representation of the plan of Table 3.11.

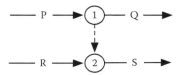

Figure 3.8 AOA dummy activity example.

the end date of the project. Consider the example shown in Figure 3.9, where activities A and B run in parallel, but A lasts longer than B. Note that Figure 3.9 extends the AON notation adding time and using the length of the boxes to represent the duration of the activities. Clearly, B, the shorter activity, can start up to four time units later than A (or, during project execution, even delay its finish date), without affecting any subsequent activity in the plan, as long as the delayed start or the extra duration does not move its end date after that of A. In fact, if it did, we would need to move the start of C, to respect the FS dependency between the two activities.

We call **free float** or **slack** the amount of time an activity can be delayed without affecting subsequent activities. In the example above, the slack of B is four time units, since we can delay its start up to four units without delaying the start of any of its successors (in the example, without delaying C). We call **total float** or **total slack** the amount of time an activity can be delayed without affecting the end of a project. In the example, A has a slack of 0 time units, but a total slack of 1 time unit, since C has a slack that can absorb a delay of A of 1 time unit, without moving E.

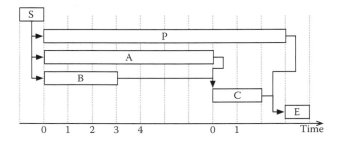

Figure 3.9 Computing the critical path.

The path in which all activities have zero total slack is called the **critical path of the plan**. Any delay in any activity in the critical path will cause a delay to the end date of the project, since the delay cannot be absorbed by any other activity in the path. Understanding what is the critical path of the plan allows a project manager to focus on those activities that are the most important to keep the project on schedule. Note that **all plans have a critical path**.

The critical path method is a technique developed in the 1960s that computes the critical path. It was developed to control the schedule of projects related to the development of the Polaris missile system. Today, the critical path computation is a basic feature of any decent Gantt charting tool. Understanding how the computation is performed, however, is interesting and useful. In particular, the method uses the AON representation of a plan and is performed by determining the earliest and the latest dates at which each activity can start (or end) without affecting the overall schedule.

The computation of the earliest and latest dates is performed in two passes:

1. A **forward pass** determines the **earliest start** and **earliest end** of each activity in the plan. The earliest start (end) date of an activity A is the earliest date at which we can start (finish) an activity, without breaking any dependency on the plan and without moving any other activity in the plan. Intuitively, it measures how soon we can start an activity.
2. A **backward pass** determines the **latest start** and **latest end** dates of each activity in the plan. The latest start (end) data of an activity A is the latest date at which we can start (finish) an activity, without delaying or moving any other activity in the plan. Intuitively, it measures how late we can start an activity without affecting the overall schedule.

The earliest and latest starts determine how much an activity can slide back and forth in a plan and are the basis for the computation of an activity's slack. The slack is in fact computed as the difference between the latest and earliest start of an activity or, equivalently, between the latest and earliest end. An activity whose latest start date (and, respectively, latest end date) is equal to its earliest start date (and, respectively, earliest end date) has a slack of zero.

The **forward pass** starts from the *start node* of the project and proceeds according to the following rules:

1. The start node of the plan is assigned the *earliest start* and *earliest end* date of zero.
2. For any other activity in the plan, the *earliest start* date is set to the highest *earliest end date* of its predecessors. The *earliest end date* is computed by adding to the *earliest start* the duration of the activity.

The calculation is best performed by analyzing the plan from left to right or, more precisely from the start node, then moving to its successors, till we reach the last

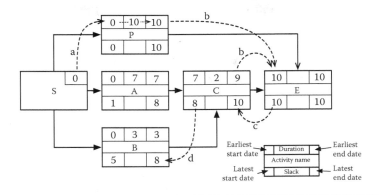

Figure 3.10   An example of critical path computation.

activity of the project.* Hence the name. Note that the *earliest end* of the plan is the *earliest end* of the last activity in the plan, that is, the *earliest end* of the end node.

When we finish the forward pass, we can start the **backward pass**. This starts from the *end node* of the plan and proceeds as follows:

- The *latest end* date of the end node is set to its *earliest end* date; the *latest start* date is set to the *latest end*.
- For any other activity in the plan, the *latest end* date is set to the lowest *latest start* of its successors, while the *latest start* is computed by subtracting the activity's duration from the *latest end*.

The computation of the backward pass is performed analyzing the plan from right to left or, more precisely, beginning from the end node, then moving to its predecessors, till we reach the start node of the project.† Hence the name.

Once we have computed the earliest and latest values of all the activities in the plan, we can determine the slack of each activity as explained before, namely, by subtracting the earliest start from the earliest end. The **critical path** of the plan is the one in which all activities have zero slack.

An example might help clarify the process. Consider the plan in Figure 3.9, for which we present the AON notation and the computation of the critical path in Figure 3.10. Note that each node uses the notation introduced in Figure 3.6, according to which the top boxes contain, respectively, the earliest start date, the duration, and the earliest end date; the bottom boxes contain, respectively, the latest start date, the slack, and the latest end date.

The handwritten numbers are the results of the computations to find the critical path, while the dotted lines show the process.

---

* Technically: breadth-first visit of the AON starting from the start node of the project.
† Technically: breadth-first visit of the AON, starting from the end node.

We begin from the start node, S: we assign an earliest start date of 0 to each activity depending exclusively on the start node. The earliest end dates are then computed adding the duration to the earliest start date. See, for instance, the computation for P—dotted line marked "a" in Figure 3.10. If an activity has more than one predecessor, we take the highest earliest end date. Thus, in the example, the earliest start date of the end node (marked E in the diagram) is 10. See the dotted lines marked "b" in the diagram. We then repeat the process till we compute the earliest start and end dates of each activity.

For the end node, the earliest end, latest start, and latest end are all set to the earliest start.

We can now start the backward pass, propagating the latest dates from the end nodes to the start. In our plan, for instance, the latest end date of activity C is 10, namely, the latest start date of the only successor of C. See the dotted line marked "c" in Figure 3.10. The latest start date of an activity is given by subtracting the duration from its latest end date. This explains why the latest start date of C is 8, that is, the result of subtracting 2, the duration of C, from its latest end date, which is 10.

Once we complete the backward pass, we are now ready to compute the slack of the different activities. Thus, for instance, the slack of A is 1, while the slack of B is 5. There is only one path having all activities with zero slack. This is the path made by just one activity, namely, P. So the critical path of the plan is composed by P. Note that this is a peculiar case; in general, more than one activity will be in the critical path. We now know that any delay to P will cause the entire project to deliver late. During the execution phase, particular attention has to be dedicated to the activity.

3.5.3 Allocate and Level Resources

So far, we determined the logic of the plan in terms of the activities necessary to achieve the project's goals, their dependencies, and the resources needed to carry out each activity. In Section 3.4, we have also seen the relationship between duration, effort, and resources. In many projects, the availability of resources is one of the most critical constraints; activities, in fact, can be carried out only when the required resources are available and at the speed determined by their availability. In this section, therefore, we look in more detail at the process of allocating resources to the plan. This will allow us to determine the duration of the project.

There are basically three constraints we need to satisfy:

1. The allocation has to comply with the estimation of the activities. If an activity requires an effort of 404 man-hours, we need to allocate sufficient resources or time to cover the effort.
2. The allocation needs to comply with the availability of resources. If a resource is available 4 h per day, we cannot create a plan in which he or she is supposed to work above that limit.
3. The constraints of the tasks must be satisfied.

This is taken care of by a three-step process composed of the following steps:

1. Qualify the resources needed for each task.
2. Verify the resources available.
3. Allocate the resources satisfying the constraints.

3.5.3.1 Qualifying the Resources Needed for a Task

As mentioned earlier, tasks require manpower, equipment, or material. Before a resource allocation can start, of course, these needs require to be made explicit.

In more detail:

- For **manpower**, we need to specify the effort necessary to carry out the activity, possibly organized per type of resource, if this is necessary.
- For **equipment**, the number of units required by each activity. For instance, the final testing activity of a software to control a robot could require the availability of two robots for 10 days.
- For **material**, the **quantity** necessary to carry out an activity. Software development plans rarely require the specification of material.

A simplifying assumption that is often made when planning is that the need for a specific resource in a task is uniformly distributed. For example, if a task requires 40 h of a designer over a period of 2 weeks, we assume a constant need of 20 h per week. Although strategies exist to deal with specific cases (e.g., a resource is available every second week; an activity requires an effort that ramps up at the beginning of the activities and slowly decreases at the end of the activity), the extra effort necessary to model such cases is usually not worth the advantages we can get.

Remark

Most entry-level planning tools allow a project manager to specify resource needs in terms of the total effort required in an activity, without distinguishing among the competences or types of resources needed.

In such situations, it is the responsibility of the project manager to allocate the actual resources in a way that is compatible with the requirements of the plan.

3.5.3.2 Specifying Resource Availability

For material and equipment, availability is expressed with quantities and units. For instance, 100 km of optic fiber; four excavators.

For manpower, resource availability is expressed as the total units of work we can allocate to our project. As we have seen, these data can be expressed, person by person, in terms of the percentage of availability. Thus, for instance, if we have one resource available at 80%, it means that he or she can allocate 32 work-hours per week.

A complex plan might abstract away the availability of individual employees. In this case, availability of resources is expressed in the form of a percentage greater than 100%. Thus, an availability of 800% means that we have the equivalent of eight people; it could be eight people full time or, maybe, six full time and four at 50%. The term **full-time equivalent** (FTE) is used to specify the availability of a person working full-time. Thus, for instance, three FTEs correspond to the availability of three people full-time or 300%.

Another aspect, to consider for resource availability are holidays and other leaves. A detailed plan will take into account such data, by specifying the nonworking days person by person. Higher-level plans typically take into account leaves by lowering the amount of work that can be performed by each resource. Thus, for instance, the maximum effort which can be expressed in a calendar-week could be set to 4.8 man-days, to take holidays into account.

Finally, note that the maximum effort available for a project is often a *theoretical* value. The actual effort a resource will be able to allocate to a task during a typical working day is much lower. In fact, we need to consider all other activities (phone calls, meetings, interruptions, breaks) occurring in a typical working day and taking time from the total availability. According to Wysocki (2011), the actual availability of resources is between 50% and 80% of the theoretical value.

> **EXAMPLE 3.4**
> In a project, we can count on the following resources:
>
> ■ Dominique, a designer, who will work full-time.
> ■ Rick, another designer, who is involved part-time, at 50%.
> ■ Elva, an analyst, who works part-time on the project, at 50%.
> ■ Giannetta, another analyst, who works part-time on the project, at 50%.
>
> Given the data above, we can say that
>
> ■ Dominique will be available 40 h per week.
> ■ Rick will be available 20 h per week.
>
> Concerning the availability of an analyst, we have two resources at 50% or, equivalently, 1 FTE.

Remark

For small/medium projects, mentally transforming percentages in actual days at the office is a good way to picture the actual involvement of a resource. For instance, a resource at 20% of his time will be able to work on the project 1 day per week.

From the previous example, it should also become clear that different types of involvements are not equally effective, due to considerations similar to those we already considered in Section 3.4. In particular, the lower the percentage of involvement, the higher the incidence of the time required to get into the task (for instance, catching up with work performed by the rest of the team).

3.5.3.3 Allocating Resources to a Plan

The third step consists in assigning resources to tasks. For manpower, this is done by allocating a percentage of a resource to the tasks.

Given an allocation of resources to a plan, a resource usage profile can be determined. The **resource usage profile** is a graph (or bar-chart) that depicts the number of hours of a resource dedicated to a given project. This is determined by summing up the hours dedicated to each activity to which the resource is dedicated in a given period.

Thus, for instance, if a resource full-time (40 h per week) in January works on two tasks, the first at 50% and the second at 25%, the resource profile in January will show 75% or 30 h per week; 20 h derive from the first task and another 10 come from the involvement in the second task.

The allocation of resources to a plan has two main effects: the first is that determines the duration of activities that have been estimated using effort. This results from the application of Equation 3.6. The second is that it introduces soft constraints in the plan. These are due to the fact that we cannot overallocate resources, that is, use resources over their maximum availability. Thus, activities that in principle could run in parallel will be sequenced if constraints over the availability of resources prevent us from doing so.

Resource leveling is the process of introducing soft constraints in a plan to ensure that no resource is overallocated. Some tools have resource leveling algorithms; others require the manager to do the job.

A resource leveling algorithm typically requires one to specify additional information for each task in the plan.

This includes:

- The **priority** of tasks, typically expressed in the form of a number. The priority determines which activities have to be scheduled earlier in case of conflicts with resource allocation. Typically, higher-priority activities are scheduled earlier.
- The **scheduling constraint** of tasks, which imposes limitations on the possible start and end dates. These are

    - **As soon as possible**, if the task has to be started at the earliest possible date, given the fact that any other constraint is satisfied. This is typically the default for planning tools and corresponds to an aggressive approach, in which we try and get done with the project as early as possible.
    - **As late as possible**, if the task has to be started at the latest possible date, given any other constraint is satisfied. This corresponds to a cautious approach, in which activities, and more important expenditures, are delayed till the very last moment.
    - **Must start on**, if the task has to start on a specific date.
    - **Must finish on**, if the task has to end on a specific date.

- **Start no earlier than**, if the task cannot start earlier than a specific date, but it is perfectly fine if it starts later than the set date.
- **Start no later than**, if the task has to start no later than a given date, but it is perfectly fine if it starts earlier than the set date.
- **End no earlier than**, if the task cannot finish earlier than a specific date, but it is perfectly fine if it ENDS later than the set date
- **Finish no later than**, if the task cannot finish later than a given date, but it is perfectly fine if it ends before the set date.

A resource leveling algorithm schedules activities ensuring that all constraints (dependencies among activities), the properties set by the project manager (priorities and scheduling constraints), resource availability, and priorities are satisfied. If the algorithm succeeds, all activities are laid out so that they satisfy the constraints.

A resource leveling algorithm can also fail. This is the case when the constraints are too tight. Consider the case of a project that must finish on a date but does not have enough resources to meet the deadline. In such cases, one or more constraints have to be relaxed. The most common strategy is adding more resources to shorten some activities. However, this does not necessarily make a project faster if coordination becomes too much of a problem, as was highlighted in Brooks (1995). Other techniques include renegotiating the project scope or compressing the schedule, as we will see in Section 3.6.

3.5.4 The Gantt Chart

The Gantt chart is a very popular notation that can be used to present schedules. Henry Gantt first introduced the notation in 1917 to control shipbuilding works.* The notation we use today is an extension of the original work, which also allows one to represent the WBS, dependencies among activities, the critical path, and various other information about tasks. Many Gantt charting tools exist, and the activities we describe in this section are often carried out interactively using these tools.

The (modern) Gantt chart notation (called a logical network in Burke (2006)) is shown in Figure 3.11. It is organized in two main parts. The left-hand side of the figure contains the list of activities, together with the start and end dates of each activity. The list can present the activities using an outline structure to highlight the hierarchical nature of the plan. The right-hand side of the chart shows the calendar time and the activities.

In particular, on the right-hand side

■ Activities are laid on the calendar as rectangles. The positioning and size of the rectangle shows the start date, duration, and end date of the activity: the

---

* The interested reader can find the description of the original work in Clark and Gantt (1923).

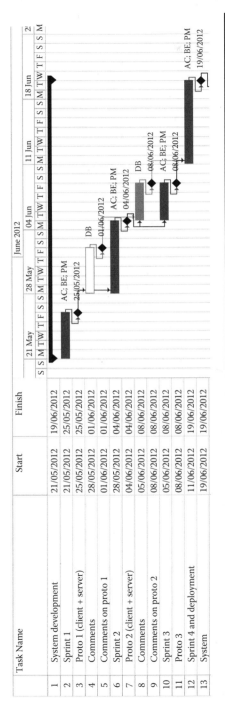

	Task Name	Start	Finish
1	System development	21/05/2012	19/06/2012
2	Sprint 1	21/05/2012	25/05/2012
3	Proto 1 (client + server)	25/05/2012	25/05/2012
4	Comments	28/05/2012	01/06/2012
5	Comments on proto 1	01/06/2012	01/06/2012
6	Sprint 2	28/05/2012	04/06/2012
7	Proto 2 (client + server)	04/06/2012	04/06/2012
8	Comments	05/06/2012	08/06/2012
9	Comments on proto 2	08/06/2012	08/06/2012
10	Sprint 3	05/06/2012	08/06/2012
11	Proto 3	08/06/2012	08/06/2012
12	Sprint 4 and deployment	11/06/2012	19/06/2012
13	System	19/06/2012	19/06/2012

Figure 3.11 An example of a Gantt chart.

left side of the activity corresponds to the start date; similarly for the right side of the activity. Activities are labeled with the initials of the people allocated to the activity.*

■ Deliverables are presented as diamonds. They have zero duration and are labeled with the date before which they are to be produced.

■ The dependencies among activities are marked with arrows starting from an activity (deliverable) and ending at another activity (deliverable). The starting and ending places of the arrow determine the constraint type. Thus, for instance, an arrow starting from the end (finish) of an activity and pointing to the start of another activity represents an FS constraint. Similarly for other kind of constraints.

■ The black lines with triangles at the ends represent work packages, grouping sets of activities.

3.6 Optimizing a Plan

In many situations, the project schedule ends up by being too long to respect the constraints set by the stakeholders, by the project goals, or by the environment. This can cause a bit of frustration to the project manager, since, as soon as he or she comes out with a realistic plan, this has to be revised and changed!

In the following, we analyze the most common techniques to compress the schedule of a plan so that it meets the customer's needs.

3.6.1 Renegotiating Goals and Deadlines

If all the project goals cannot be achieved in the required time frame, renegotiating the project scope and other project constraints can yield a satisfactory solution.

The simplest renegotiation we can try is on the **delivery date**. If the customer does not have a strong constraint on the delivery date, acknowledging the actual work that has to be done and moving the project delivery date to a more reasonable deadline is a simple and elegant solution. The actual feasibility varies. Sometimes deadlines are set arbitrarily by the customer. In these situations, using the plan to demonstrate that the deadline cannot be achieved can convince the customer to come to more reasonable terms. In other situations, deadlines are set earlier than necessary, as a padding to protect other projects that might depend on our results. In these cases, understanding the actual margins and the real risks of delivering late can help both sides decide on the most appropriate strategy. In the remaining cases, the deadline cannot be moved. In this situation, we need to use another technique.

The second kind of renegotiation is on the **project goals**. Not all goals, in fact, are equally important. We have seen in Section 3.2 how we can assign a priority to

---

* This is the default adopted by many tools, but it is by no means a standard.

different goals. Selecting with the client the most important goals reduces the work we need to do, moving the delivery to an earlier date.

If both approaches are not feasible, we need to change the logic of the plan. This is what we discuss in the next few sections.

3.6.2 Phase the Project

Organizing the project in phases allows one to organize work so that the most important goals are achieved earlier. If only some of the project goals must be achieved for a given deadline, phasing the project might help meet the requirement.

For software development projects, this can be an effective strategy, since software development accommodates relatively easily an incremental construction. Using this approach, the first phases will release an initial version of the system with basic features. The system will then be refined in subsequent project iterations. An additional advantage of this approach is that the user is given a working solution to use: this allows both users and the development team to better understand what functions are important and, consequently, how to prioritize project development.

3.6.3 Project Crashing

Project crashing is a technique that works on the project schedule trying to find an optimal balance between time and costs. Project crashing works on the assumption that shortening a project yields savings and that the duration of tasks can be reduced by assigning more resources to them (labor, material, equipment). However, since an increment in resources causes an increase in project costs, which could be nonlinear with the decrease in duration, an optimal balance needs to be found between how much a project is shortened and how much the costs are increased.

When using project crashing, the

■ **Crash costs** indicate the savings obtained by crashing the project.
■ **Crash time** indicates the time used to shorten the project.

Project crashing can be an effective method to optimize costs. The reader, however, should be aware that the technique might be difficult to apply effectively. Consider, for instance, the additional risks introduced by crashing a project. They could, in principle, cause additional rework and delays to a project that we tried to shorten instead.

> **EXAMPLE 3.5**
> Consider a project that is late and scheduled to end 4 months later than the delivery date agreed with the client. Each month of delay costs us €20K, as per the contractual agreement with the client. Thus, with the current plan, we will lose €80K. To try and recover the situation, Cathy, the project manager, has analyzed the costs to shorten the project. According to her data, reducing the duration by 1 month is relatively easy and cheap, since we can use internal personnel. However, any further

Table 3.12   Crashing costs

Crashing	Overrun	Crashing Costs
4 months	0 month	€120,000
3 months	1 month	€90,000
2 months	2 months	€60,000
1 month	3 months	€10,000
0 month	4 months	€0

shortening will require us to hire expensive consultants. The actual estimations of the costs are shown in Table 3.12.

Project crashing can be used to decide what is the optimal crashing time. This can be done by computing the crashing costs per month, which include the expenses to crash the project (data of Table 3.12) and the penalty we pay for delivering late. The data are shown in Table 3.13, where we report the costs we incur for delivering late (column "Overrun Costs"), those we incur for crashing the project ("Crashing Costs"), and the total costs, given by the sum of the previous two values.

We can now determine the optimal crashing cost, which is given by the minimum value in the "Total Costs" column. This is shown in Figure 3.12, from which we can easily see that the optimal crashing time is 1 month. In this situation, we will lose €70K, saving €10K with respect to the situation in which we do not crash the project. Any other arrangement will result in incurring higher costs.

If costs are the main or the only parameter for choosing how much the project has to be crashed, then the answer is 1 month, that is, we reduce the duration of the project by 1 month.

3.6.4 Fast Tracking

Fast tracking tries to minimize the project duration by breaking the logic of the plan. That is, some of the hard constraints in the plan are removed so that activities that would otherwise be sequential can partially overlap.

Figure 3.13 shows an example where some activities that depended on a deliverable are actually started earlier, by breaking the dependency. This allows one to end the project earlier and achieve the project constraints.

Table 3.13   Crashing Example

Crashing	Overrun	Crashing Costs	Overrun Costs	Total Costs
4 months	0 month	€120,000	€0	€120,000
3 months	1 month	€90,000	€20,000	€110,000
2 months	2 months	€60,000	€40,000	€100,000
1 month	3 months	€10,000	€60,000	€70,000
0 month	4 months	€0	€60,000	€80,000

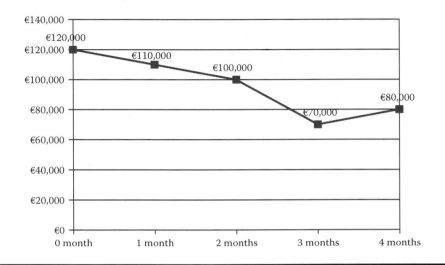

Figure 3.12   Crashing the project: Total costs over time.

Fast tracking is not odd as it might seem at first glance, if we think about the incremental nature of the work performed on this task. Work progresses in a nonlinear fashion. Thus, in many practical situations, little work and progress will remain close to the end of an activity.* Dependent activities, can thus, start on the partial results that are achieved as predecessor activity progresses, resulting in a more compact schedule.

The main risk with fast tracking is that rework might be necessary. Consider the case of writing the specification of a function and the subsequent activities related

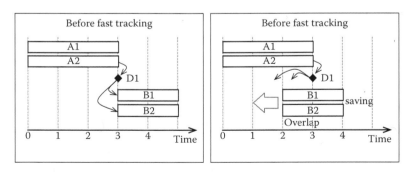

Figure 3.13   An example of fast tracking.

---

* See Section 3.6.5 for another way of looking at this issue.

to implement it. If we fast track, we start design and implementation before the specification is fully described. If important information is added after we start the implementation, we might end up implementing the wrong functions and having to redo implementation work.

Deciding what chains of activities are best suited for fast tracking is a tricky issue that depends on the tasks at hand and the project manager and team judgment. Some rules of thumb include looking at activities that will produce (stable) intermediate results and activities whose deliverables can be broken into independent pieces of work. For instance, a requirements writing activity could be fast tracked if the requirements can be organized in different and independent sections and the implementation of software can be started as each section is produced. If there are functional interdependencies, a little rework might be necessary.

Another item to consider is how rework could affect other components of the plan. One risk is propagating delays; another is producing outputs of low quality; a third is increasing the project costs.

3.6.5 *Critical Chain Management*

Critical chain project management is a technique developed at the end of the 1990s that has been successfully applied in many real projects. The technique is fairly complex and the presentation we give here is a rather significant simplification of the overall process. See Wysocki (2011) for a very nice introduction to the technique and Goldratt (1997) and Stratton (2009) for additional references.

Critical chain management starts from the assumption that estimations are random variables, as we have discussed in Section 3.4.3. Thus, if our best guess for the duration of an activity is n days, what we are really saying is that we *expect* the activity will take n days to complete. However, the activity might take longer or finish earlier. If we assume the probability distribution of the duration to be symmetric, half of the time the actual duration will be shorter than expected and half of the time will be longer.

If we take a cautious estimation, that is, an estimation that is above our best guess, *most of the time* the actual duration will be equal to or less than our cautious estimation. For instance, if we estimate the duration to be $n + \sigma_n$, where σ_n is the variance of n, the probability of the duration being lower than $n + \sigma_n$ is about 84% for normal distributions.

If we consider a sequence of activities, the guesses add up. If we consider the estimation of each activity to be independent, however, probability theory tells us that the variance of the sum of the durations is lower than the sum of the variances. In other words, the cautious estimation of the chain of activities is lower than the sum of the cautious estimations of each activity in the chain.

This is shown in Figure 3.14, where we have a sequence of two activities, A and B, for which we have provided two cautious estimations. That is, the duration we have chosen is above the mean value, as shown in the upmost diagram, by having chosen a duration right of the mean, resulting in some "padding." We can also separate, for each activity, the best guesses from cautious estimations, moving them to the end of the chain, as shown in the center part of Figure 3.14. However, if we consider the estimation of the sum of the activities, its probability distribution will have a lower variance. Even with a cautious estimation, therefore, the duration of A + B will be lower than the sum of the cautious estimations of A and B.

This is what critical chain management does: it uses best guesses to estimate each activity (rather cautious estimations) and adds cautious estimations at the ends of the chains, rather than at the end of each activity. This results in two savings. First of all, for long chains, we can expect some activities to last more and some to last less than expected: delay might be compensated for by early deliveries. The second is that the padding added at the ends of the chains is lower than that computed for each activity. When using critical chain management (CCM), therefore, we consider the chain of activities, which are estimated at their best guesses, and **contingency buffers**, which contain the *padding* (cautious estimation), as shown in the third diagram of Figure 3.14.

There are other principles that make CCM effective; one of them is that resources are allocated *greedily*, so that we can exploit any saving deriving from an activity finishing earlier than expected.

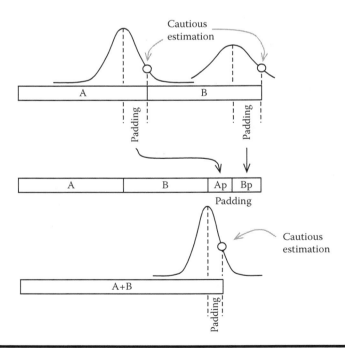

Figure 3.14   Critical chain management.

Concerning plan monitoring and management of delays, CCM assesses the execution of chains at one-third, two-thirds, and three-thirds (at the end) of their execution. In more detail, if delays were distributed uniformly during the execution of the chain, we should expect each third of the chain to delay the chain, at most, by one-third of the contingency buffer. Any worse and the chain might end late; any better and we can exploit early deliveries. Another essential element of critical chain management, therefore, is to place the contingency buffers so that they can *absorb* delays without compromising the plan. For this reason, the technique uses three types of buffers, namely, **project buffers** that protect the plan, **feeding buffers** that protect the chain of activities, and **resource buffers** that protect the plan from delays in resource availability. See Wysocki (2011) and Goldratt (1997) for more details.

3.7 Budgeting and Accounting

As pointed out in the introduction, the project manager is tasked with keeping under control three of the main aspects of a project: quality, time, and cost. This section is an introduction to the main techniques to determine the cost and price of a project and managing a project's cost over the duration of the project. Whenever possible, we instantiate the concepts to the software development domain.

3.7.1 Project Costs

Project costs are the expenses that an organization will incur into carrying out a project.

The items contributing to the expenses can be divided into in **direct costs** and **indirect costs**.

Direct costs are the expenses directly related to carrying out a project. These include

- **Personnel costs**, that is, the costs of the personnel involved in the project. This is computed from the effort and rates. Daily (or hourly) rates, for profiles or individuals, are typically determined by the performing organization and are computed by considering all the items that contribute to the cost of a resource (e.g., salary, tax, retirement funds, and fringe benefits). In some cases and countries, this can result in the cost being twice the gross salary.
- **Materials and supply**, that is, the costs of the material necessary to produce the project outputs, such as, for instance, the construction material necessary to build a house. For software development, this cost is usually very low.
- **Hardware and software**, that is, the costs of specific hardware and software necessary to carry out a project.
- **Travel**, **meeting**, and **events**, that is, the costs necessary to meet with customers and other stakeholders.

- **Consultants and subcontracting**, that is, the costs related to work that is subcontracted.
- **Other costs**, that is, all those expenses that do not fit nicely in the other categories, such as, for instance, books, training, and renting equipment.

Indirect costs include the expenses necessary to run the facility and make work actually doable. Indirect costs are also called **overhead** and include

- **General overheads**, that is, the costs necessary to run the infrastructure supporting the production team (e.g., office space rents, heating, administrative staff, consumables, and networking).
- **Project overheads**, that is, the costs necessary to run the project-specific infrastructure. Project overheads apply to large projects or to specific situations in which the accounting is performed at this level of detail. In general, all indirect costs are accounted for as general overheads and distributed uniformly among all projects that an organization is involved in.

There are three main aspects related to the management of indirect costs. The first is to determine what expenses contribute to their computation. This is usually done once and for all by analyzing the recurring expenses due to supporting operations and work.

The second is to forecast the indirect costs. This is done on a yearly basis and requires an organization to assess the fixed and variable costs, such as, for instance, costs of heating, rent, and electricity. Historical data are the basis for these kinds of estimations.

The third is to define a policy to distribute indirect costs to the different projects of an organization. A fair approach allocates indirect costs proportionally to a project's size since, in principle, larger projects will use more services and cause higher indirect costs. This can be done in different ways. One adds a flat rate to the personnel costs to take care of overhead; in this case, the overheads are computed as a percentage of the project effort. Another adds a rate proportional to the cost of each resource; the computation is like in the previous case, but resources with higher salaries will contribute with a higher overhead. A third technique computes a percentage of the overall budget of the project.

Finally, it has to be remarked that overheads can be a significant cost item of a project, in some situations even doubling the rates to be used for the personnel involved in a project.

3.7.2 Cost Element Structures

Budget should count each expense only once and no double accounting of the same costs should take place. For this reason, organizations use a **cost element structure** (CES), that is, a hierarchical structure that defines precisely what are the cost items to take into account in each project.

Table 3.14   Budget Example

	Unit Cost	Overhead	Effort/Units	Total	Comment
Personnel					
Resource A	€50	€30	100	€8000	
Resource B	€40	€30	100	€7000	
Total personnel costs				€15,000	
Hardware and software					
Hardware	€300		2	€600	Two tablets for testing the Application
Software	€80		1	€80	Library for graphs
Total hardware and software				€680	
Other costs					
Travel	€1000		5	€5000	
Meetings	€200		3	€600	
Training				€0	
Total other costs				€5000	
Total				€12,280	

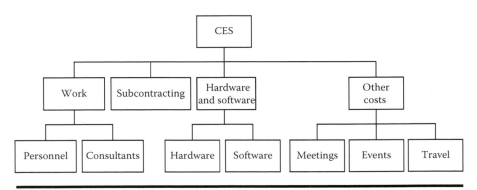

Figure 3.15   CES example.

Similar to a WBS, a CES can be presented as a tree. The advantages of a CES include no double accounting taking place. Moreover, it helps to present the budget in a standardized way and allows to aggregate and present financial data at different levels of detail.

For instance, the costs we presented in Table 3.14 could be organized as shown in the CES of Figure 3.15.

3.7.3 Determining the Project Costs

Given a CES, the rates of personnel, overhead costs, and a project plan (with the estimation of effort and other information, such as travels, etc.), the determination of the project costs can proceed by adding all the expenses foreseen in the project.

For the mathematically inclined, on the hypothesis that overheads are computed as a percentage on personnel costs

$$\text{Project budget} = \sum_{j=1}^{m} \text{Hours}_j * (\text{Cost}_j + \text{Overhead}_j) + \sum_{i=1}^{n} C_i \qquad (3.19)$$

The first part of the formula determines the personnel costs. For each of the m resources involved in the project, in fact, we determine the cost by multiplying the effort by the costs and overhead associated with the resource.

The second part of the formula includes the other foreseen expenditures.

This computation is typically performed with a spreadsheet or using a Gantt charting tool, in which case it is also possible to compute a detailed cash flow. Table 3.14 shows an example of project costs computed and presented with a spreadsheet. Whether the computation is performed on hourly costs rather than daily or monthly tariffs depends on the project size, with larger projects privileging longer periods, also to take into account the higher variability of the estimations.

For a large project, work packages are a good starting point to compute the budget. That is, the manager computes the budget for each work package and then aggregates the data. This process allows one to allocate each project expenditure in a two-dimensional matrix, made of the CES and of the WBS, as shown in Figure 3.16.* As pointed out in the Department of Defense (2011), the intersections of elements of the CES and of the WBS are the cost elements that need to be traced during project execution.

3.7.4 Managing Project Costs

A **project budget** is a view of the predicted cash flow (incomes and expenditures) of a project.

Its main goals are

1. To ensure that the money is available when it needs to be spent.
2. To monitor project expenditures so that the project remains within the budget, or appropriate actions can be taken when this is not the case.

The cash flow is built by determining, for each reporting period, the foreseen incomes and expenses. The reporting period depends on the project size and

---

* Note that we could include a third dimension, made of the organizational structure of the company involved, if the project costs have to be allocated to different departments.

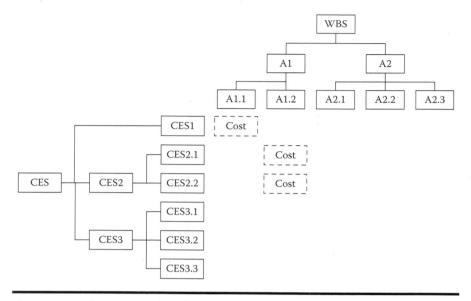

Figure 3.16   Cost accounting elements (CES and WBS).

on company policies. The allocation of incomes and expenses over time depends instead on the project plan and on contractual agreements with subcontractors, which might require an advance payment or might happily be paid after delivery. This information allows the project manager to determine the amount brought forward and the financial needs of a project, as illustrated in Table 3.15.

In the table:

- The first group collects the expenses over time, organized according to the CES.
- The second group records the expected incomes, as determined by the contractual agreement.

Table 3.15   Budget Structure

	Q1	*Q2*	*Q3*	*Q4*	*Total*
Expenses					
Expense 1	€10,000	€30,000	€50,000	€10,000	€100,000
Expense 2	€20,000	€40,000	€60,000		€120,000
Total expenses	€30,000	€70,000	€110,000	€10,000	€220,000
Incomes					
Payment	€50,000			€200,000	€250,000
Total incomes	€50,000	€0	€0	€200,000	€250,000
Balance	€20,000	−€70,000	−€110,000	€190,000	€30,000
Financial need		−€50,000	−€180,000		

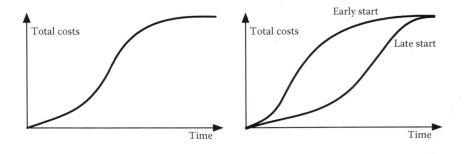

Figure 3.17   Expenditure profiles for a project.

▪ The third group determines the financial needs. In particular, the row "balance" is the net balance at the end of the period, computed as the difference between incomes and expenses. The row "financial need" indicates how much money the project needs to borrow to carry out activities. It is the result of adding the balance of the current period to the credits and debits accumulated.

Note that if we plot the accumulated expenses of a project over time, we typically get an "S"-shaped curve, with the expenditures rapidly rising when the project is in full swing and being relatively small at the beginning and end of a project. This is shown in the left part of Figure 3.17.

Since the expenditures are related to the project activities, and various activities in a plan have a slack, we can determine, for each project, two different cost profiles, one in which all activities have an early start and the other in which all activities have a late start. This individuates a **banana-shaped** region in the graph, as shown in the right part of Figure 3.17. If the project is not delayed, the actual expenditure profile will be in the "banana" region. See Burke (2006) for more details.

Determining financial needs over time establishes a simple reference framework to monitor and control project expenditures. We will see in Section 3.9 a more sophisticated technique that allows progress and costs to be controlled in an integrated way. Here, it is sufficient to remark that project and organizational constraints determine what item of the CES the project manager should monitor, what detail of accounting is necessary, and what margins of maneuver the project manager has in authorizing expenditures. For instance, personnel costs are often directly managed by the administrative offices of the performing organization. Although they concur in determining the costs of a project, it is not the responsibility of the project manager to monitor the expenditure and ensure that salaries are paid.

3.8 Project Execution

Project execution is where work takes place and deliverables are actually produced. That is, during this phase, all the activities described in Chapter 2 are actually performed.

There are three main management activities to be taken care of during this phase. These are

1. Kicking activities off
2. Collecting the output of activities
3. Collecting information about the project health.

3.8.1 Kicking Activities Off

The goal of this activity is to formalize the start of one or more project tasks with a meeting or some other communication. There are three good reasons for doing so. The first is to ensure that there is shared vision on the work that has to be performed. The second is to ensure that the project team has the necessary resources to carry out the work. The third is to make official an actual start date. This has a symbolic value, which helps everyone to get into the right mindset and actually get started with the work.

The number and type of tasks for which a kick-off is necessary, the amount of time required to prepare a kick-off, and the formality of the kick-off activity depend on the project at hand. At a minimum a **kick-off** meeting should be held to start a project. Large projects might also foresee a kick-off meeting to start each work package. Holding a kick-off meeting to start some risky or critical activity in the project is also a good idea.

Formal meetings are not always good. Small projects or projects with experienced and well-oiled teams require less formality. In these situations, a stand-up meeting or just a chat at the coffee machine could be sufficient.

See Section 5.3.3.2.1 for more information on how to structure a kick-off meeting.

3.8.2 Collect the Output of Activities

Closing activities is the second important management practice during project execution. A proper closure, in fact, ensures that activities are promptly ended when the work is completed, rather than dragging around. Moreover, it becomes possible to assess the lessons learned and to understand how to improve in the next phase. Finally, a proper closure ensures that the project outputs are properly collected.

Concerning the means and tools, we can apply considerations similar to the ones we made for kick-offs. The main *tool* is a meeting, in which the team presents the results, the lessons learned are discussed, and the project outputs are stored.

3.8.3 Collect Information about the Project Status

The goal of this activity is to assess the project status. It can be performed on a regular basis or on a need basis, like, for instance, when a critical event occurs.

Systematic collection of quantitative data about the status of activities and work can be used to monitor progress, costs, and time and thus to evaluate whether the project is running late or costing more than budgeted. This is covered in Section 3.9.

Similar to the previous case, quantitative data about the number of defects, change requests, and risks that occurred can provide information about the status of the project and that of its outputs. This is covered in more detail in Section 4.3.

Discussions and status meetings with stakeholders can provide qualitative information about team morale, progress, and other information about the project.

3.8.4 The Project Routine in Agile Methods

The agile routine is a good example of a systematic application of the practices we have described above.

Agile methodologies are based on a strict sequence of fixed-length development activities. Each development frame is called a **sprint**. The project routine for agile teams is the following:

- At the beginning of the sprint, hold a meeting highlighting the sprint goals.
- During the sprint, on a daily basis, hold a 15 min stand-up meeting to highlight the main achievements, main obstacles, and commitments for the day.
- At the end of the sprint, release a **potentially shippable product** and demo it to the team and the customer.

3.9 Project Monitoring and Control

If we were perfect planners in a completely predictable world, being a project manager would probably be rather boring. Our plans would be a perfect representation of the future and the goal of monitoring and control would be that of observing how our project develops and progresses according to the plans we set. In a completely predictable world, in fact, many other activities would be rather boring.

In practice and, maybe, also fortunately, we are not perfect planners and the world is unpredictable. We need to plan not only to tame uncertainty but also to monitor and replan to take the appropriate corrective actions when the gap between our plans and reality becomes too wide.

Monitoring and control is a structured process that helps us

1. Understand whether our projections have been confirmed by the actual execution of the plan. This is achieved by comparing our plan (called **baseline** plan) with that derived by mapping how work is **actually** progressing.
2. Understand whether any deviation has occurred and their impact in determining the future trajectory of the project.
3. Understand what actions we can or need to take to bring the project back to the nominal situation, if a deviation has occurred.

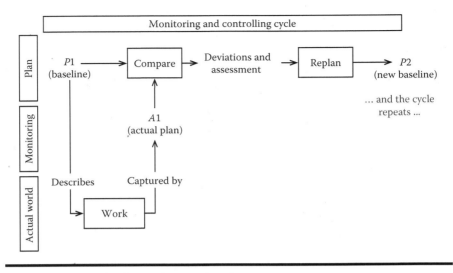

Figure 3.18 Monitoring and control cycle.

Thus, an effective monitoring and control process requires to periodically collect data, which we can compare with our plans. This generates a sequence of plans, as illustrated in Figure 3.18. The first **baseline** plan, $P1$, is generated before the start of the project. As the project progresses, data are collected in order to understand the actual progress; this can be done by building a Gantt chart, called **actual plan**, representing how the actual work has progressed ($A1$ in Figure 3.18). The baseline plan and actual progress are compared, deviations analyzed and taken care of and, if necessary, a new plan set ($P2$ in Figure 3.18). The new plan finally becomes the baseline for the next monitoring cycle.

The rest of this section is dedicated to defining what data are usually collected and what techniques are used to assess current status and make the new projections. We start by describing some simple techniques to monitor progress and time; we then continue with some basics about monitoring costs. Section 3.9 is dedicated to presenting earned value analysis (EVA), a technique that allows one to take an integrated view at the project progress, by measuring progress, time, and costs together.

We conclude the section describing the approach adopted by agile methodologies and with some information about software metrics and their role in measuring progress.

3.9.1 Bookkeeping Your Plan: Actual Start and End Dates

The simplest form of monitoring that can be performed on a plan consists in keeping track of the **actual start** and **actual end** dates of each activity in the plan. Note that variations in the start or end date of a task can propagate to other activities in the plan, if the delay (in the start or end date) is bigger than the total slack of the activity.

Many Gantt charting tools allow project managers to compare a given baseline of a plan with the actual data. Each activity is represented by two bars; the lower bar is laid down using the planned data (i.e., the data of the baseline plan), while the upper bar shows the actual data (i.e., the data derived from the last monitoring performed). An optional bar is used to show the progress performed in an activity, in terms of the effort actually spent.

An example is shown in Figure 3.19, taken from an actual project. In the upper part, we can observe two activities, A1 and A2, connected together through a deliverable. Activity A1 has been delayed. This is shown in Figure 3.19 by the upper bar, which is longer than the lower bar. The delay in the end date of A1 propagates to A2, since the plan had no slack to accommodate for any delay in A1. Thus, activity A2 starts later than planned (upper bar shifted to the right with respect to the lower bar). Activity A2, however, ends earlier than expected, compensating the delay caused by A1. This is shown in Figure 3.19 by the upper bar of A2, which ends before the lower bar.

In A3, the second case, the activity starts as planned and lasts less than expected: both bars start on the same date and the upper bar is shorter than the lower bar.

Activity A4 is only partially completed: this is shown by the fact that the upper bar is only partially filled. Many tools show the percentage of completion to the right of the bar. Thus, for instance, we can see from the diagram that A4 is 40% complete. An aspect that is less obvious is that A4 was not in the original plan when the baseline was set. A4, in fact, has only one bar and no baseline bar is shown.

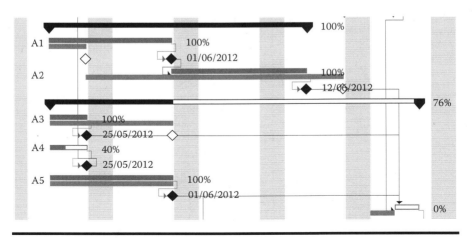

Figure 3.19 Gantt's monitoring.

3.9.2 *Monitoring Time and Work*

A slightly more complex form of monitoring measures the progress to understand whether a project is on time, early, or late. The process is bottom-up, with data collected from each activity that determines the general project status.

A simple estimation process is based on the collection of data about the *actual* work performed for each task. On the hypotheses that the estimations are accurate, the actual progress depends on the work, and that work is evenly distributed on a task, in fact, simple computations of percentages allow us to determine the progress we expected at the date, the current progress, and the estimation to the end.

In more detail, if we have a task A for which we have estimated an effort of $w_{planned}$ to complete the task and we currently have spent an effort of w_{actual} on the task, we can compute the **percentage of work completed**, p_{actual} as

$$p_{\text{actual}} = \frac{w_{\text{actual}}}{w_{\text{planned}}} \qquad (3.20)$$

For instance, if we estimated task A to require an effort of 40 h and we have already worked 20 h on A, we can estimate the task to be 50% complete, since $20/40 = 50\%$.

Note that if we determine the amount of work we *should have* produced at the monitoring date on a task, we can compare it with the actual progress and determine whether we are early or late. In fact, if the actual progress is greater than the expected progress at the monitoring date, we are early; we are late otherwise. This can be done by looking at a task's duration and planned start date.

In fact, if work is evenly distributed, we can determine how much progress we expect per calendar unit and, consequently, how much progress we should have produced at the monitoring date. For instance, if activity A is scheduled to last 5 days, we can expect to produce 20% of the work per calendar day. If 3 days have elapsed from its planned start, the progress we expect to have produced is 60%. More formally, the expected percentage of work $p_{planned}$ is

$$p_{\text{planned}} = \frac{t_{\text{now}} - t_{\text{start}}}{t_{\text{end}} - t_{\text{start}}} \qquad (3.21)$$

where t_{now} is the monitoring date, t_{start} is the start date of the task, and the denominator contains the duration of the activity, namely, $t_{end} - t_{start}$.

The data computed above can be used to determine whether each activity is early or late. We can do a bit more and also compute the new estimations to the end. The ratio $p_{actual}/p_{planned}$ gives us the *efficiency* with which we are producing effort in a task. Thus, for instance, if the ratio is less than 1, we are inefficient in the project execution, while if the ratio is greater than 1 we are producing more effort than we planned.

Given the efficiency and the hypotheses above, we can thus revise our plan and determine the new *estimated duration* of the activity and the new *estimated end date* of each task. The *estimated duration*, in particular, is the planned duration of the task divided by the efficiency. The *estimated end date* is given by adding the estimated duration of the activity to the actual start date of the task.

In formulas

$$t_{\text{estimated end}} = \frac{t_{\text{end}} - t_{\text{start}}}{p_{\text{actual}}/p_{\text{planned}}} + t_{\text{actual start}} \qquad (3.22)$$

where $t_{end} - t_{start}$ is the planned duration, $p_{actual}/p_{planned}$ is the efficiency with which we are producing work, and $t_{actual\ start}$ is the actual start date of the task.

The computation above allows one to assess the project status. Many Gantt charting tools perform the computations above, sometimes by having the user specify directly the "percentage of work complete" or "percentage of duration complete." For instance, Aksel (2008) discusses the implementation of these computation in MS Project.

It has to be remarked, however, that the hypotheses made at the beginning of the section do not always hold. In particular, it could be the case that our initial estimation of the work necessary to complete an activity is wrong. In this case, we first need to revise our estimation and then proceed with the computations described above.

The problem in the second hypothesis, namely, that progress corresponds to the work spent, is dealt with similarly to the previous case: we either revise our estimations of work to more accurately reflect the work needed or, if we have it, we find a way to measure the percentage of technical progress we expected at the monitoring date.

If the third hypothesis is false, we need to revise the computations to take into account the actual workload we expected in each activity. This, however, makes computations a lot more complex and one should evaluate whether it really makes sense to still apply the method.

Finally, before applying this method, it is always a good idea to assess the benefits and costs. For instance, in some cases, a less accurate and more informal monitoring could be equally good in terms of information and a lot more efficient in terms of the work required.

3.9.3 Monitoring Costs

Budget and expenditure monitoring can be performed using the same approach we defined above. The percentage of time elapsed determines a projection on the expense we should have performed. This is compared with the money actually spent on each item of the project's CES, in order to determine whether we are on budget, overspending, or underspending.

The process requires one to maintain an updated ledger of the project expenditures that we can use to assess the money actually spent. Since accurate financial bookkeeping is required by law, the data collection process should be simpler than in the previous case.

Similar to the previous case, however, there can be some noise in the estimations we produce and in interpreting the financial data. These can be more or less evident, according to a project's size and duration and the magnitude of expenses to be performed in the project.

The first source of noise is due to the fact that many payments happen in lump sums at specific points in time during the project. Thus, expenditure does not progress linearly with time but rather with discontinuities. As mentioned above, the relevance and importance of such discontinuities vary with a project's size and, of course, with the size of payments budgeted in the project. Consider, for instance, a project that budgets hardware for deploying a solution to the client. Any monitoring on the corresponding CES item will either show 0% or 100%, according to whether the hardware has been bought or not. (Certain planning tools allow one to specify the spending profile, in order to more closely define expenditure over time and thus simplify budget monitoring.)

The second source of noise is due to delays in payments. Subcontractors often receive delayed payment (in Italy up to 3 months) after the actual delivery of tasks. In such cases, the amount shown in the ledger containing the actual expenses will be different from the money actually available. Simple accounting practices, such as the usage of a "liability" account, address the issue.

A third (and minor) cause is the way in which various expenses get classified in the CES. Although, in principle, errors or choice in the way in which some expenses are classified should never occur, it happens sometimes in practice.

3.9.4 An Integrated Approach: Earned Value Analysis

The techniques we have seen above provide a partial view on the status of the project. If we monitor progress like we describe in Section 3.9.2, we can tell little about the costs we are incurring to achieve the technical progress. Conversely, the technique for monitoring the budget described in the previous section tells us nothing about the technical progress we achieved. Even more complex is understanding the efficiency with which we are achieving progress.

EVA is a technique that addresses the problems mentioned above by representing progress, costs, and schedule in the same measurement unit. This allows one to compare them and thus understand a project's status and derive trends and projections.

The technique was defined in the 1960s and developed subsequently over a period of 20 years. Today, it is an important methodology that is widely adopted. See Christensen (2013) for a comprehensive bibliography, which includes various historical references. Over time, technique and terminology have been standardized. In this section, we use both the historical definitions and the new standard terminology.

The concept behind EVA is relatively simple: progress and schedule are mapped in terms of money and compared with the actual expenditure measured in a project. The analysis of the absolute values, that is, where progress, schedule, and costs stand at the monitoring date, informs us about the current status of a project. The ratios among the values tell us about the efficiency of our project, which we can use to make projections to the end.

The brilliant idea of EVA is how technical progress can be measured in terms of money. This becomes obvious, however, as we measure (technical) progress in terms of the work to produce it, to which we can assign a cost. We will refine and make the definition more precise in a couple of paragraphs.

The concepts we need to introduce are

- **Planned value**, that is, an analysis of the planned progress over time. It is also known as **budgeted costs of work scheduled** (BCWS).
- **Actual costs**, that is, the actual expenditure we incurred in the project. It is also known as **actual costs of work performed** (ACWP).
- **Earned value**, that is, an assessment of the value (technical progress) we produced so far. It is also known as **budgeted costs of work performed** (BCWP).

Let us see how we compute each of these values and then how these are put into use.

3.9.4.1 Planned Value

According to the Project Management Institute (2004), "**planned value** (PV) is the authorized budget assigned to work to be accomplished for an activity or WBS component. Total planned value for the project is also known as budget at completion (BAC)."

PV can be tabulated or plotted over time as shown in Figure 3.20, defining the expenditure profile we expect from a project. The computation of PV proceeds as follows:

- We choose a reporting period (e.g., monthly and quarterly).
- We draw the Gantt chart of the project.
- We compute the costs of each activity in our project. This is the PV of the activity.
- We divide the costs of each activity according to the reporting period. That is, if an activity A has a duration of 3 months, starting from month 4 of the project and at a cost of 3000 USD, we will allocate 1000 USD at month 4, 1000 USD at month 5, and 1000 USD at month 6.
- We sum all the amounts per reporting period.

Since the PV shows the values of the costs of our plan, it provides a cost baseline of our project. If the project behaves exactly as we planned, the expenses we incur will follow exactly the profile defined by the PV.

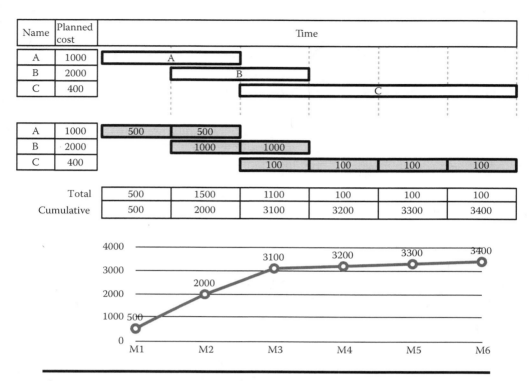

Figure 3.20 Computation of planned value.

3.9.4.2 Actual Costs

The **actual costs** (ACs) record the actual expenditures we incurred as the plan develops. ACs differ from PV for two reasons:

1. Some activities might have actual start or end dates different from those scheduled.
2. The actual effort and costs necessary to carry out an activity might be different from what was planned.

ACs are plotted similar to the PV, using, as input, the actual plan.

Comparing the PV and the ACs allows the project manager to understand how the actual plan is doing with respect to the plan defined at the project start. For instance, at any given time, we can tell whether we spent less or more than initially planned.

However, this information by itself is not sufficient, since we have no idea about the actual progress we achieved. That is, having spent more than planned could be a very good sign if the technical progress is also above the expectations, since the excessive expenditure could be a sign that our project is ahead of schedule.

In other words, in order to draw conclusions on the project status, we need to evaluate the technical progress. This is achieved with the computation of the earned value.

3.9.4.3 Earned Value

Earned value (EV) is the way in which we measure the technical progress of a project. There are two key concepts behind its definition.

The first is that we measure technical progress in terms of money. This allows one to plot EV using the same measurement unit of PV and ACs.

The second is that the value we assign to technical progress in an activity is exactly the money we *budgeted* for the activity, namely, its PV. Thus, if an activity has a PV of €3000, its EV will be €3000 when the activity is completed.

The EV of a plan is the sum of the EVs of its activities. Thus, when we complete a project, its EV will be the same as its PV. Similar to what happens with the ACs, **in the ideal plan**, the EV is an exact replica of the PV. However, during the actual execution of plans, we will have to take into account deviations from the ideal case.

In computing the EV, we are left with determining two other aspects: the first is when we accumulate EV and the second is how much we accumulate it over time.

The answer to the first question is easy: EV is accounted as the actual work to produce it. Thus, the EV of an activity that has not yet started is 0, while the EV of a completed activity is equal to its PV.

The problem is what happens in between, namely, activities that are started but not yet finished. We could have EV progress linearly with the duration of an activity. Thus, an activity at 40% of its duration could have earned 40% of its PV. The method, however, takes a simpler approach. A percentage of the planned value is accounted when an activity starts; the remaining part is accounted for when the activity ends. One simple allocation rule assigns 50% of the EV when an activity is started and the remaining 50% when the activity is completed. Another rule used very often assigns 20% when the activity starts and the remaining 80% when the activity is completed.

There are two advantages. The first is that the computation is a lot simpler. The second is that the computation is robust with respect to changes in the duration of activities started but not ended at the time of monitoring. Thus, the EV we compute at a given date does not have to be revised when we perform a second monitoring at a later date.

3.9.4.4 Assessing a Plan Health Using Earned Value Analysis

Now that we have these three values, we can assess easily the project status, since we have a way to instantly compare actual costs and actual progress (EV) with respect to our plan.

Figure 3.21 shows some of the values that allow a project manager to assess the health status of a project. Consider the following items:

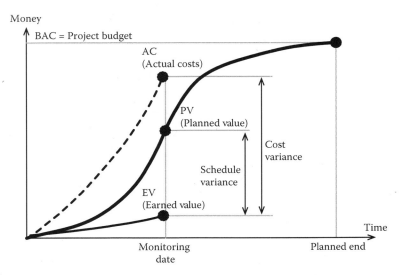

Figure 3.21 Earned value analysis.

- **Comparing PV and EV**: The difference between PV and the EV at the monitoring date tells us whether we are late or early: if EV is above PV, then we are early (we realized more technical progress than expected); the opposite will be true if EV is less than PV. The difference between PV and EV is called **schedule variance**.

- **Comparing EV and ACs**: The difference between ACs and EV tells us whether we are underbudget and overbudget. This concept might be slightly less intuitive than the previous example and deserves a bit more explanation. Consider the case of an ideal plan: PV, EV, and ACs will overlap perfectly. Now, if we are spending a bit more than expected to achieve the planned technical progress, ACs will be a bit higher than EV and PV. Similarly, if we are underachieving, EV will be less than PV and ACs. The difference between EV and ACs is called **cost variance**.

Two other measures are often taken into account to compute the efficiency. In particular, the following two measures are often used.

The **cost performance index** (or *CPI*) measures the efficiency with which we are *earning value*. It is computed as follows:

$$\text{CPI}_t = \frac{\text{EV}_t}{\text{AC}_t} \tag{3.23}$$

where *CPI*$_t$ is the cost performance index at time t, and *EV*$_t$ and *AC*$_t$ are, respectively, the EV and ACs at the same instance of time t.

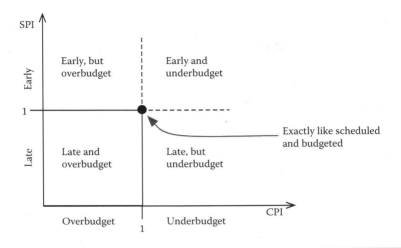

Figure 3.22 CPI and SPI tracking.

Note that $CPI > 1$ if we are achieving technical progress more efficiently than we are spending (we are earning more than one unit of EV for every unit of money we spend). If the trend is maintained, the project will be underbudget. Conversely, if $CPI < 1$, we are inefficient and the project will run overbudget if no corrective action is taken.

The **schedule performance index** (or *SPI*) measures the speed at which we are achieving technical progress. It is defined as follows:

$$\mathrm{SPI}_t = \frac{\mathrm{EV}_t}{\mathrm{PV}_t} \qquad (3.24)$$

where SPI_t is the schedule performance index at time t, EV_t and PV_t are, respectively, the EV and PV at the same instance of time t.

Note that $SPI > 1$ if we are achieving technical progress more efficiently than we planned (we are earning more than one unit of EV for every unit of money we planned to spend).

CPI and SPI can be plotted over time on a two-dimensional space, which allows one to understand whether the project is over- or underbudget and behind or ahead of schedule. This is shown in Figure 3.22.

3.9.4.5 Some Considerations about Earned Value Analysis

EVA is an effective approach to provide an integrated view on some measurements that characterize project progress. It also has some limitations. The first is that EVA does not consider the quality of outputs as it focuses only on two of the three main dimensions characterizing a project, namely, cost and schedule. The second is that the technique is best suited for larger projects, where the effort of the computation is paid back by the synthesis it produces.

The technique has been standardized (Eletronics and Department, 1998) and many resources are available. We mention the ubiquitous PMBOK, NASA, and Office-of-Management-U.S.-Department-of-Energy, from which various tutorial, publications, resources and guidelines can be downloaded.

3.9.5 Monitoring Progress, the Agile Way

All the planning techniques we have seen so far start from an estimation of the effort. During project monitoring, they measure the effort currently spent in an attempt to understand the schedule performance. As we have seen in the previous section, however, the connection between planned effort, actual effort, and technical progress is feeble. Given an actual effort, in fact, it is difficult to understand the technical progress achieved and the work necessary to finish the project. More precise approaches like EVA require a structured data collection approach and quite some work.

For these and other reasons, the agile methodologies take a different approach to measuring progress. The two fundamental differences are that the method focuses on the work left (which is always known) and on an estimation of the *velocity* required to finish the activity. Let us see the method in more detail by taking, as reference, the Scrum development methodology.

One of the fundamental differences of agile methodologies is that all project activities are organized in sprints that have a fixed time frame, that is, a project is a sequence of sprints of the same length.

During planning, rather than an estimation of the effort, the agile team produces an estimation of the size of the work to be done. This is measured in an abstract unit, called **points**. Thus, a given sprint could have allocated 45 points to develop. The value is determined by allocating points to each user story being developed and then by adding all the user stories whose implementation is allocated to the sprint. (See Section 2.1 for the definition of user story.)

Given the fact that a sprint has a predetermined fixed length, the estimation of the points to be developed (or **burned**, using the Scrum terminology) can be used to compute the **velocity** at which the points have to be burned during the sprint, that is, how many points we need to burn in order to deliver on time. These two dimensions define an *ideal* burndown.

At the start of the sprint, the *theoretical* burndown curve is set, summing all the points that need to be burned down. During the sprint, work progresses and the *actual* burndown curve is updated by subtracting the points of the user stories completed and adding those required by any rework needed. At any point in time now, by comparing the ideal and actual burndown, we can get the following information:

- **Remaining points**, that is, how many points we have still to burn down. This is shown by the current value of the actual burndown. Since the time slot is fixed, this value can be used to determine the (new) velocity needed to complete the burndown or, more realistically, what user stories the team will not be able to deliver in the time slot of the sprint.
- **Comparison with the ideal burndown**. By comparing the actual and the ideal burndown, we have a very fast way to understand whether we are early or late. If the actual burndown is below the ideal burndown, we are proceeding at a speed higher than planned; conversely, if the actual burndown is higher than the ideal burndown, we are late.

Figure 3.23 shows an example of a burndown chart. The diagram shows the ideal (line with circles) and the actual (line with triangles) burndown of a sprint lasting 10 days. As can be seen from the graph, the sprint started late and then proceeded at a higher speed than planned, bringing the sprint ahead of schedule.

This approach has two advantages over the approaches we have presented so far. The first is its *simplicity*. The second, subtler, is *focus*: the method focuses on the work left to be done, rather than on the work actually performed, and on the technical progress still to be achieved.

Some critiques have also been moved to the technique. The main problem is probably related to the abstract nature of the *points*, which makes estimation, especially for teams with little experience with agile methodologies, rather difficult. (One could argue that the same problem might arise with providing reliable estimations of the effort needed to complete a user story.) There is also a problem of consistency in the way in which points are interpreted by the different members of a team: four points for a person could be "equivalent" to nine points of another.

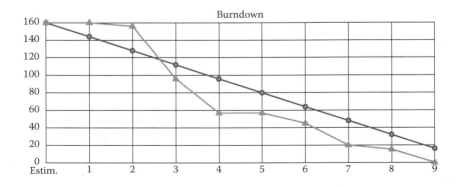

Figure 3.23 An example of a Scrum burndown chart.

3.9.6 Agile-Earned Value Analysis

The burndown chart is very simple to use and to assess the progress toward a goal. However, there are some situations in which it is important to understand how progress relates to the other dimensions that characterize a project, namely, costs and planned work. This is relevant, for instance, when Scrum is applied in contexts where people do not work full-time and with a fixed number of hours on a project, as might be the case in many situations. Moreover, the application of earned value management is suggested or compulsory for certain kind of projects. In these situations, adapting earned value management to an agile context provides a way to get the best of both worlds.

Different approaches have been suggested to apply earned value management to agile projects. Here we follow the one proposed in Rusk (2009), which works on the assumption that the product backlog (that is, the list of all the user stories to develop) must be known and estimated in advance and that the number of sprints has been decided. The hypotheses are not too strong and, as we will see, they can be further relaxed. The reader can look at Sulaiman (2007) and Rawsthorne (2010) to manage more complex scenarios.

The technique proposed in Rusk (2009) plots all data as percentages with respect to completion. The first line that can be plotted is PV, which is called the **gray line** by the method, which also emphasizes the usage of nontechnical terms to simplify the use of the technique. On the assumption of constant production speed, which is quite natural, when we use an agile methodology, the gray line is a straight line passing from the origin (no story developed) to the point having as x-value the date of delivery and as y-value 100% (everything delivered by the planned release date of the last sprint).

It is now possible to draw the other two lines, namely, ACs or **red line** and EV or **green line**, using the terminology of Rusk (2009). The first is the amount of the budget spent at the time of computation with respect to the total project budget. In a situation in which efficiency is as planned, ACs will match PV. The second is computed as the percentage of the story points actually delivered with respect to the total number of story points to develop. Similar to ACs, if the production is efficient as planned, the green curve (EV) will closely match the gray line (PV). An important aspect to highlight is the fact that value is earned when delivered and the points of a story are accrued when the functions implementing the story are actually released. In other words, a rule 0–100% is applied. The analysis will thus be accurate if the production is constant or the reporting period has a granularity that is low enough to abstract the time required for releasing a user story. If a user story requires 5 days to release, analyzing the status with EV on a daily basis will not yield any useful information till the last day: the EV, in fact, will stay the same till the function is released.

The analysis then proceeds as explained in Section 3.9.4.4. An additional advantage of agile EV over the standard analysis is that the projections are simpler, since PV is linear rather than S-shaped.

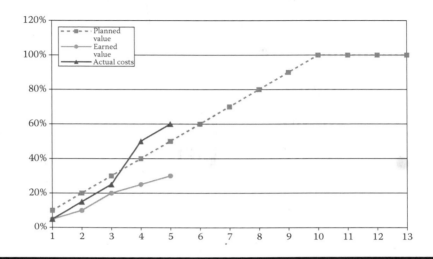

Figure 3.24 An example of agile-earned value analysis.

Figure 3.24 shows an example of an analysis, where the project is behind schedule, since the EV line is below PV, and over costs, since ACs are above PV and EV.

The initial hypothesis of an immutable backlog is quite limiting in an agile context, which embraces change. The technique, however, can be extended to accommodate changing requirements by creating a family of plots. Rusk, in particular, distinguishes between two types of changes. The first type of changes derives from an improved comprehension of the product to develop. Thus, the product backlog will increase in size as we get a better know-how on the work required to

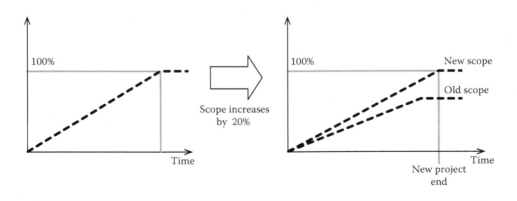

Figure 3.25 Accounting for changes in scope.

fully implement a user story. These changes, however, are residual and can be treated similarly to a systematic error in the estimations.

Different is the case of changes in scope, that is, situations in which the user changes the user stories to be implemented. Changes in scope might also trigger changes in the delivery dates. In this situation, we need to replot our gray line. The process is as follows. A new version of the backlog is the new baseline used to plot the current PV; the old PV, the ACs, and the EV can be recomputed and plotted against the new baseline. This is illustrated in Figure 3.25, where the left-hand side shows the initial status and the right-hand side the status after an increase in scope: both the new and the old PVs are shown. The new PV reaches 100%, while the old PV is at 83% (equivalent to 100%/120%).

3.10 Project Closing

All projects come to an end. According to Meredith and Mantel (2002) and Richman (2012), there are four ways in which a project comes to an end:

- **Termination by integration** and **termination by addition**. These are two successful cases in which the project outputs are integrated in an existing organization or generate a new business or a new business line.
- **Termination by starvation**. This is a case in which a project ends because resources run out.
- **Termination by extinction**. This is a case in which a project is terminated by management because it fails to meet user objectives, it has been superseded by technical advances, or it is not profitable anymore.

Project closing is the last phase of a project, when the project outputs are handed over to the stakeholders, contractual agreements properly taken care of, and project records elicited and stored for future reference. Project closing is also probably one of the most neglected phases of a project with many projects ending up spending 90% of their time with the remaining 10% of work.

There are various motivations for projects not being closed properly. Projects terminating unsuccessfully certainly do not motivate teams or project managers to invest further resources (technical, financial, and, why not, also emotional) on a proper closure. Many successful projects, however, are also not properly terminated. This is due to the following causes:

- Decreasing interest by the project team, as they might be concerned with their next assignment.
- The cost of performing closing activities, which are routine and often require little or no creativity. Consider the case of writing the installation instructions of a software system.
- Underestimation of how much implicit knowledge there is and how fast know-how of this implicit knowledge can get lost. Again, consider the case

of the installation procedure of a complex software: at the end of the project, all information is available and very clear in the project team. As time moves away, it might become more complex to recall by heart all the steps that were required.

■ Reluctance, by the project sponsor, to release resources for various reasons, among which is the fear of losing the competences needed to fully exploit the project deliverables, and so on.

For this reason, a proper management process should be enforced to ensure that a proper project closure takes places (or, if not, that the decision is an explicit management decision, rather than the result of inaction).

Project closing can be organized in the following steps (Wysocki, 2011; Richman, 2012; NASA, 2007):

■ Getting client acceptance
■ Installing project deliverables
■ Archiving old deliverables
■ Documenting the project
■ Performing a financial closure
■ Performing postimplementation audit
■ Releasing staff.

3.10.1 Getting Client Acceptance

The project is successfully completed when the customer and the project manager agree that the work performed is satisfactory. In software development projects, getting client acceptance might require some effort on the part of the project manager, since the client might be interested in keeping the project team allocated to the project.

According to Wysocki (2011), there are two ways in which acceptance is achieved. The first is a **ceremonial acceptance**, when there is no formal procedure or formal record for accepting project deliverables. Various scenarios are possible, such as a gentleman's agreement between the customer and the project manager or, simply, just reaching project deadlines.

The second is a **formal acceptance**, where there is a formal procedure for accepting project deliverables. In software development, such a procedure nearly always includes a system testing phase, in which tests are executed on the software system being handed over.

3.10.2 Installing Project Deliverables

During this phase, the outputs of the projects are installed. See Section 2.5 for the detailed list of activities to be performed here, in the case of software projects.

3.10.3 Archiving Old Deliverables

If applicable, any deliverable made obsolete by the project needs to be properly disposed of.

In software development projects, decommissioning typically requires one to archive a version of the old deliverables. It is in fact a relatively cheap operation that can bring a lot of advantages, should the new deliverables not work as expected.

3.10.4 Documenting the Project

The goal of this activity is to ensure that the documentation of the project is up to date.

It is a time-consuming activity, which is done on deliverables that might soon be archived. Still, maintaining a proper document record is not only essential in certain domains (like for the development of safety-critical applications), but also essential should a request about a project or its outputs come some time after the project closes. Consider, for instance, a request to fix a bug discovered months after the project end.

Maintaining a proper document record allows us to learn and improve, since we can use the project data and experience as a basis for our next projects. See also Section 3.10.6.

3.10.5 Performing a Financial Closure

The goal of this activity is to ensure that all expenses are paid, all credits cashed, and any remaining budget properly released.

Financial reports are generated during this phase.

3.10.6 Postimplementation Audit

The goal of a postimplementation audit, also called **postmortem**, is a critical analysis of the project in order to learn and improve and to avoid repeating the same mistakes.

According to Collier et al. (1996), a sound postmortem process requires the following steps:

1. **Conduct a project survey**, with the goal of eliciting from the project team the main issues and strengths of the project. This allows one to focus the rest of the process on the important items.
2. **Collect objective information**, with the goal of taking quantitative measures about the project. The metrics suggested by Collier et al. (1996) are shown in Table 3.16.
3. **Hold a debriefing meeting**, during which team members are given the opportunity to provide frank feedback on the project. While potentially

Table 3.16   An Example of Postmortem Quantitative Metrics for Software Development

Cost Metrics	Schedule Metrics	Quality Metrics
Planned effort and estimated SLOC	Original schedule	
Actual effort and actual SLOC	Final schedule	
History of changes to requirements and code	History of schedule slippage events	Errors at each stage

being very useful, **to be effective they require an open and constructive attitude both from the management and the team members.** If management shows a defensive attitude, in fact, the meeting will most likely yield no useful output, since the team members will not be encouraged to provide frank feedback. Conversely, if the team does not maintain a constructive attitude, the meeting risks become a dumping session in which resentful team members will monopolize time with no useful information. For this reason, it is often better to have a moderator/facilitator.

4. **Conduct a project history day**, which has the goal of understanding the root causes of problems identified at the previous steps. Each meeting is held with a selected number of participants and focuses on one specific problem among those identified at the previous steps. The meeting starts from a review of the project history, which allows participants to identify when the event under investigation started and, subsequently, what caused it.

5. **Publish the results**, during which the management team summarizes the findings of the postmortem and makes them available to the project team and relevant stakeholders in the organization. The content is structured with the following information:

   a. **Project description**: information about the project, to give context
   b. **The good**: what worked well
   c. **The bad**: the three worst factors that impeded the team's meeting its goals
   d. **The ugly**: a prescription for improvement.

A proper recording of the postmortem activities can ensure that the work carried out will also find usage in the medium/long term and become an organizational asset.

For small projects, a simpler procedure can be adopted, such as that described in Dingsøyr et al. (2005), where postmortem activities take place in a half-a-day meeting, organized with

- A brainstorming session, during which issues are elicited using the KJ method, which is based on post-it on a wall method that we saw while building WBS.
- A structuring session, during which the issues are clustered.

■ An analysis session, during which the root causes are analyzed.
■ A reporting session, where a report, containing main problems, main successes, and root causes, and the post-it used in the meetings are put together.

See Dingsøyr et al. (2005) for more practical information on structuring a postmortem and Birk et al. (2002) for a discussion of the advantages of conducting a postmortem.

3.10.7 Staff-Releasing

The transition from a closing project to new activities can be a disruptive experience from the project staff. It is an important management activity to ensure that this transition is the smoothest possible.

Two important aspects are:

1. Ensuring that proper recognition is assigned to the experience and the results obtained in the project. This is to ensure that working on a project does not turn out to be a disadvantage to the career of individuals.
2. Ensuring that proper tasks are assigned to the team members (e.g., by warning in advance the functional or unit managers about the availability of staff).

A final important aspect pointed out by Wysocki (2011) is celebrating success. Successful projects require teamwork and are a bonding experience. Showing gratitude for the work and effort your team put in a project is a good practice. In the words of Wysocki (2011), "my loud and continual message to senior management is this: Don't pass up an opportunity to show the team your appreciation."

3.11 An Example

In this section, we put into practice various notions illustrated in this chapter, by simulating the process that starts with a customer request and ends with a first plan of the activities to be performed. To do so, we imagine having been contacted by the marketing director of a group of theaters, who wants to be able to sell tickets through the Internet.

The system has to be operational at least one month before the season begins and should have the following functions:

1. View the list of shows of the upcoming season.
2. Register to the platform as owner of a seasonal ticket.
3. Register to the platform as an occasional viewer (one with no seasonal ticket).
4. Renew one's seasonal ticket, possibly choosing a new seat.

5. Buy tickets for a specific show, between one and three weeks before the show begins.
6. Access and use the system through the Internet or via smartphones.

We are asked to set up a project so that we can get started with development.

3.11.1 Initiating

The very first step is to give the project a name. We decide to name ours **Theater 3001**, as a homage to Arthur C. Clarke's *2001: A Space Odyssey*.

The first steps to get started include

1. Writing a scope document, which outlines the stakeholders, goals, budget, timing, deliverables, constraints, and risks. The scope document can be used as a basis for a contractual agreement and to ask for authorization to proceed from the management.
2. Identifying the requirements of the team that will be responsible for the development. The request could also comprehend the selection of a project manager, if this is going to be different from the person tasked with writing the scope document (unusual, but not impossible).
3. Obtaining an authorization to proceed from the client and from the performing organization.

As it is often the case in practice, the example starts with rough and incomplete information. One of the tasks in the initiating phase, in fact, is that of progressively refining and improving, so that we can come out with reliable estimations.

Some of the information we are missing from the specification given above, for instance, includes

1. The *goals of the project*, namely, what is in scope and what is not. For instance, are we being asked to deliver a product (a software system) or a service (develop a software system and operate it for our client)? This has an impact on different areas, such as

    a. *Project timing*, since additional work might be necessary for identifying a suitable hosting platform (a relatively simple task), setting the platform up (slightly more difficult), and preparing our organization to manage the service (definitely a more complex task).

    b. *Project pricing*. Although *operations* are outside the scope of the project (i.e., *outside the scope of any project*, for the definition of *project*), they might influence the project pricing. In fact, if we offer the solution as a service, subscriptions will be a source of revenue when we deliver the system. This could change the pricing schema we are willing to apply; for instance, we might be willing to charge a bit less for the project and return on investment by offering the service to different clients.

2. *Technical details about the required solution.* Various details about the requirements need to be refined. Consider, for instance, aspects related to the complexity of data the application will manage: the number of theaters we need to support, how many types of seasonal tickets there are, whether we need to integrate our solution with other existing systems, such as, for instance, an accounting system.

3. *Priorities.* Different functions have different priorities for the client. Making them explicit could help us understand what development process is best suited for the project at hand, what functions will have to be developed first, what goals are necessary to succeed. Remember the MoSCoW and SMART acronyms!

3.11.2 Building a Plan

On the hypothesis that we have collected from the client all the information required to have a clear picture of the project goals, we are now ready to build a plan. The plan could be organized as shown in Figure 3.26.

The plan is structured in four work packages:

1. **WP1. Inception**, where the system is specified
2. **WP2. Construction**, where the system is built

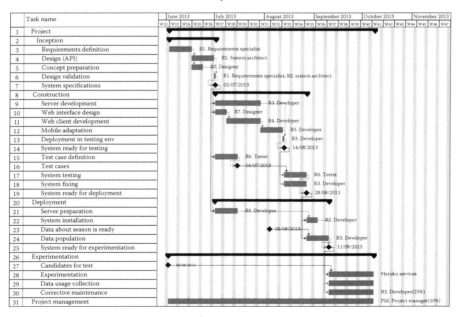

Figure 3.26 The Grantt chart of the Theater 3001 Project metrics for software development.

3. **WP3. Deployment**, which prepares the environment for a first experimentation of the system
4. **WP4. Experimentation**, where we test the system with a small group of selected users to verify the usability and interest in the application.

As can be seen, the plan is roughly scheduled as a waterfall, with work packages performed in sequence, with the exception of WP2 and WP3, which run mostly in parallel.

Two deliverables (ID 23 and 27) are required from the client. The first is the data that we need to populate the system (e.g., the shows that will be shown in the next season; the ticket prices). The second is the list of candidates for WP4, the experimentation. Note that both have a considerable slack, without providing any significant advantage to the project. A better allocation uses an "as late as possible" scheduling; this ensures that the information is collected when needed. Moreover, it minimizes the risks related to selecting candidates for the experimentation too early and then redoing part of the work to replace people who have changed their minds in between.

Another consideration is related to the effort and calendar time we have estimated for each activity. With an algorithmic technique, for instance, we could come out with an estimation of the whole plan, which we could then break down and allocate to the different activities, using the approach presented in Section 3.4.5.4. A different strategy uses reasoning by analogy or expert judgment; in this situation, we either resort to previous analogous projects or to the experience we (or our peers) have accumulated over the years.

Three milestones could be set in the project, corresponding to the main project events. The first could be set at the end of June (specifications ready), the second in the first week of September (system ready for experimentation), and the third at the end of September (system experimented). (Note that the milestones are not shown in the diagram above.)

A first analysis of the plan allows us to understand which activities are more critical. Various activities have some slack. All activities related to system development, however, are on the critical path of our plan: any delay in activities related to the development will delay our project. Thus, system development activities are those that will require more attention on our side, to ensure that the plan is not delayed.

In the plan, we have been a bit optimistic about the experimentation, for which we have not foreseen any support activity, such as, for instance, corrective maintenance that might be necessary if problems are found in the application.

Another activity that does not appear in the Gantt chart is a project management task. We decided to allocate to project management about 5% of the total project effort, since the project is not too complex. Note that the percentage for more complex projects is higher and sometimes estimated between 10% and 20% of the total effort. Whether a specific *project management* activity has to be added to the Gantt chart is a matter of personal choice. One advantage is that the management needs of a project are made explicit. Another is that the computation of the project costs can be performed using the tool.

Also note that at this stage of planning, the timing indicated by the Gantt chart is indicative as the actual availability of resources has not yet been specified. Planning tools make the assumption that the duration is equal to the effort before any resource is assigned. The actual plan could thus stretch or squeeze, according to the number of resources we will actually be able to allocate.

3.11.3 Creating a Budget for the Project

The first step to compute the budget is to define the type of expenses we will be incurring. More precisely, we need to select a CES and estimate each element of our CES. Since each organization typically has a standardized CES, the difficult part of budgeting is really that of coming out with reliable estimations of our expenditures.

In our project, the following costs will have to be sustained:

- **Personnel costs.** Cost of the personnel responsible for the development of the solution. We imagine having access to a pool of six resources, namely, R1,...,R6. Table 3.17 shows their costs.
- **Costs related to hiring a designer for the Graphical User Interface (GUI)** (R7). Note that the cost of the designer is per use and paid for upfront. This is shown by the last column of Table 3.17 that reports *Start*.
- **Costs related to hosting the application for the experimentation**, marked as WS in Table 3.17.

We do not envisage any other cost for this project: no people will travel, and no cost is necessary for meetings, no costs are foreseen for consumables or special equipment.

The budget can be computed using the estimations of the effort and on the cost of the resources, yielding a total budget of €41,000 (of which €37,000 related to producing the system and €4000 to managing the project; the management has

Table 3.17   Cost of Resources We Can Use for the Theater 3001 Project

Name	Type	Maximum Availability (%)	Cost (€/h)	Overtime (€/h)	Cost per Use	Accrue
R1. Requirements	Work	100.00	40	60		Prorated
R2. System Architect	Work	100.00	40	60		Prorated
R3. Developer	Work	100.00	30	60		Prorated
R4. Developer	Work	100.00	30	60		Prorated
R5. Developer	Work	100.00	30	60		Prorated
R6. Tester	Work	100.00	50	100		Prorated
R7. Designer	Work	100.00			€500.00	Start
PM. Project Manager	Work	100.00	60	100		Prorated
WS. Web Services		2				Prorated

Table 3.18   Budget for the Theater 3001 Project

Task Name	Resource Name	Work (Man-Days)	Cost
Theater Project		167	€41,000.00
Project		158	€37,000.00
Inception		27	€7540.00
Requirements Definition	R1. Requirements Specialist	10	€3200.00
Design (API)	R2. System Architect	10	€3200.00
Concept Preparation	R7. Designer	5	€500.00
Design Validation	R1. Requirements Specialist	2	€640.00
	R2. System Architect		
System Specifications		0	
Construction		81	€21,940.00
Server Development	R3. Developer	20	€4800.00
Web Interface Design	R7. Designer	5	€500.00
Web Client Development	R4. Developer	15	€3600.00
Mobile Adaptation	R5. Developer	10	€2400.00
Deployment in Testing Env	R3. Developer	1	€240.00
System Ready for Testing		0	
Test Case Definition	R6. Tester	10	€4000.00
Test Cases		0	
System Testing	R6. Tester	10	€4000.00
System Fixing	R3. Developer	10	€2400.00
System Ready for Deployment		0	
Deployment		25	€6000.00
Server Preparation	R5. Developer	10	€2400.00
System Installation	R5. Developer	5	€1200.00
Data about Season Is Ready		0	
Data population	R3. Developer	10	€2400.00
System Ready for Experimentation		0	
Experimentation		25	€1520.00
Candidates for Test		0	
Experimentation	Heroku Services	20	€320.00
Data Usage Collection		0	
Corrective Maintenance	R5. Developer[25%]	5	€1200.00
Project Management	PM. Project Manager	9	€4000.00

been estimated at about 5% of the overall project effort). The analytical data are shown in Table 3.18.

3.11.4 Changing the Plan to Meet External Deadlines

A common situation is one in which the plan we have built is too long, when compared with the client's constraints. That is, the project is four calendar months, but the client needs the system in 3 months. So we need to shorten the plan somehow.

As we have seen, the options we can use include

1. Changing the project approach
2. Reducing or changing the project scope
3. Allocating resources more efficiently
4. Fast tracking.

Let us see each option in more detail, after reminding that shortening a plan typically increases the risk profile of a project. Thus, a full analysis always needs to consider the possibility that the project is not feasible, given the constraints.

3.11.4.1 Changing the Project Approach

It might be the case that not all functions are equally useful for the client and that the waterfall is not the best process for the project at hand.

For instance, on the hypothesis that "buying a seasonal ticket" is more important than the other functions, we could revise the project and adopt an incremental approach, splitting the project into two cycles. The first cycle could be dedicated to implementing the most important functions; the implementation of the other functions could be postponed to the second stage. This option might reduce the estimated effort and duration by the amount necessary to achieve the project deadline. As an additional bonus, the contract (or payments) could be broken into two distinct parts (one for each cycle), with the option for the client (or supplier) to abandon the project, if the results achieved at the end of the first iteration are not satisfactory.

An alternative is to replan the project using critical chain management. In this scenario, a revision of the project durations and the allocation of feeding and project buffers might end up in a project that can meet the client's deadline.

3.11.4.2 Reducing or Changing the Project Scope

Changes in scope are also possible. For instance, eliminating the experimentation from the plan would spare us one calendar month, moving the delivery date to September 9, which might be good enough for the client, although not as good as the desired deadline. In addition to canceling the experimentation, giving up the implementation of the web client would allow us to squeeze the plan by another 10 days, thus meeting the client deadline, on the hypothesis that the web client is not important for the client. Note, however, that the resulting plan has significant risks, among which:

■ The project has no buffer and many important activities are on the critical path. Any small delay could end up being catastrophic for the client, since it would most likely move the delivery date after the expected deadline.
■ Canceling the experimentation might lower the quality of the end-product, which we will not be able to test on the field.

3.11.4.3 Allocating Resources More Efficiently

A quick analysis of the plan will show that developers are underutilized and that allocating more developers to the activities might shorten the plan a bit.

Consider, for instance, activities 9, 10, and 11, two of which are on the critical path and, therefore, if shortened, will cause the plan to shorten (till a new critical path kicks in). If we allocated all developers to these activities, activity 9 would be shortened to about 7 days, and activities 10 and 11 to about 8 days, together. This could shorten the plan a bit.

Trying the same approach for other activities has less effect: for instance, allocating more developers to activity 18 does not yield any saving, since it is not on the critical path; the overall duration of that portion of the plan depends on activity 17, which cannot be shortened.

3.11.4.4 Fast Tracking the Plan

Another possibility is to break some dependencies from the plan. We need to analyze the plan in detail, understanding what dependencies are "weaker" than others.

Some opportunities in the plan include the following:

- The "data population" activity, which requires one to populate a database with the data about the upcoming theater season, does not require a fully functional system. As long as the database structure is stable, the work can be performed with little or no risk of rework. Thus, we could break the SF dependency between activity 19 and activity 24 and save 1 week.
- Activity 12, "Mobile adaptation," consists in adapting the web interface for mobile clients. Also, in this case, we could break the dependency and run the activity in parallel with activity 11, either by developing a completely independent interface for the two worlds, or by using an approach in which activity 11 feeds activity 12 as soon as any portion of the web interface is ready (rather than waiting for the whole interface to be ready). This allows us to squeeze the plan by another 10 days, by introducing some risks related to rework.
- Similar to the previous case, we could interleave development and testing. The possibility of rework in this case, however, is rather high. An excellent synchronization is also required between the development and testing teams, increasing the complexity of the activities, stress, and the probability of delivering late.

3.12 Questions and Topics for Discussion

1. Consider the introduction of a market information system in a developing country. A market information system collects and sends information to subscribers about prices of vegetables in local markets, so that farmers can decide

when and where to sell their produce. The information is sent through SMSs. Farmers in developing countries, however, live on a tight budget. What could be the sustainability model of such a solution?

2. Perform the stakeholder analysis of a project to build a motorway connecting two cities.

3. Imagine we want to pilot a software system to track personal finances with a restricted set of users. Try and imagine some SMART goals for the project.

4. Build a WBS for a business reengineering project to automate the enrollment of students in courses. Define also the WBS dictionary.

5. What are the main advantages and disadvantages of algorithmic estimation techniques?

6. What could be the value of mixing different techniques when evaluating the effort required for the development of a software system?

7. What is the impact on the schedule of doubling the effort, according to the COCOMO model?

8. Define a CES for a software development project. Do the same for a house construction project. Look for CES on the Internet, if necessary, and compare the differences.

9. What are the main advantages of earned value analysis? What are the limitations?

10. What are the possible ways in which a project terminates?

11. Consider a ticket reservation system for Greyhound buses. Try and replay the Theater 3001 example, outlining the goals, a plan, and a budget of this new project.

References

Aksel, J. E., 2008. Defining White paper, Celeris Systems. Last retrieved June 21, 2013.

Albrecht, A. J., 1979. Measuring application development productivity. In *Proc. IBM Application Development Symposium*, pp. 83–92. IBM Press.

Birk, A., T. Dingsoyr, and T. Stalhane, 2002, May/June. Postmortem: Never leave a project without it. *Software, IEEE 19*(3), 43–45.

Boehm, B. W., 1981. *Software Engineering Economics*. Englewood Cliffs, NJ: Prentice Hall.

Boehm, B. W., 1984, January. Software engineering economics. *IEEE Transactions on Software Engineering SE-10*(1), 4–21.

Boehm, B. W., C. Abts, A. W. Brown, S. Chulani, B. K. Clark, E. Horowitz, R. Madachy, D. J. Reifer, and B. Steece, 2000. *Software Cost Estimation with COCOMO II*. Prentice Hall, Englewood Cliffs, NJ, USA.

Boehm, B. W. and K. J. Sullivan, 2000, June. Software economics: A roadmap. In *Conference on the Future of Software Engineering at the International Conference on Software Engineering*, Limerick, Ireland, pp. 319–343. Technical report available at http://www.cs.virginia.edu/people/faculty/pdfs/p319-boehm.pdf. Last retrieved November 15, 2013.

Brooks, F. P. J., 1995. *The Mythical Man Month* (Anniversary ed.). Addison-Wesley: Boston, MA, USA.

Burke, R., 2006. *Project Management, Planning and Control Techniques* (4th ed.). John Wiley & Sons, New York, NY, USA.

The Business Model Generation, 2013. The business model canvas. Available at http://www.businessmodelgeneration.com/downloads/business_model_canvas_poster.pdf. Last retrieved June 14, 2013.

Cameron, W. S., 2005, March. Lessons learned again and again and again. *Ask Magazine* (Issue 12). Available at http://askmagazine.nasa.gov/issues/12/features/ask12_features_lessonslearned.html. Last retrieved April 3, 2013.

CDC, 2013. Work breakdown structure dictionary. Available at http://www2.cdc.gov/cdcup/library/templates/CDC_UP_WBS_Dictionary_Template.doc. Last retrieved June 15, 2013.

Center for Software Engineering, 2000. Cocomo II model definition manual. Available at http://csse.usc.edu/csse/research/COCOMOII/cocomo2000.0/CII_modelman2000.0.pdf.

Christensen, D. S., 2013. Earned value bibliography. Available at http://www.suu.edu/faculty/christensend/ev-bib.html. Last retrieved April 2, 2013.

Clark, W. and H. L. Gantt, 1923. *The Gantt Chart—A Working Tool of Management* (Second printing ed.). The Ronald Press Company, New York, USA.

COCOMO 81, 2013e, April. Available at http://csse.usc.edu/csse/research/COCOMOII/cocomo81.htm.

Collier, B., T. DeMarco, and P. Fearey, 1996, July. A defined process for project post mortem review. *Software, IEEE 13*(4), 65–72.

Department of Defense, 2011. Work breakdown structure for defense materiel items. Technical Report MIL-HDBK-881C, Department of Defense Standard. Available at http://www.everyspec.com/MIL-STD/MIL-STD-0800-0899/MIL-STD-881C_32553/. Last retrieved November 15, 2013.

Dingsøyr, T., T. Stålhane, and N. B. Moe, 2005, August. A practical guide to lightweight post mortem reviews. Available at http://www.uio.no/studier/emner/matnat/ifi/INF3120/h05/studentarbeider/Prosjektoppgave/PMA_practical_guide.pdf. Last retrieved January 5, 2013.

Government Eletronics and Information Technology Association Engineering Department, 1998, May. Earned value management systems. Technical Report ANSI/EIA-748-1998, Electronic Industries Alliance.

Friesner, T., 2013. History of SWOT analysis. Available at http://www.marketingteacher.com/swot/history-of-swot.html#. Last retrieved January 5, 2013.

Goldratt, E. M., 1997. *Critical Chain*. The North River Press, Great Barrington, MA, USA.

Hamilton, L. R., 1964, June. Study of methods for evaluation of the pert/cost management system. Technical Report ED-TDR-64-92, MITRE Corporation.

International function point user group, 2013c, Available at http://www.ifpug.org. Last retrieved April 9, 2013.

Jørgensen, M. and M. Shepperd, 2007, January. A systematic review of software development cost estimation studies. *IEEE Transactions on Software Engineering 33*(1) p. 33–53.

Longstreet, D., 2008. Estimating data. Available at http://www.softwaremetrics.com/Articles/estimatingdata.htm. Last retrieved April 9, 2013.

Maylor, H., 2010. *Project Management* (4th ed.). Harlow, England: Pearson.

Meredith, J. R. and S. J. Mantel, 2002. *Project Management: A Managerial Approach*. New York, NY: John Wiley & Sons, Inc.

Merlo-Schett, N., M. Glinz, and A. Mukhija, 2002. COCOMO (constructive cost model). Working notes of Seminars in Software Engineering, Available at https://files.ifi.uzh.ch/rerg/arvo/courses/seminar_ws02/reports/Seminar_4.pdf.

NASA, 1994, May. *Work Breakdown Structure Reference Guide*. Program/Project management series. NASA.

NASA, 2004. Software assurance standard. NASA TECHNICAL STANDARD NASA-STD-8739.8 w/Change 1, NASA.

NASA, 2007, December. Systems engineering handbook. Technical Report NASA/SP-2007-6105 Rev1, NASA.

NASA, 2012. Earned value management (EVM). Available at http://evm.nasa.gov/tutorial.html. Last retrieved October 13, 2012.

NPS, 2013. COCOMO II calculator. Available at http://csse.usc.edu/tools/COCOMOII.php. Last retrieved April 20, 2013.

Office of Management, U.S. Department of Energy, 2012. Earned value management. Available at http://energy.gov/management/office-management/operational-management/project-management/earned-value-management. Last retrieved October 13, 2012.

PERT Coordinating Group, 1963. *PERT Guide for Management Use/PERT Coordinating Group*. Number NASA-TM-101864. U.S. Government Printers, Washington, D.C.

Project Management Institute, 2004. *A Guide to the Project Management Body of Knowledge (PMBOK Guides)* (4th ed.). Project Management Institute, Newtown Square, Pennsylvania 19073-3299 USA.

Quantitative Software Management, 2013. Function point language table. Available at http://www.qsm.com/resources/function-point-languages-table. Last retrieved April 20, 2013.

Rawsthorne, D., 2010. Monitoring scrum projects with agileevm and earned business value (EBV) metrics. Available at http://danube.com/system/files/CollabNet_WP_AgileEVM_and_Earned_Business_Value_Metrics_032510.pdf. Last retrieved June 3, 2013.

Reifer, D., 2000. Web development: Estimating quick-to-market software. *Software, IEEE* 17(6), 57–64.

Richman, L., 2012. *Improving Your Project Management Skills*. American Management Association (AMACOM).

Ruhe, M., R. Jeffery, and I. Wieczorek, 2003. Using web objects for estimating software development effort for web applications. In *Software Metrics Symposium, 2003. Proceedings. Ninth International*, pp. 30–37, Sydney, Australia.

Rusk, J., 2009. Earned value for agile development. Available at http://www.agilekiwi.com/EarnedValueForAgileProjects.pdf. Last retrieved June 3, 2013.

Space Division—North American Rockwell, 1971, June. Space shuttle program—space shuttle phase c/d baseline volume 3: Work breakdown structure dictionary. Technical Report N76-71555, Space Division—North American Rockwell. Last retrieved June 15, 2013.

Stratton, R., 2009. Critical chain project management theory and practice. In *POMS 20th Annual Conference*. Last retrieved June 16, 2013.

Sulaiman, T., 2007, October. Agileevm: Measuring cost efficiency across the product lifecycle. Available at http://www.infoq.com/articles/agile-evm. Last retrieved June 3, 2013.

Tomczyk, C. A., 2005. *Project Manager's Spotlight on Planning*. Harbor Light Press, San Francisco, CA, USA.

University of Southern California, 2013. COCOMO® 81 intermediate model implementation. Available at http://sunset.usc.edu/research/COCOMOII/cocomo81_pgm/cocomo81.html.

Wysocki, R. K., 2011, October. *Effective Project Management: Traditional, Agile, Extreme* (6, illustrated ed.). John Wiley & Sons, New York, NY, USA.

Yang, Y., M. He, M. Li, Q. Wang, and B. Boehm, 2008. Phase distribution of software development effort. In *Proceedings of the Second ACM-IEEE International Symposium on Empirical Software Engineering and Measurement*, ESEM '08, New York, NY, pp. 61–69. ACM.

Yu, E., P. Giorgini, N. Maiden, and J. Mylopoulos, 2011. *Social Modeling for Requirements Engineering*. The MIT Press, Cambridge, MA, USA.

Chapter 4

Making IT Better: Managing Changes, Risks, and Quality

In the previous chapter, we have introduced the basics for managing a project. In fact, goals, time, and costs establish the characteristics of the products to build, the work to be performed, its timing, and its costs.

In the scenario, we set in the previous chapter, we followed the process end-to-end, but little space was dedicated to the unpredictability of projects. We discussed uncertainties of estimations and hinted about variations in Section 3.9, where we saw how to evaluate progress in a project.

It is time to start all over! In this chapter, we introduce two main sources of perturbations in the plans we defined in the previous chapter. The first main source of perturbation is a request for changes; the second is project risks. Both are necessary and unavoidable. Fortunately, we also have techniques to control and tame these sources of entropy. They are change control and configuration management, risk management, and quality management.

4.1 Managing Changes

During a project, requests to change the work to be performed or some of the characteristics of the deliverables to produce will originate from internal and external stakeholders, for the most diverse reasons, such as

- **Incompleteness** or **incoherencies** in the project requirements or in the description of work, which were not apparent when the project started
- A **better comprehension** of the system to be developed, which provides an opportunity for a smarter construction of a project deliverable
- A **technical opportunity**, which could yield a more efficient or a more feature-rich deliverable
- A **technical challenge**, which makes the construction of the deliverable impossible with the approach chosen when the activity started
- A **change in the external environment**, including an influent stakeholder changing his/her opinion or a change in the business landscape, such as the launch of a new competing product*
- **Noncompliance**, if a deliverable does not conform to its specifications.

A request for changes and changes in a project have a cost, provide an opportunity, and constitute a perturbation and a risk.

That a request for changes has a cost should be relatively intuitive, although not obvious at first. After all, software is extremely flexible: change a function here, modify something else there, and you are done. This is, however, a simplification. Work is needed to follow up on the change request and ensure that all changes are propagated to the relevant artifacts. As we pointed out in the introduction, the cost of changes in a project, in fact, increases as the project develops. For instance, Figure 4.1 shows the increasing cost of fixing a bug during different phases of software development.

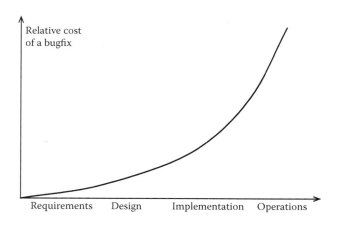

Figure 4.1 The cost of change.

---

* Notice that important and influential stakeholders, similar to politicians, never change their opinion: it is our perception of their thoughts that changes.

With costs also come opportunities. There are many situations in which a change to the planned course of action gives an opportunity to improve the quality of deliverables at little or no cost or improve other project metrics, such as cost and schedule.

The medium- and long-term effects of changes, however, need to be carefully analyzed and constitute a risk. Introducing a modification in agreed work and taking a new route introduces uncertainties. Under the pressure of project execution, forgetting some initial hypotheses on which a specific choice is based or underestimating the impact of a change can be a significant source of trouble.

Another important consideration is that changing a course of action while the work is not complete requires a lot of discipline and attention to make sure we do not get stuck in the middle of the road, failing to fully implement the new route, and having difficulties going back to the initial situation.

For the reasons mentioned above, it is a good idea to have a controlled process to manage changes. This should be done in the early phases of a project, by adopting or defining a standard to manage changes that are agreed on by all stakeholders.

The process should achieve the following goals:

1. **Ensuring that all stakeholders agree on the fact that a request for change has occurred**. This is to avoid what is called **scope creeps**, namely, a steady flow of small changes that causes a project to drift out of control. A typical example is a flow of clarifications on the work statement occurring directly between the developers and the customer, which slowly changes the initial formulation of the work to be performed.
2. **Ensuring that changes are beneficial and agreed on by all stakeholders**. Different stakeholders might have contrasting views on the system. If changes are incorporated as soon as they are elicited from one stakeholder, they might disagree with the vision of other stakeholders. We might thus end up building a system that is different from the one some stakeholders expected. This can potentially lead to significant rework, adding and removing features.
3. **Protecting the coherency of a project and of its outputs**. Projects produce many deliverables whose content is interrelated. Every time we introduce a change, we need to ensure that changes propagate to all relevant artifacts. If this is not done, the quality of artifacts will degrade over time causing failures or making a system more difficult to maintain.

Many processes have been proposed to manage changes. They all share four characteristics.

The first is that they **formally record and document that a request for a change has occurred**. This requires one to document requests, possibly with additional information, such as the originator and motivation. Note that the documentation of request for changes simplifies project acceptance. In fact, even if there is complete agreement between the client and the project team, it might as well be that the reference people change during the project and that the person (or people) in charge of accepting project outputs are different from the ones with whom the changes to the project scope have been agreed with. If such changes are not documented, the situation might be difficult to handle.

The second is that they define how to **decide whether a request for a change will be accepted or not**. The decision process typically includes an evaluation of the request (e.g., importance and relevance), an evaluation of the ways in which the request can be incorporated, an evaluation of the impact of the request (namely, what has to be changed to accommodate the change), and the approval or rejection process (namely, who decides).

The third is that they all **record the life cycle of change requests**, so that it can be established whether a change request has been approved and, if so, when it has taken place. The process also ensures that there is accountability for the decisions that are taken in a project.

Finally, all processes **specify who has to be involved or informed about the change**. This is to ensure that everyone is informed about the current status of a system. When information does not flow as expected, in fact, difficult situations might occur. A very nice example comes again from Cox and Murray (2004). In an early launch of one vector of the Mercury program, a vector failed to lift off from the launchpad. A series of subsequent events, such as the automatic deployment of Mercury's parachute (which could work as a sail and cause the vector to crashland) and the fact that the vector was fueled and in an unknown status contributed to raising various concerns, till the situation was recovered with no incident. The cause of the failure was traced back to a small change to one of the prongs of one plug connecting the missile to the umbilical tower. One technician had removed a quarter of an inch from one of the prongs of a plug, to ensure that it would fit more easily into the plug; he did not tell anyone. During the launch, however, the shortened prong detached a bit earlier than the longer one, determining a nonnominal situation and causing the onboard computer to decide that it was safer to shut off the engine.

In the following two subsections, we look at two different approaches to change management in software development projects.

4.1.1 Managing Changes in the Traditional Approach

Figure 4.2 shows an example of change management process. It is a simplified version of the one defined (NASA, 2007).

The first step is the creation of a request for a change. Requests are filed by the stakeholders (including the project team) when the need arises. Special templates can be used to file requests, to ensure that a minimal set of information is entered.

Change requests are then assigned a priority and organized as

■ **Nonconformance reports**, in case a released item is not compliant with some of its specifications. They can be further classified according to their severity, for instance, by using a three-level classification (critical, major, minor).

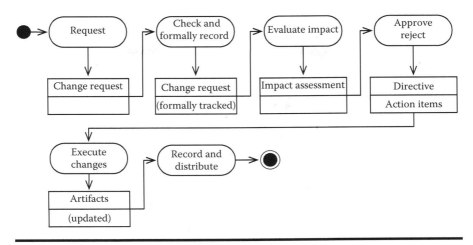

Figure 4.2 A typical configuration control workflow.

- **Concessions**, in case an item is compliant with its specifications, but a change of the specification offers an opportunity to meet some needs better.
- **Waivers**, in case an item is intentionally released without meeting its specifications (because, for instance, the specifications were wrong or irrelevant).

The possible impacts of the change request are then analyzed and the information used to decide whether the change has to be considered further or not. The actual decision procedure varies. In many cases, it is based on a consensus by the members of a **control board**, which authorizes or rejects a change. In formal environments, an aspect to consider for the operations of the control board is the management of conflicts and situations in which a consensus cannot be reached. A simple solution is based on majority voting. Other solutions include more articulated processes, in which the motivations for a choice are further refined and discussed till an agreement is reached.

Once the decision is taken, a formal record of the decision is kept and the appropriate actions taken. These include doing the technical work to incorporate the changes, properly supervising activities to ensure that all changes take place, and informing all stakeholders. Failing to inform the relevant stakeholders might cause significant trouble, since unaware stakeholders might do work based on obsolete information, compromising the integrity of the system.

As mentioned earlier, other processes have been defined and used. See, for instance, Northwestern University Information Technology (2011) and Fermi National Accelerator Lab (2010).

Change requests are very common in software development. Issue and bug tracking systems are used to keep a record of the change requests and to support the change management process. See Section 6.4 of the Bugzilla Development Team (2006) for a change management process related to software products.

4.1.2 Managing Changes in the Agile Methods

The change management process in agile methodologies is a simplified version of the process described in the previous section.

It is a three-step process composed of the following steps:

1. Solicit potential change requests from any project stakeholder, including the project team, clients, and sponsors. If the request originates from the project sponsor or customer, also elicit the potential payoff (how much the change is important for the customer).
2. Document the change request, using the most appropriate mean, given the project size and level of formality. Anything from an email to a signed scope request change document can do. Assign the change the status "open" and put it in the product backlog, together with the other feature requests that are planned for the system.
3. When the sprint ends, the change request is treated like any other system feature in the backlog.

4.1.3 Configuration Management

Software systems are composed of many different items and artifacts: documents describing requirements and architectures, test plans, test outputs, source code files, manuals, and support scripts (for instance, for managing packaging and deployment), to mention the main ones. These artifacts are the building blocks that need to be assembled together to build an application. Unfortunately, they are also extremely simple to change. These two facts pose two challenges.

The first challenge is that changes to an element of a software system typically impact various other artifacts of the system. Consider, for instance, a modification to a requirement performed after the release of a system, that is, when the source code and other project artifacts are already available. The change to the requirement might cause a modification to the architecture and it will most likely require some portions of the source code to be changed, namely, those that implement the requirement that has changed. This is not all, however: test plans might need to be updated, so that the new test cases test the new version of the requirement (rather than the old version); the user manual might also need to be updated. If the change has a major impact, other system artifacts such as conversion and installation scripts might also need a revision.

The second challenge is that applications live in different configurations and states. For instance, we could have a *base* version and a *pro* version, sharing various artifacts or releasing different versions of our product over time. As our system evolves, we will have different versions in use. Our development and support plans will thus have to take into account all the different versions in use.

For instance, as of May 1, 2013, at least four versions of Internet Explorer are in use. The newest and the oldest version, namely, IE10 and IE6, have roughly 6% of the total users, while IE9 and IE8 have, respectively, 18% and 23% of the market share. Other browsers account for the remaining 53% (NetMarketShare, 2013). When Microsoft releases a fix of a critical security bug, it has to do so for all the different versions currently in use.

This is where change and configuration management (CM) come into play. CM is, in fact, a set of activities running in parallel with the development process, whose goal is to establish and maintain the system's coherency over time. According to NASA (2007), "The impact of not doing CM may result in a project being plagued by confusion, inaccuracies, low productivity, and unmanageable configuration data." CM clearly interacts with the change management workflow, ensuring that approved changes are dealt with. To support CM activities, **versioning systems** are used often.

In the rest of this section, we will look at these activities in more detail, starting from some considerations about evolutionary models for software.

4.1.3.1 Configuration Management Goals and Practices

According to the ESA Board for Software (1995), a CM process needs to achieve eight different goals, which are meant to ensure that we have control over our system, its evolution, and that we can properly manage changes that have been approved.

The first four goals focus on **ensuring that we can identify the components of our system**, that we can **build a system from a consistent set of components**, that the **software components are available and accessible**, and that the **software never gets lost**. These four requirements are not as trivial as they sound. Let us look at some scenarios in which the requirements are not met.

Consider, for instance, a case in which a software system uses a database to store data. The database needs to be populated with an initial set of data that is essential for the system to run. The team uses a setup script to perform this task. As the system evolves, however, most of the development work focuses on other areas. The script is not needed anymore and the team forgets about it. Various releases later, a new fresh installation of the system is required. However, the setup script is not available anymore and needs to be rewritten.

Another very common situation occurs when a system depends upon external libraries and components. If we do not keep them under control, we fail to satisfy the second requirement, namely, that the system is built from a consistent set of components. Think of a situation, for instance, in which we fail to realize that a developer has introduced some incompatible changes to a library that we use to build our system and we do not pay much attention about what version of the library we use.

Finally, ensuring that the software components and the software itself are always available and accessible is sometimes difficult to achieve. Some readers might recognize a situation occurring during software development, in which certain artifacts might reside only on the computer of a developer. Equal attention has to be taken after a system release. Think of a case in which the sources of a system developed years before have to be retrieved to fix a bug. Good data archival procedures and keeping the storage media functional can make the difference.

The points mentioned above are taken care of by a **configuration identification** activity, which has the goal of defining what artifacts constitute a system. Its outputs include

1. The **list of items that constitute a product**. In the case of software development, the items that typically need to be put under configuration control include the source code, support documents (e.g., requirements and architecture documents), support scripts (e.g., testing and data migration scripts), and manuals. In case of software that requires special components or compilers to be built, it is also a good practice to include the tools necessary to build the software.
2. The **characteristics of the items**, including the relationships among these items, performance, interfaces, and other attributes.
3. An appropriate **identification and numbering scheme**, to uniquely identify an item. The numbering scheme and the list of items are used to define a product baseline, where the **baseline** is a set of configuration items, that has been formally approved and that can be used as a basis for further development.

The second set of goals of ESA Board for Software (1995) deals with changes. In particular, it states that in a good CM process, **every change to the software is approved and documented, changes do not get lost, it is always possible to go back to a previous version**, and **a history of changes is kept**, so that it is always possible to discover who did what and when.

To satisfy this second set of requirements, we need to establish proper procedures for **configuration status accounting**. In fact, they define how to formally record the item characteristics, history of changes, status of proposed changes, and **baseline records**, where a **baseline record** lists, for each baseline, the corresponding version of each configuration item composing the product identified by the baseline. (Baseline records are automatically stored by version control systems.) Configuration status accounting is the responsibility of a designated member of the project team. For software projects, the configuration status accountant is also called the **software librarian**.

An important operation to keep track of is the release process. **Release** occurs when a product is released externally to the project. For software systems, the operation occurs when a system is put in production or made available to the public. The artifacts typically associated with a release are the product itself and **release notes**, that is, a document that lists the most notable (or all the) changes that occurred since the previous release. See Section 2.5 for more details about the release process.

4.1.3.2 Versioning Systems and Software Evolution Models

A versioning system is a tool to support part of the CM process. To present how they work, we start from the discussion about the different versions of Internet Explorer and look at the way in which software evolves. Software, in fact, evolves according to a linear or a branching model.

When we have only a single running version of our application, a system can evolve linearly. Each new version of the artifacts to build an application replaces the previous ones. We can maintain copies of the older version of the artifacts—and this is usually a very good practice—or simply forget about them: the only important version is the last one.* This is shown in Figure 4.3. The linear development model works for many different types of applications, including all those web applications offered whose owners retain the code (think, e.g., Google Documents); another example are one-offs.

Things become more complex if our system lives in different configurations (e.g., a *base* version and a *pro* version; a version for Linux and one for Mac) or different versions of the same application (like in the case of the Internet Explorer, above). In this situation, we need to keep track of all versions in use and support the parallel evolution of the different versions of our system.

This changes the evolution model from a linear model to a branching model, in which the relationships between different versions of a system can be represented by a tree or, as we will see shortly, a graph. This is shown in Figure 4.4, where the evolution of a system takes into account the fact that each release can evolve

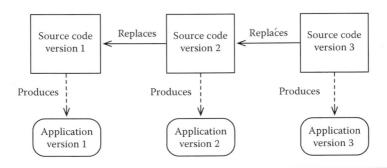

Figure 4.3 The linear development model.

---

* Things are slightly more complex. Sometimes, it is necessary to retrace our steps and restore an old version. This happens, for instance, if we introduce a critical bug. A simple solution is to revert and start all over again.

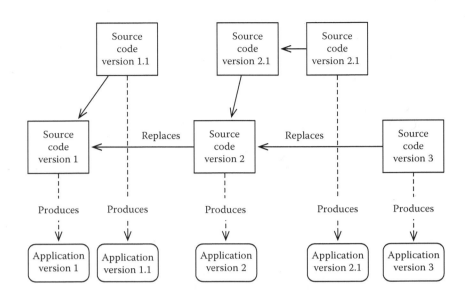

Figure 4.4   The branching evolution model.

independently. Each different version of our system lives in a **branch** of our tree of configurations.

When using a branching model, new versions of a system generate new branches. In some cases, it is possible or necessary to **merge branches**, that is, build a new system that includes all the features of two different versions of our software. Various tools automatically manage branch merging, if the branches being merged have a common ancestor. This is shown in Figure 4.5.

A **versioning system** is a tool that allows one to manage software evolution both in the linear and the branching models. Versioning systems are typically based on two concepts: a **repository**, where all the versions of a system reside, and a **working**

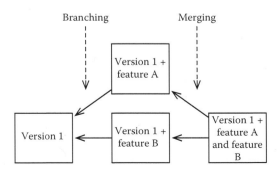

Figure 4.5   A merge of software branches.

copy, which is the copy currently used for development. Commands allow one to commit (i.e., store) artifacts in the repository and retrieve branch, and merge old versions. Versioning systems can be **distributed**, if there are many repositories that can be branched and merged, or **centralized**, if there is only one repository. Distributed versioning systems are very popular in open source development.

In modern software development practices, versioning and branching are used extensively: in some development models, a branch is created for every new feature being developed. Merging commands then allow one to put together the different functions being developed in parallel. This development model allows one to separate concerns, since each branch focuses on one set of changes to the code.

A standard way to identify a specific version of a system is to use a numbering system. A popular approach uses three numbers, $N.M.P$, where P is incremented every time we make a small change to the system, M is changed if we modify a more significant part of the system, and N is changed when the system undergoes major modifications. The version number can be labeled by strings identifying special system states. For instance, "**alpha**" and "**beta**" can be used to denote early releases of a system, and "RCX" (where "X" is a number) to denote a "**release candidate**," that is, software nearly ready for a public release. Werner (2013) provides clear and simple conventions for version numbering.

4.2 Risk Management

Various definitions of risk exist, according to the domain and the standard adopted. Similar to many other definitions given in this book, we use that of Project Management Institute (2004), where a **risk** is defined as "an uncertain event or condition that, if it occurs, has a positive or a negative effect on a project objective. A risk has a cause and, if it occurs, a consequence."

Thus, a risk in project management might either have a positive or a negative effect. We speak of **menaces** to identify risks that might negatively affect a project and **opportunities** to identify those risks that might positively affect a project.

Many of us are bad at perceiving risks and uncertainty. Unexpected events exert pressure and cause stress and, under stress, we distort reality and take the wrong decisions—the phenomenon is known to psychologists under the term of **cognitive distortion**; see, for instance, Forensic Psychology Practice Ltd. (1999).

Defining a project that considers risks from the early phases of a project and manages them throughout the project life cycle is therefore a very good idea. There are, in fact, two good uses. First, it gives the project manager and the other stakeholders more tools to understand whether a project is worth undertaking and what factors have to be taken into account and monitored. Second, it gives the project manager the possibility of defining a strategy to manage risks when there is neither the pressure nor the stress coming from a project in full swing.

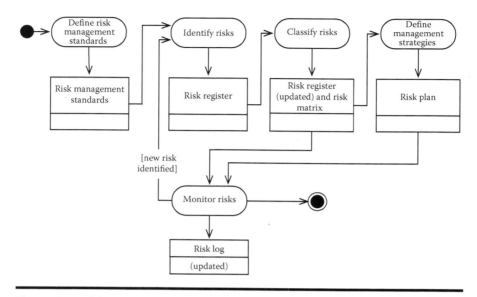

Figure 4.6   Risk management process.

With little variations, the process generally agreed for managing risks is shown in Figure 4.6 and is composed of the following five steps:

1. **Define standards for managing risks.** During this phase, the project manager defines the process according to which risks will be identified along with the procedures for managing risks where they occur.
2. **Identify risks.** During this phase, the project risks are identified.
3. **Classify risks.** During this phase, the project risks are classified by assigning a probability and an impact. This is the basis for understanding the most important risks to track in the project. Different techniques exist to classify risks, some of them qualitative and others based on a quantitative approach.
4. **Define a management strategy.** Given the classification of risks in the previous step, a management strategy is defined for each risk or, better, for classes of risks. This allows the project manager and the stakeholders to agree on the policies to apply should a risk occur.
5. **Monitor risks.** During project execution, the risks are monitored and the appropriate strategies applied should a risk occur.

In the rest of this section, we look at the main techniques and methodologies to implement the different steps.

4.2.1 Define Standards

The first step in this process is the definition of the standards that will be applied during the other phases. The main output of this activity is the definition of a **risk**

management plan, which identifies what are the procedures to monitor and update risks and who is in charge of what operations.

As we will see in the next sections, the management of a risk involves the activation of a contingency plan, defined to properly deal with the risk. The risk management plan defines **who is responsible for raising a warning** and **who is to be warned**; **who is responsible** for approving the activation of the contingency plan; and **what are the formal steps** to record the activation of the plan.

Note that projects differ greatly in the level of formality and, consequently, on the procedure to activate the contingency plans. For small teams and small projects (or low-risk projects), the procedure might be as simple as a democratic decision. Similar considerations apply to the contingency plans, which could be additional actions that are taken in parallel to the main plan or, in more complex situation, alternative paths of actions that replace the nominal plan.

Another aspect that is often considered by the risk management plan involves the **procedures to revise risks and contingency plans**. These include both the frequency with which the process will be conducted and, similar to the previous step, the roles and responsibilities.

A good example of a risk management plan can be found in Jones (1998).

4.2.2 Identify Risks

The goal of this activity is to identify all the risks pertaining to a specific project. One of the criticalities related to this activity is to come out with a list that is specific and complete where by **complete** we mean that all the project risks have been identified, and by **specific** we mean that the risks apply to the project at hand (rather than applying to any project in general).

Risk identification can be organized in two steps. A **collection** step allows the project manager to collect all the potential risks of a project. The most common ways of collecting risks include *meetings*, which can be structured in different ways (see Section 5.3.3.1), *analysis of project documents*, and the use of *checklists*, which list common risks for a category of projects.

An **analysis** steps is then performed to structure the information gathered at the previous point and identify, among all potential critical items, the risks that have to be monitored. The main goal is to avoid common mistakes, such as misinterpreting effects as causes. For instance, the loss of 10,000 euros for a late delivery in a project could be wrongly evaluated as a cause, rather than as the effect of another more fundamental project event, such as poor team performance, which is the actual menace to monitor. There are several analysis techniques and Project Management Institute (2004) provides a rather complete reference on the matter. Here we mention **root cause analysis**, which progressively identifies the elementary events contributing to a potential risk.

The output of this activity is a **risk register**, namely, a list of the risks that are applicable to the project at hand. The risk register comes in the form of a table, with one risk per row, and in which the risks are at least annotated with

- A **description**, which describes and qualifies the risk
- A **risk category**, to classify the risk as an opportunity or a menace
- A **time frame**, which corresponds to the period in which the risk can occur
- A **root cause**, which identifies the root cause of a risk.

Other information, such as **probability** and **impact**, is attached to the risk as the analysis progresses (see the next sections).

4.2.3 Some Common Risks in Software Development

Many software development projects have similar features. Starting from general considerations about the risks most often occurring in software development projects can thus be used as an inspiration to determine what are the actual risks that apply to the project we have at hand.

Barry Boehm developed the first and probably most famous list of risks for software systems (Boehm, 1988). His analysis includes the following main reasons why projects fail:

1. **Personnel shortfalls**, due, for instance, to difficulty in getting personnel with adequate skills and maturity.
2. **Unrealistic schedules and budgets**, due to the difficulties we have discussed in the previous chapter.
3. **Developing the wrong software functions** and **developing the wrong user interface**, due to the difficulties related to understanding correctly the requirements.
4. **Gold-plating**, namely, developing nonimportant functions. This risk originates both from the client, who might ask for features that are not really needed, and from the team, which might engage in lower priority activities that are more fun to develop.
5. **Continuing stream of requirement changes**, as we have discussed in Section 4.1 with the scope creep.
6. **Shortfalls in externally performed tasks**, that is, the quality of the work of subcontractors is lower than that expected and required.
7. **Performance shortfalls** and **straining computer science capabilities**, when the technical difficulty of the system to be built is considerable.

Various other lists are available on the Internet. Many highlight risks very similar to those identified by Boehm. However, it is also worth mentioning the **lack of involvement of stakeholders**, the **inadequate management of changes**, and the **lack of an adequate project management methodology**. See, for example, Wallace and Keil (2004), Schmidt et al. (2001), and Arnuphaptrairong (2011) for a survey on the matter.

Sommerville (2007) provides a different and higher-level starting point. Risks, in fact, are organized in three main areas: **project-related risks**, which include all risks related to the development process of a software system, such as schedule and costs; **product-related risks**, which include all risks inherent in the solution being developed, such as performance and quality; and **business-related risks**, which include all risks related to the environment in which a project develops, such as the marketability of a solution. Risk identification can thus proceed by analyzing what risks we could have in each area.

4.2.4 Classify Risks

Once we have identified the risks of our project, the next step is to understand what risks are worth monitoring. Risks are usually classified along two dimensions:

1. The **probability** that the risk will occur
2. The **impact** that the risk will have

The combination of probability and impact determines if a risk is worth further attention or not. There are two main approaches to determining probability and impact: **qualitative** and **quantitative**.

In the qualitative approach, the project manager (or the person/team responsible for evaluating the risk) gives a rough evaluation of the probability and impact of each risk. The evaluation is given in terms of values chosen out of a predefined scale. A very common classification is given in Table 4.1, where both probability and impact are classified with one out of five values. Different representations can be adopted, such as, for example, text, integers, or real numbers. Their meaning, however, is the same: it is a *qualitative* measure of the *perceived* likelihood and impact of a risk.

Remark

A mistake that is often made is to believe that representing impact and probability with numbers makes the method quantitative. That is, using 4, rather than *severe*, moves the assessment from qualitative to quantitative.

Different from what we are doing in this section, however, quantitative methods provide a (mathematically) precise way of determining probability and impact, something that we do not do with the methods we described above.

Probability and impact define the relevance of a risk for a project. Such relevance can be highlighted in two different ways.

In the first approach, the risks can be shown on a two-dimensional space, in which one axis represents the probability and the other axis represents the impact. Given the fact that we are dealing with finite values, we can present the risks using a **risk matrix**, in which rows represent the probability and columns the impact.

This is shown in Figure 4.7, where we show six different risks with a different probability and impact. "Risk 1" and "Risk 3," for instance, have low probability and very low impact.

Table 4.1 Common Probability and Impact Ranges

	Probability			Impact	
As Text	As a Real Number	As an Integer	As Text	As a Real Number	As an Integer
Very low	0.2	1	Negligible	0.2	1
Low	0.4	2	Small	0.4	2
Normal	0.6	3	Significant	0.6	3
High	0.8	4	Severe	0.8	4
Very high	1	5	Catastrophic	1	5

In the second approach, the risks are assigned a weight, computed as a function of the probability and impact. The main requirement of the function is that it is monotonic with respect to both probability and impact (e.g., it gives higher values when probability or impact increase). A very simple function to compute the weight is

$$\text{Weight} = \text{probability} \times \text{impact} \qquad (4.1)$$

Different from what happens with the risk matrix, probability and impact contribute equally to determining a risk's weight. That is, a risk with probability 3 and impact 5 has the same weight and importance of a risk with probability 5 and impact 3. Whether this is true for the risks of a project is a decision for the project manager to make. The advantage, however, is that it is faster and simpler to manage.

This is shown, for instance, in Table 4.2, where we list the same risks of Figure 4.7. Notice how "Risk 4" and "Risk 5" have the same weight, in spite of belonging to two different cells in the risk matrix of Figure 4.7.

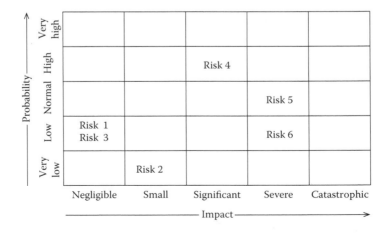

Figure 4.7 A risk matrix highlighting menaces.

Table 4.2 Classification of Menaces Using a Risk Register

Risk Description	Probability	Impact	Weight
Risk 1	2	1	2
Risk 2	1	2	2
Risk 3	2	1	2
Risk 4	4	3	12
Risk 5	3	4	12
Risk 6	2	3	6

4.2.5 Risk Management Strategies

The strategies to deal with menaces aim at reducing probability or impact. More formally, we talk of

1. **Avoidance**, if the project plan or other project conditions are changed in such a way that the risk will not occur. This is thus the most cautious approach, but often it is impossible to use for all risks.
2. **Mitigation**, if the project plan or other project conditions are changed in such a way that the probability or the impact of the risk is reduced. Notice that avoidance is a special case of mitigation in which the probability of occurrence is set to zero.
3. **Transferral**, if the risk is transferred onto another party, who is willing to deal with the menace if it occurs. An example of transferral is preparing an insurance. It can be thought of as a way to reduce the impact of a menace to zero, at the cost required for the transferral.

In the case of opportunities, the approach is similar and we talk of

- **Exploitation**, if the project plan or other project conditions are changed in such a way that the risk will certainly occur.
- **Enhancement**, if the probability or the impact of the risk is increased.
- **Sharing**, if the risk is shared with other stakeholders so as to increase the probability (or the impact) if it occurs.

Finally, a strategy that works with both menaces and opportunities is to **accept**, namely, just deal with the problem (or favorable chance) if it occurs.

From the discussion in the previous section, it should be clear that not all strategies apply equally well to all risks. For instance, accepting a high probability and high impact menace is calling for trouble. A widely used approach, therefore, is that of organizing risks in three different areas, according to their weight. This is shown in Figure 4.8, where we have organized the risk matrix in three zones. A **green zone** includes all those risks that are considered acceptable, a **yellow zone** includes all those risks that require special treatment and special monitoring, and the **red zone** includes risks that are not acceptable. Projects with risks in the red zone will not be

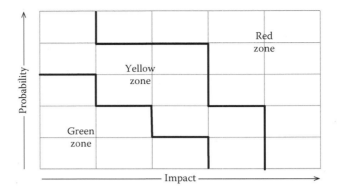

Figure 4.8   Risk management strategies.

started. Note that the actual boundaries are arbitrary and depend on the inclination to risk of the performing organization.

We can now define how to deal with different classes of menaces. In particular

1. **Menaces in the green area are simply accepted.** Some variability and uncertainty is inherent in any project and the burden of defining a management strategy to deal with the risk could not be worth the time it takes to deal with the risk if it occurs.
2. **Menaces in the red area need to be removed from the red zone.** We need to apply one of the three strategies we have introduced above, namely, avoidance, transferral, or mitigation. Independent of the strategy adopted, the output of the activity is moving the risk to the yellow zone, to the green zone, or to remove it altogether from the table.
3. **Risks in the yellow area need to be dealt with.** Here we need to reason case by case to find an appropriate strategy for each risk. Avoidance, mitigation, and transferral are all viable options. Acceptance might also be a proper strategy, as long as it is not a passive acceptance, but, rather, adequate measures are foreseen if the risk occurs.

A similar discussion can be made for opportunities; we leave it to the reader.

Defining a strategy, however, is not enough, since we also need to ensure that risk occurrences are properly recognized and dealt with. Together with the strategy chosen for a given risk, it is a good practice to define the **person responsible for monitoring the risk**. This is the person who has the ultimate responsibility of notifying the project manager that a given risk has occurred. Risk recognition could happen through **indicators** that could, for instance, measure certain aspects of the project.

4.2.6 *Budgeting for Risks*

Projects should allocate a specific budget to deal with risks and to effectively implement the contingency plans. The budget for risks is added on top of a project budget; when this is not done, costs associated with risks reduce the profit.

There are three approaches to define a budget to deal with risks, which greatly differ depending on the level of complexity and accuracy they provide. These can be chosen according to the information available and according to the other project constraints.

The simplest approach is the allocation of a lump sum, which is computed as a percentage of the project budget. The percentage is calculated according to historical data and, in some cases, it can be up to 30% of a project's budget.

A slightly more complex approach is illustrated in Figure 4.9, where the budget is allocated according to the probability and impact of a project's menaces. In particular, if each risk can be assigned a monetary value (for instance, the costs of additional resources to deal with the risk), the following strategies can be identified:

1. *High-probability and low-impact risks* require the whole amount of the risk to be budgeted, since the risk is more likely to occur than not and not having enough money would result in not being able to properly manage the risk.
2. *Low-probability and low-impact risks:* If our project has several risks in this area, the expected monetary value can be used. The **expected monetary value** of a set of risks is defined as the sum of the impact of each risk multiplied by the probability of occurrence. See below for an example.
3. *Low-probability and high-impact risks* have to be dealt with by special agreements, like, for instance, an insurance or other special funds. Adding them to a project budget, in fact, would not make sense.

See also Northumbria University (2004) for a more thorough discussion on the matter.

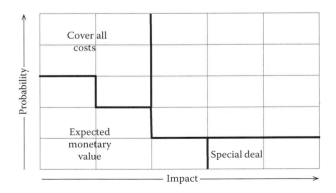

Figure 4.9   Budgeting for risks.

Table 4.3   An Example of Risks in the Green Zone

Risk	Probability	Impact
R1	0.10	€500.00
R2	0.10	€1000.00
R3	0.20	€400.00
R4	0.15	€1000.00
R5	0.10	€200.00

EXAMPLE 4.1

Suppose we have a project with five risks in the green zone, for which we have managed to quantify probability and impact as described in Table 4.3.

The expected monetary value of the risks is computed as follows:

$$\text{EMV} = \sum_{i=1}^{n} p_i * c_i \tag{4.2}$$

Substituting the data in Table 4.3, we get

$$\text{EMV} = 0.10 * 500 + 0.10 * 1000 + 0.20 * 400 + 0.15 * 1000$$
$$+ 0.10 * 200 = 400 \tag{4.3}$$

which is the amount we can allocate to manage risks in the green area. Note that the amount allows us to cover R3 and R5 and most of the costs of R1. If R1, R2, or R3 will occur in the project, we will need to find the money from another source.

A more cautious approach in the example we have made could allocate €1000, enough to cover R2 or R4 and any other risk. However, given the probabilities, all the risks in the table are far more likely not to occur than to occur and the money reserved for these risks is more likely not to be used than to be used. Thus, like in many similar situations, the techniques provide a good reference framework, but the project manager always has the responsibility of understanding situation and context and take the appropriate choice based on all these information.

4.2.7 Risk Monitoring and Control

During project execution, the risk management machinery we have set-up in the previous sections is put into practice. The process is composed of three main activities: reviewing, sharing, and applying contingency plans.

4.2.7.1 Review and Share

With the frequency required, the risk registered is assessed and the risk status is reviewed and updated. For instance, risks can be assigned a status, such as "occurred," "closed," "active," "inactive," to indicate, respectively, that a risk has occurred (and we are currently dealing with), a risk has been dealt with, a risk is active (and it could occur), and a risk is inactive (and cannot occur anymore). The status is typically shared with the project stakeholders. One way of doing this is, for instance, defining different alert levels ("green," "amber," "red"), which encode the level of criticality of the project at a given time in space.

4.2.7.2 Apply Contingency Plans

The procedures for activating the contingency plans and related actions are then started for all those risks that occurred. According to the project size, risk, and formality, the procedures could be very easy and agile or require formal approvals from management. The appropriate resources (including budgetary resources) are then released and allocated to deal with the risk.

An important remark is that the contingency plans should be applied as defined during the risk planning phase. Any run-time change, in fact, poses various criticalities, such as taking the wrong decision under pressure and not activating the proper communication channels to ensure that all the relevant stakeholders are warned.

4.2.7.3 Revise and Iterate

It is important to observe that the project stakeholders might become aware of new risks as the project progresses.

During project monitoring and control, therefore, on top of managing the existing risks, the overall process has to be repeated for each new menace and opportunities identified as the project progresses.

4.3 Quality Management

Intangible as it is, software can fail in many spectacular ways, causing inconveniences significant economic damages, and, in some cases, the loss of human lives. Garfinkel, for instance, in Garfinkel (2005), presents his top ten list of the worst software bugs in history. Among them there is the Ariane 5 software failure, which caused the loss of the rocket and its payload, valued at 500 USD millions.*

Compliance with requirements in software development is often considered a synonym of software testing. Software testing, however, covers only some aspects that determine the overall quality of a software project and its products. For this reason, a sound software quality assurance (SQA) process should be part of any software development project. Thus, SQA process is the **planned and systematic set of activities that ensures the conformance of software life cycle processes and products to requirements, standards, and procedures** (NASA, 2004).

---

* To be more precise, the failure is due to a combination of a software glitch and a management error, which led ESA to reuse the Ariane 4 software for the new Ariane 5 rocket. Unfortunately, the software did not correctly handle the higher input values provided by the more powerful Ariane 5.

Following Project Management Institute (2004), a good SQA process is composed of three steps:

1. **Quality planning**, which identifies the relevant standard and practices and the way to implement them
2. **Quality assurance**, which focuses on ensuring that the project applies and follows the quality standards identified at the previous step
3. **Quality control**, which ensures that the products respect the quality standards identified during the planning phase.

Quality control for software can be particularly complex.

Indeed, various nonfunctional characteristics might be part of a software's specification, and their quality assessment might be particularly tricky. For instance, Rosenberg (2002) mentions nine different nonfunctional characteristics of a software system that might be difficult to assess. Three of them, **efficiency**, **integrity**, and **usability**, refer to product characteristics related to the use of a system. Four others, namely, **flexibility** (can I change it?), **maintainability**, **portability** (will I be able to use it on another machine?), and **reusability** (think of the Ariane example above) highlight qualities related to how easy it is to change and adapt the system to new environments. The remaining two, namely, **testability** and **reliability**, highlight features that are important for safety-critical applications.

Another important aspect is that the input and number of different behaviors of a software system is huge and always outside the range of exhaustive testing (including automated exhaustive testing): defining which test cases and what techniques are necessary and sufficient to get reasonable confidence in a system is difficult.

The third motivation involves safety-critical applications, a domain in which quality control is particularly important and software is required to be fail-safe or fail-operational. Specifically, in case of malfunctions, the software has to maintain the functions or degrade gracefully, without compromising any other component or the general system safety.

4.3.1 Quality Planning

A good quality management plan ensures that the goals of quality management are met in a project.

Goals defined in the scope document and any constraint related to regulations and standards that have to be met are the starting point of a quality plan. All the information thus collected defines the **quality assurance and control requirements** of a (software-development) project. For instance, a project might require software to be developed according to DO-178B, a standard that regulates the development of safety-critical software. A good project needs to find the right balance between quality, costs, and time. Thus requirements have to be analyzed to understand their impact and their importance. To this purpose, for instance, NASA (2009) identifies eight different classes of software systems with different criticality and therefore different quality assurance requirements.

The requirements defined at the previous step allow the project manager or the quality team appointed to ensure that the quality goals are met to define the **quality assurance and control activities** that will be performed in the project. An important aspect is to ensure that sufficient time is allocated to these activities.

For software systems, quality assurance activities include inspections, reviews, walkthroughs, testing, and formal verification. Together with the activities, it is always a good practice to define the actors and responsibilities. See the rest of this section for more details about the activities that are most commonly used. In certain cases, quality assurance activities can be conducted by the project team (**V&V**); in other cases, they might require an independent validation (**IV&V**).

Quality control is equally important, since it helps measure the progress we are achieving and whether we are meeting the goals we set. The simplest way to perform quality control is through a **quality measuring program**, which quantitatively monitors progress and infers information about the effects of quality assurance and control on improving quality. Thus, the quality plan should specify what metrics are collected, with what means, and with what frequency.

Table 4.4, inspired from the NASA Software Assurance Guidebook, recaps the main project deliverables that should be verified with SQA activities, together with some minimum quality criteria.

4.3.2 Quality Assurance

The main tools to perform quality assurance are **quality audits**, that is, independent reviews to determine whether project activities are being performed in compliance with the standards set in the quality plan. Quality audits are conducted analyzing the documentation, by conducting interviews, and by conducting audit and review meetings, which are described in Section 5.3.3.2.3. The output of a quality audit is a report that describes the main findings and, if specific issues have been found, indicates the need for corrective actions.

More information about how to conduct a review can be found in NASA (1990). Some of the warning signs of troublesome projects, according to NASA (1990), include frequent changes in milestones, unexplained fluctuations in personnel, continued delays in software delivery, unreasonable number of nonconformance reports, or change requests.

4.3.3 Quality Control

Techniques for quality control can be organized in three main classes: inspections, analyses, and tests.

Table 4.4 SQA Activities

Phase	Deliverable	Goal
Software concept and initiation phase	Management plan	Ensure that processes, procedures, and standards identified in the plan are appropriate, clear, specific, and auditable. Ensure that there is a QA section.
Software requirements phase	Software requirements	SQA assures that software requirements are complete, testable, and properly expressed as functional, performance, and interface requirements.
Software preliminary design phase	Architectural (preliminary) design	Assuring adherence to approved design standards in the management plan. Assuring that all software requirements are allocated to software components. Assuring that a testing verification matrix exists and is kept up to date. Assuring that the interface control documents are in agreement with the standard in form and content. Reviewing preliminary design review documentation and assuring that all the action items are resolved. Assuring that the approved design is placed under configuration management.

Software detailed design phase	Architectural (detailed) design	Assuring that the approved design standards are followed. Assuring that the allocated modules are included in the detailed design. Assuring that the results of design inspections are included in the design. Reviewing critical design review documentation and assuring that all the action items are resolved.
Software implementation phase	Implementation	Results of coding and design activities including the schedule contained in the software development plan. Status of all deliverable items. Configuration management activities and the software development library. Nonconformance reporting and corrective action system.
Software integration and test phase	System	Assuring readiness for testing of all deliverable items. Assuring that all the tests are run according to test and procedures and that any nonconformances are reported and resolved. Assuring that the test reports are complete and correct. Certifying that testing is complete and software and documentation are ready for delivery. Participating in the test readiness review and assuring that all action items are completed.
Software acceptance and delivery phase	System	Assuring the performance of a final configuration audit to demonstrate that all deliverable items are ready for delivery.

Inspections include all those activities to analyze a particular project product and verify whether the product has the required characteristics or not. Checklists are often used to proceed systematically in the review process. For a requirement document, an inspection checklist might prescribe to verify various syntactic and semantic qualities of the requirements. For instance, it could require to verify that each requirement has a unique identifier and a priority, as well as being easily comprehensible and testable.

For source code, **walkthroughs**—peer reviews performed by analyzing the source code—are a common type of inspection. Some automation can also be achieved using **static checkers**, which allow one to verify the compliance of source code with predefined (or custom) coding conventions, such as, for instance, the fact that the assignments are not used as test conditions in conditionals.

Analyses include all those activities that are meant to probe and demonstrate that a system has the required quality characteristics. Analyses include, for instance, analysis of control flow, formal verification of the properties of a system, and simulation. See Bozzano and Villafiorita (2010) for more details.

Testing includes all those activities that are meant to verify the behavior of a system under specific conditions. See Section 2.4 for more details.

Figure 4.4, inspired from the NASA Software Assurance Guidebook, recaps the main SQA activities and outputs to verify in a software development project.

4.3.4 Establishing a Metrics Program

Establishing a measurement program allows one to collect quantitative data, which can be used to understand how well a specific quality assurance and control program is working.

Many different measures can be taken and tools exist to automate the collection process. Metrics can be collected about various aspects of a project. In particular, we can collect **process metrics**, which are meant to measure different significant events in our project, and **product metrics**, which are meant to measure different characteristics of our system. For software systems, the product metrics can be further organized in **size metrics**, which are meant to measure the size of a system, and **complexity metrics**, which are meant to measure the complexity of a system.

An important aspect of a metrics collection program is that often trends are as important as the absolute values. That is, for each measurement we decide to take, we get a lot more information from analyzing its evolution over time, rather than by looking at a specific value at a point in time. To make things a bit more concrete, it is more useful to understand whether the number of bugs is increasing or decreasing over time, rather than to say that our system has, let us say, 42 bugs.

A sound metrics collection program establishes, where possible, automated means for the computation of metrics. For software systems and software-related metrics, this can usually be achieved using source code repositories and specific applications. See Chapter 9 for more details.

4.3.4.1 Size Metrics

Size metrics are meant to measure the size of a system. As we have seen in Section 3.4.5, there are two different approaches to measuring a system's size: **size-oriented metrics** count the physical lines composing a software system, while **function-oriented metrics** provide an indication about the size of a system using an abstract measurement of the system's functions.

Size metrics are commonly used for quality assessment. Simple measures that are taken include **source lines of code**, **delivered source lines of code** (defined in Boehm (1981) as the lines of code delivered to the client—i.e., excluding tests, conversion procedures, etc.), **blank lines**, and **comment lines**, that is the number of lines in the source code that are comments. The **number of classes** and the **weighted methods per class** are two other metrics commonly collected when using object-oriented languages.

4.3.4.2 Complexity Metrics

Complexity metrics are meant to measure the complexity of a system and how difficult it might be to test and maintain a system.

Some metrics, like **cyclomatic complexity**, are meant to measure the complexity of algorithms (e.g., how many tests and loops there are). They provide an indication of the possibly different states a system can be in and, consequently, of the difficulty of testing and grasping all the possible behaviors.

Other metrics, such as **coupling between objects**, **depth of inheritance**, **fan-in** and **fan-out**, are meant to measure how coupled different components of a system are; these metrics provide an indication of the difficulties people might encounter in maintaining a system.

Complexity metrics are direct indicators of the quality of a system, since they provide information about various nonfunctional characteristics (such as maintainability) and about a system's testability.

4.3.4.3 Quality Metrics

Various indicators can be derived from the previous metrics and other information in order to get an idea of the quality of a system. They include

- The **ratio between lines of comments and lines of codes**. This is an indication of the maintainability of a system, on the hypothesis that the comments in the code will help other developers get a better understanding of what a specific portion of a system does.

- **Cumulative number of open issues**. This is the total number of problems that have been signaled and that have not yet been solved. This allows one to measure whether our process is "converging". If the number of open issues continues to increase (in spite of our effort of closing them), for instance, this could be a sign that our system is doomed to remain plagued by bugs.
- **Error density**. This is the number of errors found per source line of code. The error density is computed by counting the ratio between the number of errors found during testing and the system size, possibly organized by error severity. Looking at the trend of error density—whether it is increasing, remaining stable or decreasing—can help one understand whether the development process has some systematic faults.

4.4 Questions and Topics for Discussion

1. What are the advantages of a change management process? And those of a quality management program?
2. What are the differences between change management and configuration management?
3. Perform a risk assessment analysis on the Theater 3001 project.
4. What metrics could we use to highlight a scope creep?
5. Discuss the merits and difficulties of setting up a metrics program.

References

Arnuphaptrairong, T., 2011. Top ten lists of software project risks: Evidence from the literature survey. In *Proceedings of IMECS 2011*, pp. 732–737, Hong Kong, March 2011. Newswood Limited. Last retrieved November 2, 2013.

Boehm, B. W., 1981. *Software Engineering Economics*. Prentice Hall, Englewood Cliffs, NJ.

Boehm, B. W., 1988. A spiral model of software development and enhancement. *IEEE Computer 21*(5), 61–72.

Bozzano, M. and A. Villafiorita, 2010. *Design and Safety Assessment of Critical Systems*. CRC Press (Taylor and Francis), an Auerbach Book, Boston, MA.

Bugzilla Development Team, 2006, October. *The Bugzilla Guide—2.18.6 Release*. Bugzilla. Available at http://www.bugzilla.org/docs/2.18/html/lifecycle.html. Last retrieved April 3, 2013.

Cox, C. B. and C. Murray, 2004, September. *Apollo*. South Mountain Books, Burkittsville, MD.

ESA Board for Software, 1995, May. Guide to software configuration management. Technical Report PSS-05-09, Issue 1, Revision 1, ESA.

Fermi National Accelerator Lab, 2010, December. Change management process and procedures. Technical report, Fermilab. Available at http://cd-docdb.fnal.gov/cgi-bin/RetrieveFile?docid=3530;filename=ChangApril 3, 2013.

Forensic Psychology Practice Ltd., 1999. Cognitive distortion—A practitioner's portfolio. Available at http://www.forensicpsychology.co.uk/wp-content/uploads/2011/10/WebCD.pdf. Last retrieved August 30, 2012.

Garfinkel, S., 2005, August. History's worst software bugs. Available at http://www.wired.com/software/coolapps/news/2005/11/69355. Last retrieved November 15, 2013.

Jones, D., 1998. Project zeus—Risk management plan. Available at http://sce.uhcl.edu/helm/ZEUS/rmpzeus.pdf. Last retrieved June 21, 2013.

NASA, 1990, November. Software quality assurance audits guidebook. Guidebook NASA-GB-A301, NASA. Available at http://www.hq.nasa.gov/office/codeq/doctree/nasa_gb_a301.pdf. Last retrieved June 8, 2013.

NASA, 2004. Software assurance standard. NASA Technical Standard NASA-STD-8739.8 w/Change 1, NASA.

NASA, 2007, December. Systems engineering handbook. Technical Report NASA/SP-2007-6105 Rev1, NASA.

NASA, 2009. Nasa software engineering requirements. NASA Procedural Requirements NPR 7150.2A, NASA. Available at http://nodis3.gsfc.nasa.gov/. Last retrieved June 1, 2013.

NetMarketShare, 2013. Desktop browser version market share. Available at http://www.netmarketshare.com/browser-market-share.aspx?qprid=2&qpcustomd=0. Last retrieved May 1, 2013.

Northumbria University, 2004, November. Risk management. Available at http://www.jiscinfonet.ac.uk/infokits/risk-management/. Last retrieved June 22, 2013.

Northwestern University Information Technology, 2011, June. Change management process. Technical report, Northwestern University Information Technology. Available at http://wiki.it.northwestern.edu/wiki/images/1/1b/Change_Management_Process.pdf. Last retrieved April 3, 2013.

Project Management Institute, 2004. *A Guide to the Project Management Body of Knowledge (PMBOK Guides)* (4th ed.). Project Management Institute, Newtown Square, Pennsylvania 19073-3299, USA.

Rosenberg, L. H., 2002. Software quality assurance. Available at http://sstc-online.org/2002/SpkrPDFS/MonTracs/p460.pdf. Last retrieved June 8, 2013.

Schmidt, R., M. K. Kalle Lyytinen, and P. Cule, 2001. Identifying software project risks: An international Delphi study. *Journal of Management Information Systems 17*(4), 5–36.

Sommerville, I., 2007. *Software Engineering* (8th ed.). Addison-Wesley, Redwood City, CA.

Wallace, L. and M. Keil, 2004, April. Software project risks and their effect on outcomes. *Communication of the ACM 47*(4), 68–73.

Werner, T. P., 2013. *Semantic Versioning*. Available at http://semver.org/, 2013. Last retrieved May 1, 2013.

Chapter 5

Making IT Perfect: Managing People and Organizing Communication

---

Two main resources contribute greatly to making good software: people's intellect and people's ability. The techniques we have seen in the previous chapters help to control the software production environment, but people turn ideas into requirements and requirements into software. Thus, it is not surprising that managing people and teams effectively is a big component of software development projects. To be fair, managing people and teams is important in any kind of project. In no other engineering domain, however, can people contribute so much to determining the success or failure of a project.

In this chapter, therefore, we will have a look at the main activities related to managing teams and organizing work. We will look at the topic from two points of view. On the one hand, we will look at the activities that are necessary to manage people. On the other hand, we will hint at some of the theories and studies behind the management of people, to understand what motivates people and what a manager can do to create a favorable environment to carry out work. A look at organizational structures for projects and at managing communication completes the overview, by suggesting how work can be organized and how information flows.

5.1 Managing People

There are four main steps related to human resource management in a project. They are

1. **Define staff requirements**. This is the activity during which the project requirements, in terms of human resources, are identified. It includes both numbers and, more importantly, skills and competences.
2. **Select staff**. This is the activity during which the people who will work in the project are selected. The selection process can include personnel already working in the organization or it might require new resources to be hired.
3. **Manage staff**. During a project, the manager has three main goals. The first is to make a team out of the individuals participating in the project. The second is to provide resources and motivations to the team so that it can perform well. The third is to ensure that people acquire skills and capabilities, so that the time they invest in the project is spent not only in achieving project results but also in creating new career opportunities and self-growth.
4. **Release staff**. All projects come to an end. When a project nears completion, it becomes necessary to manage the transition of the team to their next assignments. A management concern in this phase is to ensure that proper recognition is given to the work performed in the project and, when possible, that the know-how built in the project is not dispersed.

Actual scenarios in which projects live and teams form are most diverse. In some organizations, teams consolidate and the same people will end up working in different projects. In other structures, each new project requires the formation of a new team.

Some of the activities described in this section are sometimes carried out with the support of the human resources department, if the organization is big enough to afford one. For instance, part of the staff selection process could be the responsibility of human resources. On some occasions, human resources might support a project manager in strengthening a team and improving teamwork. On others, human resources set the organizational standards and limit the margins a manager has, for instance, in granting bonuses.

Good project managers, however, have good people management skills.

5.1.1 Define Staff Requirements

As soon as the goals, assumptions, and boundaries of a project are clear (see Section 3.2), it is necessary to start defining the requirements of the project team. One approach identifies the hard and the soft skills that a project requires.

Hard skills are those that refer to specific technical abilities that can be taught and are measurable; for instance, the ability to write software in C, knowledge about statistical methods, and being able to read and write Portuguese.

Table 5.1   An Example of a Skill Matrix

Activity	Skills
Requirements	Good know-how of the automotive domain. Experience in questionnaire management.
Design	Experience in the use of the IBM Rational suite of modeling tools.
Implementation	Very good know-how of the C++ and WxWidget GUI environment. Experience with test-driven development.

By contrast, **soft skills** (or **emotional intelligence**) are capacities that are difficult to teach and difficult, if not impossible, to quantify. Soft skills usually depend on personality traits and include the capability of getting along with other people, empathy, thoroughness, and creativity, to name a few. In general, all projects will require both hard and soft skills.

To become systematic, one can use a **skill requirements matrix**, as suggested in Tomczyk (2005). The matrix is a table that lists, for each project activity, the main hard and soft skills that are required. Table 5.1 shows an example of a skill matrix: each row corresponds to a project activity; for each project activity, the matrix highlights the main requirements. Focusing on specific skills, rather than generic ones, of course, can make the definition of the skill matrix more effective.

Note that soft skills take time to develop. Hard skills, by contrast, can be taught. Certain projects might have a time frame for which appropriate training activities and specific skills might be acquired.

5.1.2 Selecting Internal Staff

The skill matrix defines our main personnel requirements to carry out the project. Once we have the requirements, we can start individuating the personnel who fulfill these requirements.

The first step is to look for personnel already available in the organization. There are three elements that need to be taken into account.

The first consideration is that policies and practices might limit the actual possibility of selecting resources. For instance, some organizations do not favor moving resources from one department to another, even on a temporary basis. Thus, the internal resources that can be actually selected for a project do not necessarily correspond to those potentially available.

The second is that experienced resources are limited. In many situations, if a skilled resource is required, part-time involvement might be inevitable.

The third consideration is the timing and priority of our project. Both could limit or enlarge, for different reasons, the pool of resources we can select from.

In all the situations mentioned above, good negotiation skills with peers and bosses can help quite a bit in drafting the right people for your project.

5.1.3 Selecting External Staff

When the internal selection process does not yield the people with the required characteristics or availability, it might be necessary to **hire personnel** for the project.

The hiring process requires the following:

1. Defining a job description
2. Advertising the position
3. Waiting for an appropriate amount of time
4. Analyzing the received résumé
5. Interviewing the candidates
6. Selecting the personnel to hire.

A **job description** is a short document that describes the context for which a position is sought, information about the company hiring and the project, the skills and experience required, and the salary range. Sometimes, companies do not want to make their recruitment needs public. In these cases, the job description lists only the skills required and the salary range. The advertising and the pre-selection processes are delegated to a recruitment company, which finds the most appropriate candidates. An advantage is the speed with which personnel with the right skills are found, since these companies manage a big network of potential candidates.

Job descriptions are advertised through specific and generic channels. Professional associations, mailing lists, and websites are some starting points. One's professional network and friends are another source of support.

The goal is to collect a list of potential candidates. These will answer the call providing a résumé, in some cases reference letters, and an accompanying letter, motivating the reason for the application. The résumé will highlight the hard and soft skills, together with the work experience and education; the accompanying letter might explain where the interest for the position comes from.

Human resources and the project manager will then analyze the résumés received, identifying the most promising candidates, who will then be interviewed.

The most diverse interview styles have been proposed and used. Some focus on the technical skills. The interviewers, in this case, will test the proficiency and competency of the candidate by posing a technical problem, like, for example, writing a bubble-sort algorithm in C++, if programming in C++ is one of the skills required for the position. Others prefer to test general problem-solving abilities, posing questions that probe the analysis and synthesis skills. Administering questionnaires or adopting specific interviewing strategies can be used to assess personality traits and verify the performance of people under stress.

In any case, an initial exchange with the candidate about the résumé, working experience, and motivations helps provide basic information about the candidate and sets the ground for more specific questions. Work experience, in fact, might provide details about technical skills and personality traits; education provides insights on the fundamentals, but it becomes less important for people with long experience on the field. Feedback from previous bosses (where this is feasible) or from people providing references can also help in getting a frank and sincerer assessment of the candidate.

The selection process can be very structured. Larger organizations, for instance, use a multistage process in which a potential candidate is interviewed by different people, each assessing different traits of the candidate.

Independent of the specific technique, the analysis of the résumé and the interviews should end up with the manager having a clearer picture about the hard and soft skills of the candidate.

5.1.4 *Managing Staff*

A range of soft skills, such as the capacity to motivate, mediate, and solve conflicts, clearly helps one be a good manager. Thus, we might be happy enough stating that good managers have good soft skills and those who do not should be doing something else.

Moving one step further and understanding what drives and motivates people can have a huge impact on the science of management. In fact, it can make one a better manager and, more importantly, it moves people management from art to science, making it teachable in the process.

Researchers have tried to explain people drivers and, consequently, the management styles that make teams more productive and effective. These are shown in Figure 5.1, which depicts a timeline of the main studies in the area.

Taylor formulated one of the first theories about management and workers' motivations; it is known as **scientific management** (Taylor, 1911). Taylor does not have a particularly positive view of workers. Some of his findings are that workers perform at the slowest rate that goes unpunished and that workers cannot be relied on for talent and intelligence. The solutions Taylor proposes to make work more efficient are high control from the management and, maybe a bit surprisingly, better

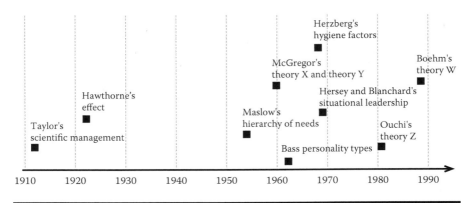

Figure 5.1   A timeline of management theories.

pay and rest periods. However, the first is connected to outputs and the latter allows workers to regain strength and make the work subsequent to the rest period more efficient.

In the 1950s,* **Maslow** proposed a **hierarchy of needs** (Maslow, 1943, 1954). According to his work, people are wanting animals and, as soon as they achieve a need, they start craving for something else. Maslow thus organizes the needs in a hierarchy, which represents the order in which these cravings materialize. At the lowest level of the hierarchy, we find physiological needs, such as, for instance, the **need for safety**. As we satisfy our basic needs, we start desiring higher level needs. The top level of the hierarchy is constituted by **self-actualization**, in which workers are free to fully express themselves. Thus, according to the theory, good managers will create an environment that allows workers to be driven by higher levels of the hierarchy.

McGregor conducted the next relevant studies that are summarized by the **theory X and theory Y** work. According to **McGregor**, there are two different theories that explain how workers behave. The first, called **theory X**, describes workers as little motivated, similar to Taylor. The second, called **theory Y**, recognizes work as a natural activity, assumes people are very creative, and considers self-realization and self-esteem as motivating drivers, similar to Maslow's hierarchy of needs. The key point is that two different management styles will have to be applied in the two contexts. If the manager thinks she is dealing with a "theory X" person, she will adopt an autocratic management style. In contrast, if the manager believes she is working with a "theory Y" person, she will prefer a style that entails a climate of delegation and trust. See McGregor (1960, 1966), McGregor and Cutcher-Gershenfeld (2005) for more information.

The **situational leadership** theory, proposed by **Blanchard** and **Hersey**, elaborates on McGregor's work. According to the two researchers, in fact, the best management style is a combination of **direction** and **support**. Four different styles can be defined: **low support and high direction**; **high support and high direction**; **high support and low direction**; and **low support and low direction**.

The management style a manager should adopt is one of the four and depends on the person being managed. People with *low skills* and *low motivation* are best managed with a highly directive and low support management style. This, in fact, will be the only way to achieve results. As the motivation of an employee grows, management will benefit from increasing support and decreasing the directive behavior. As skills improve, so can delegation. In fact, people with *high skills* and *high motivation* are better managed with low direction and low support.

---

* There is a bit of discussion about the dates. Maslow published his first work in the 1940s, but the book that made his work famous got published in the 1950s.

Choosing the wrong management style yields to friction and failure. For instance, applying a highly directive management style to a skilled person underpins competency and undermines motivation. More to the point, modulating one's management style can help personnel move from a low skills/low motivation status to a high skills/high motivation status. The theory, originally published in Hersey and Blanchard (1969) is nicely described in Hersey et al. (2012).

Another good, effective, and simple characterization is that proposed by **Bass** according to whom people are **task-oriented, interaction-oriented**, or **self-oriented** (Bass and Dunteman,1963; Bass et al., 1963; Bass, 2008). Different personalities prefer and work better on different types of tasks. Thus, assigning the most appropriate task increases individual and team performances. Task-oriented people will be more interested in tackling intellectual challenges, while interaction-oriented people will thrive in collaborative environments; finally, self-oriented people will have to find a return in what they do.

A more recent theory, proposed by **Merrill** and **Reid**, distinguishes personality traits in two main dimensions: how much a person is task- rather than people-oriented and whether a person is an introvert or an extrovert. The quadrants of this two-dimensional space define four different personality traits: **analytical** (introvert and task-oriented), **driver** (extrovert and task-oriented), **expressive** (extrovert and people-oriented), and **amiable** (introvert and people-oriented). Different personality traits have different needs and, consequently, different stimuli to which they react better. Thus, for instance, the amiable type needs personal security and sincere appreciation and performs better in situations in cooperative group work. See Merrill and Reid (1981) for more information.

Other relevant works focus on the drivers.

Hawthorne Works, in the 1920s, commissioned one of the first studies to improve workers' efficiency. In particular, the study tried to evaluate the effect of different lighting conditions on workers' performances. To the surprise of the researchers, it turned out that increasing or decreasing lighting conditions had the same effect: workers increased their performances. One explanation is that being observed and the motivation deriving it were the actual causes of the increased performances. The studies had a significant impact in the field of organizational behavior (Zhong and House, 2012). See, however, (Kolata, 1998, 2009), for some recent critiques about the rigorousness of the study and its results.

Frederick Herzberg, in the 1960s, presented his **theory of hygiene factors**, which was based on the consideration that *the opposite of job dissatisfaction is not job satisfaction*. In more detail, Herzberg analyzes various factors contributing to job satisfaction and job dissatisfaction, realizing that some of them systematically contribute mainly to job dissatisfaction, while others contribute mainly to job satisfaction. Factors in the first group are called **hygiene factors**, while factors in the second group are called **motivational factors**. Hygiene factors are necessary but not sufficient to create the conditions of a good working environment. If the hygiene factors are not satisfied, a worker will be unsatisfied. However, if the hygiene

Table 5.2   Herzberg's Hygiene and Motivational Factors

Motivational Factors	Hygiene Factors
Achievement	Company policy and administration
Recognition	Supervision
Work itself	Relationship with supervisor
Responsibility	Work conditions
Advancement	Salary
Growth	Relationship with peers
	Personal life
	Relationship with subordinates
	Status
	Security

factors are satisfied, the worker will not be satisfied unless one or more of the motivational factors are present. Table 5.2 shows the motivational and hygiene factors and (Herzberg, 2003; Herzberg et al., 1957, 1959) provide more information about Herzberg's work.

Finally, Boehm and Ouchi focus their work on motivations and win-win conditions (Ouchi, 1981). In slightly more detail, Ouchi's **Theory Z**, close to the lean manufacturing theories, focuses on keeping workers motivated and creating an environment in which people report mistakes.

Boehm proposes **theory W**, according to which it is necessary to create **win-win** conditions for all stakeholders. Thus, a good manager will focus on understanding the winning conditions of his/her team, setting the right expectations, and assigning *achievable* tasks, based on a person's capabilities (Boehm and Ross, 1989).

5.1.5 Management Styles

If you are not at the top of your organization's pyramid, you will have a boss. So, taking a different point of view, we can also have a look at the styles a manager has, in order to better comprehend behaviors and drivers. We will focus on two main theories. The first characterizes management styles on a one-dimensional continuum, while the second uses a two-dimensional space.

The one-dimensional theory distinguishes five different management styles:

1. **Autocratic**, when the manager takes all the decisions. A subcase is the **paternalistic** management style, when the manager pays a bit more attention about the opinions and feedback of subordinates, but the ultimate decision remains with the manager. Autocratic managers can be further classified as **permissive** or **directive**, according to the degrees of freedom they allow the subordinates to carry out the work.

2. **Persuasive**, when managers tend to convince subordinates to do the work and implement the decisions they have taken. While still autocratic in the

decision-taking process, persuasive managers tend to be more aware of the needs of personnel and to motivate their decisions.

3. **Consultative**, when managers involve the personnel in the decision process while retaining control over the decision process. Emphasis is given to ensuring that the needs of personnel are taken into account.
4. **Democratic**, when managers allow personnel to take part in the decision process. This management style requires extra effort on the part of the manager, for example, to have the appropriate information flow, but might end up in environments that are nicer to work in.
5. **Laissez-faire** and **chaotic** environment managers are those whose employees are given complete freedom on the decisions they take. The style embraces flexibility and creativity, with the managers playing the role of a mentor and guide.

The two-dimensional theory, proposed by **Blake** and **Mouton**, uses **concern for production** and **concern for people** to characterize five different management styles (Blake and Mouton, 1964).

Four styles are suboptimal. They are

1. The **impoverished style**, when both concern for people and production are low. The main goal of the manager is to avoid troubles, keep a low profile, and try to preserve jobs and seniority.
2. The **country club style**, when there is a high concern for people, but a low concern for production. The style is characterized by a friendly atmosphere, but production might not derive as a consequence of the nice environment.
3. The **produce or perish style**, when concern for production is high, while concern for people is low. This is a scientific management environment, where money is the justification for the employee to work and the manager uses rules and punishments to achieve the company goals.
4. The **middle-of-the-road style**, when concerns for people and production are somewhere in between. Managers who use this style hope to achieve acceptable performance.

With all due respect to the theory, the best management style is something we could expect. It is, in fact, the **team style**, where both concern for people and production are high. More interesting is the fact that this style is implemented using McGregor's theory Y and by making the employee feel as a constructive part of the company.

We conclude this section by highlighting some common mistakes that a manager can do to demotivate people (Amabile and Kramer, 2011). According to the study, there are, in particular, two conditions that need to be avoided. The first is one in which *work is stripped of its meaning*. The second is one in which managers become *micromanagers*.

Signs that work is being stripped off its meaning include situations in which managers dismiss the importance of employees' work or destroy employees' sense of ownership of their work. Other demotivating factors concern attitude on plan and priorities. In particular, giving the message that the work one is performing will never end, keeping on changing priorities, and neglecting to inform employees that priorities have changed are three mistakes to avoid.

Micromanagement is the second way of demotivating people. Micromanagement is a form of autocratic management, in which the manager closely directs and monitors the work of employees. Lack of delegation and a zeal for monitoring without providing any help are two signs that one is micromanaging. The other two characteristics are withholding information and taking credit for results and shifting blame onto subordinates.

5.2 Project Organization Structures

The level of influence a project manager and other project stakeholders can exert depends on the organizational structure of a project. Choosing an adequate structure for the project can thus simplify or hamper a project.

Various organizational structures have been experimented with. As usual, project size and formality, together with external constraints, determine what organizational structure can be adopted for a specific project.

A good organizational structure has to define, at a minimum, the following information:

■ Where responsibility and accountability are
■ How information flows
■ How conflicts are solved.

Some rules of thumb help make organizational structures more effective. We mention, for instance, ensuring that the responsibility is set where influence can be exerted and there is an interest in exerting it; keeping the decision process simple, so that decisions are taken fast; and making sure information flows.

In the following section, we review some of the most common structures, highlighting, for each one, the main positive and negative characteristics.

5.2.1 Hierarchical

Figure 5.2 shows different types of hierarchical structures.

In its simplest form, the project manager has control over technical and managerial matters and organizing the work of the project team, which might be structured in different groups. This is shown in Figure 5.2a.

The hierarchical structure works well in small projects. As the project size increases, however, the project manager becomes a bottleneck. In larger projects, therefore, the identification of a middle layer (e.g., work-package leaders) helps

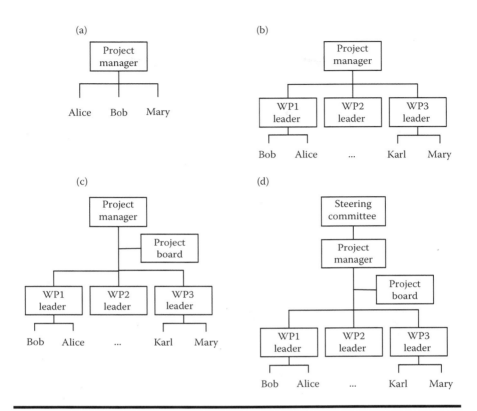

Figure 5.2 Hierarchical organizational structure. (a) The project manager manages the team; (b) the project manager interacts with work package leaders, who manage the team; (c) a project board supports the project manager; (d) a steering committee provides strategic guidance.

ensure that activities proceed more autonomously, while, at the same time, an effective coordination is kept. This is shown in Figure 5.2b.

When a project involves different functions or units of an organization, another common structure is one in which the middle layer is made by the people responsible for the organization's division or units. In such cases, the organization of the project structure is by function, rather than by task.

Another point of attention with the hierarchical structure is that it requires the project manager to have both managerial and technical competencies to properly deal with a project. In another common variation, therefore, technical and managerial leadership is distinct. The technical leader supervises the technical work, while the manager maintains control of the overall process. The level of autonomy can vary greatly, from situations in which the technical leader works as a counselor to situations in which the technical leader has large autonomy over the project.

In large projects, technical or managerial advice can also be provided by a **project management board**. The board can be composed by the work-package leader, providing a better integration among the work conducted in the different work-package levels. This is shown in Figure 5.2c.

In projects involving various organizations or a large number of stakeholders, often a **steering committee** is also appointed. The **steering committee** provides strategic guidance about the project by defining the strategies to apply and supporting the project manager in their implementation.

Advantages exist both for the project manager and the stakeholders. The first, in fact, can share some of the project liability or obtain support that would otherwise be difficult. The others have a chance to have their ideas and goals represented in the project. This is shown in Figure 5.2d.

5.2.2 Matricial Organizations

The hierarchical structure assumes that the manager can freely organize the work of the team. In many situations, however, projects borrow team members from the existing functional structures of a company and project managers need to negotiate assignments with the functional managers. Even if both managers work for the same company, the goals and interests of the project manager often differ from those of the functional managers. The first, in fact, focuses on taking the project home, while the others are more concerned with continuing operations in the departments they lead. They look at the project activities carried on by *their* personnel as a distraction.

In this case, allocating the responsibility of the team exclusively to the project manager or to the functional managers leads to solutions that are equally unrealistic. The **matricial structure** can mitigate this problem. In the matricial structure, personnel are assigned both to the project manager and to the functional manager. According to who has priority when conflicts on assignments arise, we can distinguish a **weak matrix**, a **strong matrix**, or a **balanced matrix**. In the first case, the functional area manager has priority in solving conflicts; in the second case, the project manager has such a privilege; in the third case, the situation is something in between.

Figure 5.3, for instance, shows a matricial organizational structure.* We distinguish, in particular, between four functional units, namely, "design," "engineering," "production," and "administration" (shown in the columns of the matrix), and three projects (shown in the rows of the matrix). At the intersection of a functional unit and a project, we find the personnel of the functional unit who are working for a project. Thus, for instance, "Project 1" has two people working from the "Design" unit and three people of the "Production" unit. Similar is the case for the other projects.

---

* The pictures of the people in this and other diagrams are taken from Morville and Callender (2010) and distributed under a Creative Common License.

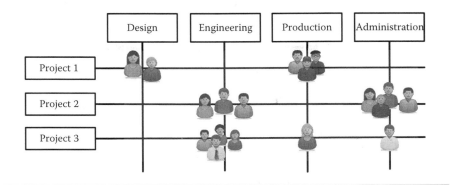

Figure 5.3 **Matricial organizational structure.**

One of the strengths of the matricial structure is that it favors pooling of competencies. For instance, it accommodates very well a **project management office**, which pools the management competencies of an organization.

The main drawback is the so-called *two bosses syndrome*, in which personnel report to two bosses.

Note that the matricial structure can also be used to organize the work within a project, if this is large and complex enough to justify such structuring.

5.2.3 RACI Matrix

The **RACI** matrix is a useful tool to represent the role and responsibilities in a project. RACI is an acronym, which stands for **responsible** (who carries out the work), **accountable** (who liable for the work performed), **consulted** (who is consulted), and **informed** (who is kept informed).

In a RACI matrix, rows include the list of work packages or tasks of a project and the columns contain the team or the organizational structures involved in the project. At the intersection of each row T and column P, the letters "R," "A," "C," and "I" indicate the role P has in task T. The only constraint is having exactly one "A" per row. All other allocations depend on the project.

This is shown, for instance, in Table 5.3, where we show the RACI matrix of a large project involving eight different partners (labeled $P1, \ldots, PN$) and seven different work packages. Cells define the role of each partner in the different work packages. Thus, for instance, $P3$ is accountable (and responsible) for the work in WP5. All other partners are consulted.

5.2.4 Agile Teams

Agile software development moves away from the structures we have just presented, favoring smaller structures and a more democratic approach to decision taking.

Table 5.3   An Example of an RACI Matrix

Work Package	P1	P2	P3	P4	P5	P6	P7	P8
WP0. Project Management	AR	C	C	C	C	C	C	C
WP1. Case Study Requirements	C	C	C	AR	R	C	C	R
WP2. Network Architecture Definition		AR			C		C	C
WP3. Software Development	AR			R	C	R		C
WP4. Assessment and Evaluation	C	C	R		AR	R	R	R
WP5. Sustainability and Exploitation	R	R	AR	R	R	R	R	R
WP6. Dissemination	R	R	R	R	R	AR	R	R

Concerning the first point, for instance, Scrum teams are usually between five and nine people. Concerning the second point, all members of the team are empowered and participate in the decision-taking process. Thus, rather than focusing on the chain of responsibilities, agile teams talk about roles, which can be interchanged from one iteration to the next.

Scrum teams define the following three roles:

1. The **Scrum master**, who is the person responsible for measuring project progress and solving issues.
2. The **Customer**, who is the person responsible for the overall implementation of the Scrum process. Note that since teams are self-organizing, the Scrum master ensures that activities and artifacts are produced, that no impediments hinder work, and that the development can proceed. The Scrum master is also the interface with the *external world* and *shields* the team from external influences. By contrast with "traditional" project management, work is (self)assigned by the team.
3. The **Team**, which is responsible for the work. The team is self-organizing, with roles decided and fixed by the team at the beginning of each software development project. Programming in agile teams is often conducted in pairs, with one person writing code and the other advising and supervising the work. The person writing the code is called the **driver**, while the other is called the **navigator**.

A critique that is often made of agile teams is how they can be scaled up to manage complex projects. The standard solution is to use teams of teams. A **team of teams** is essentially a hierarchical structure with a twist. The lowest level of the hierarchy is, in fact, composed of agile teams. Higher levels of the hierarchy are agile teams composed by taking one person from each team at the lower level. In this way, teams are kept small and all teams participate in the decision-taking process, through the representatives appointed to participate in the teams of teams. This is shown in Figure 5.4.

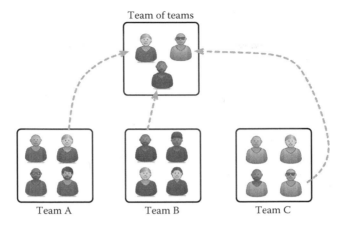

Figure 5.4 Teams of teams.

5.3 Managing Communication

A proper management of communications in a project ensures that information flows in a timely manner and reaches the appropriate stakeholders.

The types of information that are exchanged in a project include

- **Technical information**, which is necessary to carry out the work in the project. For software systems, one of the challenges in this area is to ensure that all stakeholders form a shared view about the system being built. This might require some attention to take into account the different skills and competencies of the stakeholders involved.
- **Project status information**, which is necessary to understand whether activities are being carried out as planned. This information is essential to evaluate and take action if any deviation occurs and to make sure that all stakeholders are aware of such changes. One of the points of attention in this area is to establish good and reliable data collection practices.
- **Project decisions**, which are necessary to ensure that the proper choices are taken and the project moves in the right direction.
- **Project action items**, which include all the information necessary to ensure that the plan is implemented, activities are actually started, and project outputs are actually collected and stored.
- **Project advertisement**, which is necessary to ensure that stakeholders are informed and engaged. Although not necessary in any projects, ensuring that a project gets proper publicity and dissemination can help create a favorable environment. Internal meetings, updates to senior management, and dissemination to the public, conferences, and workshops are some of the means.

5.3.1 Planning a Communication Strategy

Communication always happens through a **noisy channel**. That is, what we say is not always what we intend and what our listeners perceive is not always what we said. Simplifying a bit, we intend *ABC* and people perceive *ACD*. Various factors can influence the amount of *noise* we have to deal with in a discussion, including **cultural differences** (think, e.g., different etiquette in use by different cultures), **language barriers** (think, e.g., teams for which the project official language is not their mother tongue), **personality traits** (think, e.g., the different personality types we discussed in Section 5.1.4), **capacity to assert and listen** (which might depend on personality traits or the project environment, or circumstances), and **communication means** (think, e.g., the different impact a formal letter has with respect to the same topic sent by email or discussed in person).

The second consideration is that a good communication plan delivers the **right information**, to the **right people**, at the **right time**. The goal, in fact, is to make certain that the information raises the correct level of attention in the right stakeholders, when the moment arrives.

To make the point clearer, consider the opposite scenario, a situation in which all project information is distributed to all stakeholders, regardless of type and role. Since many pieces of information will turn out to be irrelevant to many stakeholders, they will soon lower their attention and miss the important information. Similarly for timing: send a communication about an internal meeting 4 months in advance and few will remember it (or, more likely, so many things will happen in between that the chosen time slot will have to be changed). Send it 1 h before the meeting and no one will be able to attend.

Another important aspect to consider is the **means**. The same information, in fact, can be delivered in different ways: meetings, workshops, emails, letters, document repositories, chats, and phone calls, to mention a few.

An appropriate mean can be chosen by looking at the following factors:

- The **recipients** and, in particular, whether the recipient will be able to use the information with the mean we have chosen.
- The **logistics** and, in particular, the cost, in terms of time and resources, of delivering the information with the mean we have chosen.
- The **formality** and, in particular, the kind of impact the mean could have on the recipient. In fact, some information is better exchanged with traceable means and is better written than spoken. The opposite also holds, however, and some communications are better spoken in person, rather than written.

Bigger projects, therefore, will benefit from writing a **communication plan**. At a minimum, a communication plan defines

- **Information to be exchanged**. Starting from the *project plan* and the *list of deliverables*, the project manager defines what information is exchanged.

Associating a *level of confidentiality* to each deliverable, as we have seen in Chapter 3, helps to highlight the possible constraints.

- **List of stakeholders to be involved and lines of communication**. Starting from the *project roster*, the *stakeholder map*, and the *RACI matrix*, the project manager defines the line of communications, namely, who is made aware of what.
- **Communication means**. According to the project constraints and available infrastructure, the project manager will define how information flows and is made available to stakeholders. Digital assets might be distributed through **websites/wikis**, **mailing lists**, and **document repositories**, to mention a few. **Workshops** and **meetings** are also commonly used. Note that some of the means *push* the information to the stakeholders, while others require the stakeholder to be more active and *pull* the information they need.

More detailed plans will also include a specification of the **communication timings and triggers**, which specify the strategy chosen to deliver information. The simplest strategy is **event driven**: when a specific piece of information is available, it is distributed to the relevant actors. Deliverables are best distributed on an event-driven basis. Another possibility is to distribute the information **periodically**. On a regular basis, all new pieces of information are distributed to the project participants. Project status information is often made available periodically.

5.3.2 Communication Styles

Individuals have different **communication styles**. Understanding one's communication style helps to establish a good communication channel.

A common characterization distinguishes among

- The **aggressive** communication style, in which opinions are expressed clearly but without regard for other people's feelings or opinions. It is a communication style that can cause resentment and stress; on certain occasions, for instance, when a decision has to be taken quick, it can be an effective way to take an action.
- The **passive** communicators, who tend to hide their opinions and feelings or open up possibilities for others to disregard one's rights. It is an ineffective form of communication because it does not help to convey opinions and information.
- The **assertive** style—the most direct form of communication—in which opinions are clearly expressed without disregarding other people's feelings and opinions. It is the most effective form of communication.

Another characterization distinguishes between **open, reserved, indirect**, and **direct** communicators, according to whether one tends to express feelings openly or not (open/reserved) and focuses more on data rather than ideas and opinions. See, for instance, Rampur (2012).

See also Newton (2013); Academic Help (2013); Blume (2013) for some more resources on the topic.

5.3.3 Meetings

If you have ever worked in the IT industry, you probably know that meetings can become a consistent part of your work. Unfortunately, many meetings end up being useless or less efficient/effective than they could have been. Various books have been written on how to try and make meetings more effective. A recent search for "meeting management," in fact, showed 26,302 hits in Amazon's book section.*

In this section, we look at some common meeting types and some techniques to try and make them more effective.

5.3.3.1 Managing Meetings

Some general rules of thumb can help make your meeting a bit more effective.

The first and most important rule is to define the **meeting goals**, decide who has to **participate** to make the meeting effective, and **select a format** of the meeting so that the goals can be more easily achieved. (We will look at some common formats in the next subsections.)

Participants at meetings might have goals different from yours; some may be related to the project, like discussing a specific issue about a technical choice, and some may be just related to other agendas. To prevent a meeting from being *hijacked* and drifting, a second good rule is to ensure that the meeting remains on track. Thus, a good idea, is to define an **agenda of the items** to be discussed, possibly planning in advance a timing for each item, so that we fix both the start and the end time of a meeting. To make sure that the agenda is followed, another good practice is to appoint a **moderator** who takes responsibility for keeping the agenda and ensuring a good interaction among the participants.

When the goals, participants, and agenda have been defined, a **convocation** is sent out. The convocation should at least contain the goals of the meeting, participants, agenda, time, and location. If relevant information is required during the meeting, it is also a good practice to tell participants how to get prepared for the meeting.

The second rule is to stick to the agenda and goals during the meeting. First of all, ensure that each participant is provided sufficient context—in advance, if possible, or during the meeting otherwise—to actively participate in the discussion. Then, following the agenda, the participants discuss the different items. At the end of the discussion, a brief recap of the main findings and of the decisions taken helps share and agree on the findings and results.

---

* Search performed on April 28, 2013. This book might have increased the count by one.

The third rule is to maintain a track of meetings, outputs, and follow-up actions. This can be done in different ways. In brainstorming sessions, where notes are scribbled on a whiteboard, a picture of the whiteboard might be sufficient. Audio recording is another option.

Writing **meeting minutes** that recap the meeting outputs and actions is a more formal approach. Meeting minutes usually contain the following information:

- Coordinates of the meeting: time and location.
- Goal and agenda.
- Participants and, if required, whether the absentees are justified or not.
- When required, for each item, a recap of the discussion/main findings.
- Main outputs (findings) and actions decided during the meeting. These should include a description of the action, a person responsible for the action, a deadline.

Meeting minutes are an important record of a project, and sometimes drafting, commenting, and approving the minutes can be a delicate and tricky matter. Thus, in general, a good practice is to ask participants to approve the meeting minutes or to propose changes. In some cases, the approval is a formal requirement of the project.

Keeping a formal/written track of meetings and meeting outputs is also an important step in tracking actions and establishing effective change and configuration management practices. In fact, since meetings will be held to clarify or modify project requirements, choices, and so on, meeting minutes become an essential input to keep a consistent and clear vision of the project and project outputs.

5.3.3.2 Types of Meetings

5.3.3.2.1 Kick-Off Meetings

Kick-off meetings are held to get started with a project, a work package, or a significant task of the project. The goal is to ensure that all relevant stakeholders are provided the information necessary to carry out the activities about to start.

For this reason, the meeting can be structured in three parts:

1. An introduction of the participants and relevant stakeholders.
2. A presentation about the context and the specific goals that have to be achieved with the activity about to start. The presentation includes all relevant information, including constraints, standards to be followed, allocation of responsibilities, and timing.
3. A final question and answers session allows one to clarify any doubt or remaining issue.

5.3.3.2.2 Decision-Taking Meetings

An essential task of project managers is to establish a good context for taking decisions. We have already seen in Section 5.1.5 different management styles and how they influence the decision-taking process. In this section, we recap some rules of thumb for establishing an effective and participated decision-taking environment; see Harvard Business School (2006) for more details.

According to the Harvard Business School (2006), good decision making requires

- **Establishing a context for success:** providing time for ideas to form, creating an environment in which an open discussion can take place, and agreeing on the decisions taken.
- **Framing the issue properly** and **finding alternatives:** making sure that the process does not stop at the first formulation of the problem or the first solution encountered. Including opponents and skeptics in the discussion can help take different perspectives and points of view and find alternative solutions.
- **Choosing** the alternative that appears to be the best. Solutions can be measured according to qualitative and quantitative parameters. When choosing what alternative to take, both positive and negative impacts should be debated. The agreement on the decision can be in one of many different forms: **general consensus** and **majority** occur when everyone or the majority of participants agree; **qualified consensus** occurs when key selected stakeholders agree; and **directive leadership** can be the last resort, when no consensus can be found.

5.3.3.2.3 Audit and Review Meeting

Audit and review meetings are held to assess the status of a product or project.

These meetings are usually organized by identifying three roles:

1. The **auditors**, who are responsible for analyzing products or project documentation in order to form an opinion and an evaluation. Good characteristics of auditors include adequate proficiency to carry out the work, independence (so that no interests can influence one way or another the auditing process), and professional care in conducting the audits and in reporting it (EPA, 2000).
2. The **project members**, who are responsible for providing clarifications and explaining the choices and status.
3. The **moderator**, who ensures that the agenda is followed and the meeting environment remains productive. In fact, since auditors and the selected project members have seemingly conflicting goals, ensuring that a good attitude is kept also ensures that the meeting remains productive.

Audit meetings can be triggered by various causes, among which a periodic evaluation, a project deliverable, a potential problem, accidents, and improving performances.

An auditing process might include the following activities:

- Definition of the goals and boundaries of the audit
- Identification of the auditing committee
- Distribution of all the relevant material to the auditors
- Preparation of the auditing by the auditors
- The conduct of the analysis and auditing activities during the meeting
- Preparation of the final report.

Examples of auditing activities include quality inspections (e.g., code walk-throughs), accident investigations, and project progress assessment, to mention a few.

5.3.3.2.4 Brainstorming

Brainstorming is a technique described by Alex Osborn in Osborn (2008), a book first published in 1948, in which the author describes the techniques used in the creative firm where he worked. Although today the term **brainstorming** is used simply to denote a meeting to collect ideas, **brainstorming meetings** have a precise structure and precise rules.

Concerning the structure, following an opening session, where the problem is framed and rules explained, brainstorming meetings are structured in rounds to collect ideas, possibly stimulated by the meeting organizer, or solicited by having each participant propose at least one idea. A wrap-up session allows one to collect all the information in a structured way.

Concerning rules, to ensure that ideas are properly elicited and collected, Obsorn suggests the following:

- **Focus on quantity** and **welcome unusual ideas**. The more ideas that are generated, the more chances there are of finding good ones; for this reason, unusual ideas are to be welcomed in the brainstorming process.
- **Withhold criticism**. In brainstorming, criticism should be withheld. Instead, participants should focus on extending or adding to ideas, reserving criticism for a later stage of the process. By suspending judgment, participants will feel free to generate unusual ideas.
- **Combine and improve ideas**. The underlying assumption is that the sum is bigger than the individual contributions, and therefore combining ideas yields better results.

An important aspect of the technique is highlighting associations among ideas, so that they can then be grouped and combined at a later stage. Brainstorming meetings can be conducted in many different ways. See, for instance, Colwell (2004) for a discussion about the organization of brainstorming sessions and Mittleman (2013) for some variations to the technique.

Researchers have criticized some of Obsorn's assumptions, among which, ironically, the fact that criticisms have to be withheld. More radical criticisms question the need for the rules described above and attribute the effectiveness of the technique more to the interaction of different minds and mindsets than to other contributing factors. See Lehrer (2013) for a very nice recap on the matter.

5.3.3.2.5 Other Creative Techniques

Many other creative techniques have been proposed and are largely applied. We mention the **six hats technique**, according to which six different mindsets are defined, represented by hats of six different colors. People participating in the meeting are asked to take a hat and provide feedback according to the corresponding mindset. Mindsets are then shifted while the meeting continues; see Bono (2013) for more details.

Several references on the web mention techniques to foster creativity, among which are CreatingMinds.org (2013).

5.3.3.3 Delphi

The Delphi method was devised in the 1960s by Helmer et al. (1967) to improve the effectiveness of meetings. One of the goals was create an environment in which nonscientific factors such as "who has the loudest voice," "stubbornness," or "supposed authority" would not be allowed to bias data. The methodology focuses on collecting data, but the format is general enough to accommodate other kinds of information gathering.

The method is composed of the following steps:

- Deliver a set of question to the experts (best if in the form of a questionnaire), such as, for instance, the effort required for each activity of the plan.
- Have the experts use their techniques to come out with an answer (the original paper emphasizes the importance of simulation, but in general, any technique is fine).
- Collect answers and highlight the median value and the interquartile range, that is, the interval containing the majority of opinions.
- Ask the experts to reconsider their opinion and, if the estimations are still out of the interquartile range, have them, motivate their choices.
- Iterate, presenting also the motivations for outliers, till the closest match to the consensus can be derived.

5.3.3.4 Planning Poker

Planning poker is a modern (and fun) version of the Delphi technique, adopted by agile methodologies for the estimation of the difficulty associated with the development of user stories and tasks. The technique can, however, be used for other purposes.

Planning poker takes its name from the fact that participants at the meetings are given a deck of cards and seem to be playing a card game. In more detail, the cards are organized in colors and each color contains all the possible estimations a person can give to a given user story. Note that the values are a limited set of numbers, for instance, following the Fibonacci series (e.g., 1, 2, 3, 5, 8, 13, ...); two special values, "**infinity**" and "**?**," mean, respectively, *extremely complex* or *"I don't know."* Each person is given all the cards in a color.

The game proceeds as follows. For each user story, users are asked to provide their estimations. Following the Delphi approach, they do so in secret, by picking one card from their decks. Then everyone shows their cards at the same time. If the evaluations agree, the user story is assigned the weight chosen by the team. However, if there is significant disagreement in the evaluations, a discussion follows so that the players can justify their choices. Similar to Delphi, other rounds then follow till an agreement is reached.

As a curiosity, the technique also considers the case in which an agreement is not reached. Following the words of Grenning, the inventor of the technique, "the team can then discuss their different estimates and try to get to consensus. If you can't get consensus, don't sweat it. It is only one story out of many. Defer the story, split it, or take the low estimate" (Grenning, 2002).

5.4 Questions and Topics for Discussion

1. Discuss the commonalities and differences among the motivational theories presented in the chapter.
2. What are the motivations for micromanaging, if any? What are the risks of micromanagement?
3. Consider the different personality traits presented in the chapter. How would you position yourself? What software development better suits your characterical traits?
4. Discuss the merits and limitations of the different organizational structures we have seen in the chapter.
5. Define a communication plan for the Theater 3001 project.

References

Academic Help, 2013. People should enhance their communication skills. Available at http://academichelp.net/samples/annotated-bibliography/people-should-en%hance-communication-skills.html. Last retrieved April 28, 2013.

Amabile, T. M. and S. J. Kramer, 2011. The power of small wins. *Harvard Business Review* (5), 77.

Bass, B. M., 2008. The Bass Handbook of Leadership: Theory, Research, and Managerial Applications (4th edition). Free Press, New York.

Bass, B. M. and G. Dunteman. May 1963. Behavior in groups as a function of self-interaction, and task orientation. *The Journal of Abnormal and Social Psychology* 66(5), 419–428.

Bass, B. M., G. Dunteman, R. Frye, R. Vidulich, and H. Wambach, 1963. Self, interaction, and task orientation inventory scores associated with overt behavior and personal factors. *Educational and Psychological Measurement* 23(1), 101–116.

Blake, R. R. and Mouton, J. S., 1964. The Managerial Grid. Gulf Publishing Company, Houston, TX, USA.

Blume, L., 2013. Communication skills bibliography. Available at http://www.lilblume.ca/communication. Last retrieved April 28, 2013.

Boehm, B. W. and R. Ross. 1989. Theory-w software project management principles and examples. *IEEE Transactions on Software Engineering* 15(7), 902–916.

Bono, E. D., 2013. Six thinking hats. Available at http://www.debonogroup.com/six_thinking_hats.php. Last retrieved April 28, 2013.

Colwell, B., 2004. Brainstorming, influence, and icebergs. *Computer*, 37(4), 9–12.

CreatingMinds.org, 2013. Tools for creating ideas. Available at http://creatingminds.org/tools/tools_ideation.htm. Last retrieved April 28, 2013.

EPA, 2000, January. Guidance on technical audits and related assessments for environmental data operations. Technical Report EPA/600/R-99/080, United States Environmental Protection Agency.

Grenning, J., 2002, April. Planning poker or how to avoid analysis paralysis while release planning. Available at http://renaissancesoftware.net/files/articles/PlanningPoker-v1.1.pdf. Last retrieved March 4, 2012.

Harvard Business School, 2006. *Decision Making: 5 Steps to Better Results*. Harvard Business Essentials. Harvard Business Review Press, United States.

Helmer, O., O. Helmer-Hirschberg, and Rand Corporation, 1967. *Analysis of the Future: The Delphi Method*. P (Rand Corporation). Rand Corporation.

Hersey, P. and K. H. Blanchard. 1969. Life cycle theory of leadership. *Development Journal* 23(5), 26–34.

Hersey, P., K. H. Blanchard, and D. E. Johnson. 2012. Management of Organizational Behavior (10th Edition). Prentice Hall, NJ.

Herzberg, F., January 2003. One more time: How do you motivate employees? Harvard Business Review. Available at: http://hbr.org/2003/01/one-more-time-how-do-you-motivate-employees/ar/. Last retrieved Nov 2, 2013.

Herzberg, F., B. Mausner, R. Peterson, and D. F. Capwell. 1957. Job Attitudes: Review of Research and Opinion. Psychological Service of Pittsburg, Pittsburg.

Herzberg, F., B. Mausner, and B. B. Snyderman. 1959. The Motivation to Work (2nd edition). John Wiley, New York.

Kolata, G., December 1998. Scientific myths that are too good to die. The New York Times. Available at: http://www.nytimes.com/1998/12/06/weekinreview/scientific-myths-that-are-too-good-to-die.html. Last retrieved Nov 2, 2013.

Kolata, G., June 2009. Light work. The Economist. Available at: http://www.economist.com/node/13788427.

Lehrer, J., 2013, January. Groupthink—The brainstorming myth. *The New Yorker*. Available at http://www.newyorker.com/reporting/2012/01/30/120130fa_fact_lehrer. Last retrieved November 15, 2013.

Maslow, A., 1943. A theory of human motivation. *Psychological Review* 50, 370–396.

Maslow, A., 1954. *Motivation and Personality* (1st edition). Harper & Brothers, New York.

McGregor, D., 1960. *The Human Side of Enterprise*. McGraw-Hill, New York.

McGregor, D. and J. Cutcher-Gershenfeld, 2005. *The Human Side of Enterprise* (Annotated Edition). McGraw-Hill, New York.

McGregor, D., 1966. The human side of enterprise. In W. G. Bennis and E. H. Schein, editors, *Leadership and Motivation, Essays of Douglas Mc-Gregor*, Volume 2. MIT Press, Cambridge, MA.

Merrill, D. W. and R. H. Reid, January 1981. *Personal Styles & Effective Performance*. CRC Press, Boca Raton, FL.

Mittleman, D. D. and Briggs, R. O., 2013. Directed brainstorming: New techniques to improve idea generation. Available at http://www.midwest-facilitators.net/downloads/mfn_20000128_mittleman_briggs.pdf. Last retrieved November 22, 2013.

Morville, P. and J. Callender, 2010. *Search Patterns: Design for Discovery*. O'Reilly, Sebastopol, CA, USA.

Newton, C., 2013. The five communication styles. Available at http://www.clairenewton.co.za/the-five-communication-styles.html. Last retrieved April 28, 2013.

Osborn, A., 2008. *Your Creative Power: How to Use Your Imagination to Brighten Life, to Get Ahead*. University Press of America, United States.

Ouchi, W. G., 1981. *Theory Z*. Avon Books, New York.

Rampur, S., 2012, March. Communication styles in the workplace. Available at http://www.buzzle.com/articles/communication-styles-in-the-workplace.html. Last retrieved April 28, 2013.

Taylor, F. W., 1911. *The Principles of Scientific Management* (1919 edition). Harper & Brothers, New York and London.

Tomczyk, C. A., 2005. *Project Manager's Spotlight on Planning*. Harbor Light Press, San Francisco, CA, USA.

Zhong, C.-B. and J. House. 2012. Hawthorne revisited: Organizational implications of the physical work environment. *Research in Organizational Behavior* 32(0), 3–22.

Chapter 6

Software Project Pricing

6.1 From Cost to Pricing

Project pricing is how much we charge the client for a project. As excellently pointed out by Sommerville (2007), there is no simple relationship between cost and pricing, since broad organizational, contractual, political, and business considerations influence the price charged.

To understand better some pricing strategies for software products, a good starting point is to look at a product life cycle and understand what are the sources of costs and revenues for a software system. This is shown in Figure 6.1, where we distinguish four different phases:

1. **Inception** (or feasibility) is the phase during which an organization analyzes the opportunities and risks related to the development of a new software system and authorizes its development. In some cases, the process is initiated internally. This is the case of products that will be sold or deployed internally to improve the organization's efficiency or capabilities. In other cases, the process is initiated externally. This happens, for instance, if a prospective customer asks for the development of a one-off software system or specific services related to a product of the performing organization. The activity is organized as one or more projects, using the project selection techniques we have seen in Section 3.1.

2. **Development** is where the actual development of the software system takes place. Software development is organized with one or more projects, as illustrated in the previous chapters.

3. **Operation** and **maintenance** is where the system is used and updated to meet old requirements, which were implemented wrong, and new

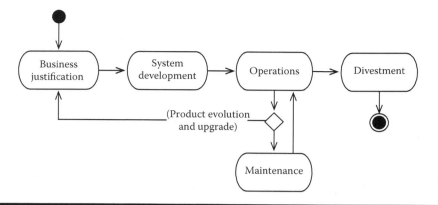

Figure 6.1   The life cycle of a product.

requirements coming from changed conditions in the operations or business environment.

4. **Divestment** is the phase during which a system is retired. Divestment costs might be significant; consider the case of stopping a nuclear power station. For software systems, however, the situation is rather different and the costs related to the divestment of a software system are mainly related to migrating the application data to a new operating environment.

All phases of the process mentioned above are a source of costs for an organization. They are also a form of investment and a source of revenue, according to the project goals and the destination of the product being developed. To exemplify, let us consider two different scenarios.

The first is a situation in which a software house decides to develop a new product to be sold to users. Inception and development of the system is an investment; during these phases, in fact, the software house will be spending money without getting any revenue for the work being performed. During operations, the situation is partly reversed: money will start flowing in from selling the software. For business to make sense, the revenues should sustain the operational costs (e.g., maintenance and support), cover the inception and development costs of the system built (or the inception and development of a new system), and allow for some profit.

The second is a situation in which a customer requires services for the development of a one-off system. We can take two different points of view, that of the customer and that of the contractor. From the customer's point of view, inception and feasibility are a cost; the first may be as an internal investment (e.g., to evaluate the benefits of the system); the second may be in the form of services requested of the contractor. During operations, the client will save money or possibly make more money by using the system developed. When the system is retired, the customer will bear the expenses. The contractor is in the opposite situation. Inception and development will be a source of profit. During operations, various situations occur. The contractor might incur unexpected expenses if a low-quality delivery, for instance, requires extensive corrective maintenance. Conversely, the contractor could incur additional revenues if the client asks for new functions to be added to the system.

The scenarios above are quite common and apply to different kinds of projects and products, not necessarily software systems. Software and the characteristics of the software business, however, introduce novel possibilities in the arrangements between the client and the supplier.

Software, like any other digital good, is extremely cheap to reproduce: thus, most of the costs related to the software business are for the production of the first copy. Software is also cheap to distribute through the Internet. This, and the fact that the software industry is more internationalized than any other sector, fuels a global competition like no other (Bruxam et al., 2013).

This chapter introduces some basic concepts about project and product pricing. It is a vast subject, whose surface we can only scratch. Here, we will look at some of the basic principles and concepts.

6.2 Software Pricing

6.2.1 Software Pricing Models

According to Bruxam et al. (2013), there are three ways to determine the price of software:

1. Based on cost
2. Based on value
3. Based on competition.

Cost-based pricing determines a project price based on the costs. Costs related to software, as we have seen, include production and distribution. Production costs can be estimated using the techniques we have seen in Section 3.4 or, more simply, accounted for once a system is production-ready. Operating costs include distribution, maintenance, and customer support and are sometimes underestimated.

Things are not so clear-cut, though. To provoke the reader, Davidson (2012) suggests that production costs are **sunk costs**, that is, money already spent and therefore unrecoverable. Thus, according to the author, only operating costs should be part of the pricing equation. We elaborate a bit and say that cost-based pricing should *at least* cover the operating costs; otherwise, it would not even make sense to distribute a software system. Cost-based pricing should thus carefully analyze what are operating costs, which are often hidden; consider the time spent on customer support. If we want our business to grow, on top of that, cost-based pricing should allow a sufficient profit to pay for the development of new systems.

Value-based pricing determines the cost based on how much the customer is willing to pay. This allows one to define a pricing strategy more flexibly, since it is based on the *perceived value* of a system. The perceived value can be changed in different ways. For instance, Davidson (2012) suggests using the company's reputation, offering a better service, and creating a community or a sentiment behind a specific brand or product.

Finally, **competition-based pricing** determines the cost based on how much the competition is charging for a similar system.

6.2.2 Selling and Licensing Software

Ownership is another important factor in determining the value and the price of a software system.

In principle, three possible schemas are applicable: licensing, leasing, and selling.

When a company **licenses** a software system, it grants the right to use the software to a customer, while retaining the ownership. The license is usually sold and the money made with the licenses is used to pay for the development and maintenance costs, as described above.

Licenses are sold in different ways. The most common is **selling by the copy**. Larger organizations often benefit from **bulk** purchases, with which they buy, at a discount, the right to use multiple instances of the software. Bulk purchases, in turn, can be **by user**, **by seat**, or **by instance**, according to whether the number is bound to the people who have the right to use the system, to the computers on which the software can be run, or to the maximum number of instances that can run at any given time.

Leasing is another schema in which the right to use the software is sold for a limited period. Users need to renew their licenses on a regular basis. Similar to many other markets, in some cases, the entry cost is set low to reduce the barrier to entrance. Leasing is very popular with web applications, since access to a system is directly controlled by the company leasing the software, which can grant it or revoke it as needed. Some desktop applications also use or offer a leasing mechanism. This, however, requires specific protections to be in place, so that the software does not run if the lease has expired.

With respect to the previous model, leasing has some advantages both for the client and the seller. The first, in fact, can get the product at a lower entry cost. The second has a revenue model that guarantees more steady revenues.

Finally, software can be **sold**. Although this is seldom (if ever) the case for off-the-shelf software, for one-offs, the client might be interested in taking ownership of a system.

6.2.3 Open Source Software

A very peculiar type of license is that of **open and free software**. The concept has its roots in 1983, when **Richard Stallman** started the **GNU project** with the goal of building an operating system that would be free for users to use and for developers to collaborate on (GNU Software Foundation, 2013). In the process, he also started a movement that has led to the development of industrial-strength software used by millions of people, such as the **Firefox** browser, the **Linux** operating system, the Apache **HTTP Server**, the **LibreOffice** office suite, and the **Ruby On Rails** development framework, to mention a few.

Today, the term **free software** has a relatively broad meaning, with different rights and obligations for users. Some free licenses simply allow one to use an application without paying any fee. Other approaches, which we call **open source software**, also make the source code available for anyone to improve and use. Even if we restrict our attention to open source software, more than 60 different licensing schemas are available Open Source Initiative (2013). Of these, according to Open Source Resource Center (2012), two of the most popular are the **GNU General Public License** and the **MIT License**. The former protects original and any derivative work, which has to be made available under the same license (Free Software Foundation, 2007). The latter is a very liberal schema that allows the software to be reused and relicensed as one wishes (MIT, 2013).

There are different motivations for developing a system using an open source license. Ideals are the main driver of many like Stallman. Others use it as a way to build a critical mass and foster the development of applications for which there are not enough resources. This is the case, for instance, of **Netscape**, which released the source code of its browser, **Netscape Navigator**, as an attempt to resist the increasing pressure set by Microsoft with Internet Explorer (Kornblum, 1998; Lewis, 1995).

Open source software can also be a source of revenue. The main models include

- Donation and gadgets
- Service providing
- Advertisement
- Market segmentation and freemium services.

Various organizations behind the development of open source systems base their revenue on **donations** or by selling **gadgets**, such as T-shirts or mugs. This is the case, for instance, of Mozilla and the GNU Software Foundation.

Another way to make a living out of open software is by selling services. RedHat, for instance, distributes a custom version of Linux for free.* The company makes a profit by selling customer support, training, and other services.

Revenues can also come from showing **advertisements** while the application is running. The schema is used mostly with web applications and with applications for smartphones. In both cases, specific developer kits are available to try and customize the advertisements based on the user characteristics. In some cases, companies also offer an ad-free version at a price, a case of **market segmentation**.

---

* Linux is distributed with the GNU License, which makes the software and any derivative work open source. RedHat could, in principle, sell the software as long as it made available all source code.

Various companies offer a base version of a system for free and charge users for additional services. This is an example of **market segmentation** or **freemium** services, a contraption of the *free* and *premium* words. For instance, Github, a source-code hosting company, offers a freemium service. Similar to the previous case, freemium systems break the barrier to entrance by making it easier for a user to try a new system, switch to it, and eventually pay for the additional services which the platform offers.

We conclude by noting that some for-profit companies developing closed-source software support and profit from open source systems. In a typical scenario, an open source component might be the basis for closed-source extensions. The company licenses the closed-source extensions while making available its contribution to the open source component, on which their system is based. This is done both to fulfill open source licensing obligations and to keep a community working on the open source component. This is the case, for instance, of **Apple**'s operating system (**OSX**), whose operating system is partly based on **BSD Unix**, released under an open source license.

In other situations, the open source component might be made available to foster integration and extensions by a community of volunteers. This is the case, for instance, of **Ruby On Rails**, a web application framework made available under a very liberal open source license. **David Hansson** developed the first version of Ruby on Rails, while he was working at **37Signals** on **BaseCamp**, the flagship product of the company. Today, Ruby on Rails is a very popular web applications development framework. Releasing Ruby On Rails in open source fostered the growth of a large community. Thus, additional effort required to make a system open source was richly rewarded by the vibrant community it created and the visibility obtained by the company and its products. Thus, even if the initial release was not motivated by self-interest, it created a win-win situation.

In synthesis, companies and foundations alike support the development of open source software. Projects developing software in open source have produced hundreds of millions of source lines of code and systems as large as 30.7 million source lines of code (Black Duck Software, 2013). It is therefore an opportunity and a model to consider with attention.

6.3 Project Pricing Strategies

In the previous section, we have seen some techniques to determine the price of a software system. On many occasions, however, this can be very difficult or irrelevant.

In these situations, looking at the **project costs** is a second good strategy. We can take two points of view, that of the client and that of the supplier. Basically, the strategies described in the following sections allocate financial risks between the supplier and the client, trying to find the equilibrium that makes it convenient for both parties to achieve the project goals, given the constraints. Given the fact that the client and the supplier often have different goals, this process is difficult, challenging, and very interesting.

6.3.1 Determining the Project Price

From the supplier's point of view, given the basic equation:

$$Price = profit + costs \qquad (6.1)$$

we can end up with different project pricing strategies, according to which one of the elements we fix in the equation (Maylor, 2010).

We can fix the **price**. Setting the price of a project to how much a client is willing to pay, for instance, can be an effective way to get a contract. The strategy, called **pricing to win**, however, constrains every other project aspect around the price. Risks include the possibility of not making any profit or delivering at a loss. If the price is set too low, another risk is compromising the quality or the delivery of the project outputs.

To mitigate the problems above, a **target costing** strategy can be put in place. According to this strategy, both price and profit are determined. The first is based on a value that makes the project competitive, the second according to the desired margin of profit. The costs are then met by elaborating on the other project constraints. The management, for instance, can evaluate different implementations; it can make project activities more efficient, or it can push the cost constraints to suppliers of project components.

The technique, applied systematically by Japanese companies, is today popular in the aerospace and automotive fields (Maylor, 2010). See Feil et al. (2004) for a nice historical overview.

An alternative schema **fixes the profit** and determines the price based on the actual costs incurred on a project. The profit is typically in the form of a percentage of the actual costs. The schema increases the probability of achieving the time and quality goals one desires. However, one risk for the client is that costs spiral out of control. Another consideration is that there are no incentives, from the economic point of view, to deliver efficiently or according to the required quality and schedule.

Finally, it has to be remarked that an organization may deliberately choose to be not profitable in a project to achieve a more strategic goal, such as entering a new market, getting a new important client, and limiting competition from other companies. In these situations, project costs need to be covered internally.

6.3.2 Contractual Agreements

Given the constraints above, we can come with different contractual agreements that try and allocate project risks between the client and the supplier.

Fixed price contract is a kind of agreement where the price is fixed at the beginning of the project for a given set of services or products to be delivered.

For the supplier, this contract requires accurate estimations and sufficient margins to accommodate for changes in the effort and other unexpected expenditures. It suits better projects in which the requirements are very clear. The client will end up paying an extra price (the margin imposed by the vendor to accommodate for unexpected events), but the price will be known before starting the project.

If estimations are inaccurate or the price is set too low, one risk is compromising project deliveries, as explained above. As pointed out in Wysocki (2011), "all potential suppliers might agree on a fixed price, but this could be a way to just get in the door and work the details later."

In specific cases, for instance, if the requirements volatility becomes unexpectedly high, additional agreements might be set to deal with unforeseen expenses. A "cost-plus" contract, however, might be more appropriate if the risks are known in advance—see below.

Time and materials is a kind of agreement in which the supplier exposes the costs to the client and bills according to the actual costs incurred. It requires the vendor to track the activities and actual time spent on the project. An additional effort might be required to check the *eligibility* of expenses, some of which might not be covered by specific agreements.

An initial estimation can be set to give a rough estimation of the project costs. The contractual agreement, however, corresponds to the *fixed profit* pricing strategy, since additional expenses are covered for, if the initial estimations are not met.

The agreement works well in situations with a high uncertainty or volatility of requirements, since it shares the project risks between the two contracting parties.

Retainer is a kind of contract in which a fixed price is paid to the vendor in exchange for a fixed amount of time provided.

It is equivalent to renting manpower to achieve a specific goal and, similar to the *time and materials* agreement, it works better when the requirements are not clear and have a high variability.

Finally, **cost plus** is a kind of agreement in which the buyer pays a contractor for all the allowed expenses up to a set limit. An additional payment is foreseen to allow the contractor to make a profit if certain conditions are met.

This kind of agreement is applied by government agencies for larger projects when it is difficult to come out with a price and the project execution risk is shared between the buyer and the vendor.

There are various kind of cost-plus agreements, among which we mention

- **Award-fee contracts**, if the additional payment is bound to the final quality of the product.
- **Incentive-fee contracts**, if the additional payment is bound to contracts that meet or exceed the performances. Incentive fee contracts reward efficiency.
- **Fixed-fee contract**, if the fee may be adjusted as a result of changes in the work to be performed under the contract. This permits contracting for work

that might otherwise present too great a risk to contractors. However, it provides the contractor only a minimum incentive to control costs (Government, 1998).

Cost-plus can be used when efficiency, quality, or improved performances are a desirable feature. Think, for instance, of the U.S. space program.

However, cost control becomes more difficult. Moreover, similar to time and materials, additional bookkeeping is necessary, for example, to verify that all the expenditures exposed by the contractor are eligible.

6.3.3 Contractual Agreements and Project Budget

From the financial point of view, the client and the supplier have contrasting goals in setting a schedule for payments. The client typically would like to pay as late as possible, while the supplier tries to be paid as soon as possible.

A reasonable compromise must be found between the client and the supplier to show a reciprocal commitment, reduce the financial exposure of the supplier, and minimize the risks of the client paying for services or products that will not be delivered.

To demonstrate the balance that needs to be established between the supplier and the client, consider Burke (2006), who discusses the future and past or **sunk** costs. In economics, only *future* costs and profits have to be considered when taking a decision. Any decision we take, in fact, will not allow us to change the past: we can make new money, but nice as it would be, we cannot "unspend" the money we have already spent.

Thus, if *financial consideration is the only element to decide whether a project has to continue or is better stopped*, the supplier has a simple equation: it has to determine how much the project will cost to complete and how much money the project will award at completion. If the amount is positive, then the project is worth continuing; if not, there is no financial reason to continue a project. Thus, the agreement between the client and the supplier should be such that the money awarded at the end of the project is higher than the cost to complete it.

However, if payments are awarded only at project delivery, a significant investment might be required on the supplier side. The required financial exposure might be impossible to bear or the risk of not being paid at the end of the project could be considered too high to actually get started with the work.

Two main types of agreements are achieved to solve the problem above: payments based on deliverables or time billing.

When adopting a **payment structure based on deliverables**, the client awards the customer a percentage of the total project price on achievement of specific deliverables or an important project milestone.

The actual payments have to be agreed case by case. An approach fixes the payments based on the costs to achieve a milestone. The schema ensures that, in nominal conditions, the costs to complete it are always lower than the money awarded. Moreover, the financial exposure for the supplier is limited, since payments are performed milestone by milestone.

To reduce the risks of the supplier, an **advance payment** might be requested at project start. This has the advantage of showing the commitment of the client to the project. For software development projects, the advance payment is often between 20% and 30% of the project total budget. A large number of projects require an advance payment on contract signing.

To simplify the process, organizations working in specific sectors standardize both the milestones for which they ask a payment and the payment structure, in the form of a percentage of the total amount charged for the project.

Stack Overflow (2008) and Hunt (2010) describe the payment structures actually used by some software consultants. One of the schemas described there, for instance, requires a 20% advance payment, followed by a 70% payment on software delivery, and a final 10% awarded on project completion.

A second approach, called **time billing/reimbursement**, requires payments on a regular basis according to the expenses the supplier has actually incurred.

When using this schema, at the end of every reporting period, the supplier bills the client based on the time actually spent on the project and, if allowed by the agreement, for the expenses actually incurred. If the agreement does not include the reimbursement of any expense, the client bills only for the time. In this case, an overhead is added on top of the hourly rates to cover for the other project expenses. See Section 3.7. Additionally, a percentage might be added on top of the invoice as a profit by the organization.

An important aspect characterizing time billing is the required amount of formality. Some public bodies, such as the European Union, require a detailed account and actual proofs of the expenses sustained. In other situations, the level of formality might be lower. The paperwork required for both parties changes a lot.

Finally, in specific cases, an analysis of the cash flow can be used to determine the actual financial needs of a project and, based on that, decide on a payment structure. This is particularly important if the project has to self-sustain financially.

The four diagrams of Figure 6.2 show the impact of different payment structures on the cash flow of a project. The first diagram (Figure 6.2(a)) shows a retainer agreement, in which payments for services to be provided (marked P1, P2, and P3) ensure the project is self-financed. The second diagram (Figure 6.2(b)) shows a time billing agreement, in which regular payments (marked P1, P2, and P3) reimburse for the actual expenses incurred. The project needs a continuous investment from the supplier. The risks are lowered by regular payments that cover the actual costs.

Figure 6.2(c) and (d) show payment structured by milestones. In the first case, shown in Figure 6.2(c), the project is largely self-financed. This is made possible by an advance payment (P1) and a milestone payment (P2) that also cover some future project costs. The last case, shown in Figure 6.2(d), is a project that requires an investment from the supplier, which is nearly covered on payment P1 and finally covered at the end of the project, with payment P2.

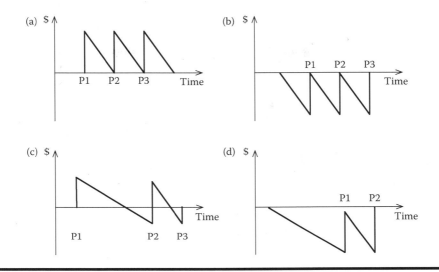

Figure 6.2 The impact of different payment structures on a project cash flow. (a) Using a retainer payment structure; (b) using time billing payment structure; (c) with an advance payment by milestone; (d) without an advance payment by milestone.

6.4 Procurement and Outsourcing

Projects require different competencies and abilities, and often their success is the result of a joint effort of different companies and consultants.

Procurement management is the set of activities to effectively manage vendors and contracts with vendors. It spans different phases of a project life cycle, including planning, execution, and project closing.

The procurement process can be organized in the following four activities:

1. **Identify needs**, during which the actual procurement needs are made clear.
2. **Identify vendors: solicitation, selection, award**, during which the most appropriate vendor is individuated. Different approaches can be used. We will have a look at the main ones below.
3. **Manage contract execution**, during which the project manager will monitor and control the project by ensuring that the procurement activities are proceeding as agreed.
4. **Accept final product**, during which the product is accepted.

When we outsource we start a (sub)project in which we take the role of the client. The techniques we have seen in the previous chapters therefore help us set up the main activities required for a sound management of the procurement activities.

For instance, the needs identification phase can use the assessment techniques we have seen in Section 3.1. If we need to choose between externalizing some activities or performing them in-house, for instance, we can use a *make or buy analysis* to analyze the benefits and risks and select the best alternative.

A similar consideration applies to managing contract execution. The monitoring and control techniques we have seen in Chapter 3 help in establishing clear goals and analyzing subcontractors' performances. One aspect to consider is that visibility over the actual project data of subcontractors might be limited. Thus, it becomes more important to define reporting duties and what metrics and data the subcontractor should make available.

The acceptance of the final product can be conducted using the quality assurance and testing techniques illustrated in Chapter 4.

More interesting are the considerations related to the vendor selection process, which we describe in more detail in the following two sections.

6.4.1 Vendor Solicitation

Vendor solicitation is the process according to which potential vendors are contacted and informed about your business needs.

This is usually done with an **invitation to tender**. The invitation to tender contains a specification of the products and services to be provided, together with other constraints related to the proposal.

At a minimum, an invitation to tender will include the following:

- A **specification of the products or services to be provided**. Think of a scope document. Attention should be paid to ensure that the document clearly states the goals and constraints related to the contract, such as, for instance, timing, quality, and costs; required reliability and compliance with standards; type of support to be provided after the contract ends; and management of intellectual property rights.
- **Procedure to submit a proposal** and the **selection criteria that will be used to award the contract**. Best price is a selection criterion. Other considerations might be equally important, as we saw when we discussed contractual agreements—Section 6.3.3. The selection criteria are typically required for contracts awarded by public administrations.

Contractors distribute invitations to tender through various channels, such as advertisements in newspapers, websites, mailing lists, and specialized journals; governments make available their tenders in official documents (e.g., Official Gazette); some companies and some websites provide services of collecting tenders by type and sector.

Tenders can either be **open**, when any subject can participate, or **restricted**, when only the supplier can be contacted by the buyer to participate in the bidding phase.

In some situations, a **direct call** or **negotiated procedure** to a single vendor might also be used. Restricted and direct calls are used when there are specific project concerns. In these cases, the selection process includes only the vendors who satisfy certain constraints, like having adequate or specific technical competencies. Concerns about financial solidity and the capacity to support the delivered solution after the project ends might also be taken into account. The standard bidding procedure for public administrations is the open tender. Restricted or negotiated procedures can be chosen in specific and motivated situations. The risk is, in fact, that of using public money to favor certain contractors.

For open and restricted tenders, once the proposals are collected, the buyer will select a vendor. This is done by evaluating how the different proposals meet the criteria identified. According to the size and procedures in place, a commission might be appointed with the task of evaluating the proposals.

Evaluations often use score matrices (Section 3.1.3.2) to measure the relative merits of each proposal. In this case, the bid with the highest score is awarded the contract. For score matrices to be fair and effective, of course, the criteria have to be defined before any evaluation actually starts. The problem of fairness, of course, remains in the way in which scores are assigned.

Table 6.1 shows a score matrix to evaluate and select different vendors. The example is taken from the criteria used by the European Union to finance a class of research projects (The Secretariat of the African, C. and P.A.G. of States, 2012). In particular, the evaluation proceeds along two main dimensions, the *relevance of the proposal* (called *action* in the table) and its *design*. Four criteria are identified for assessing the relevance of the action; two for its design. Each criterion has a weight of 1 and a maximum score is set for each criterion.

Note that making the evaluation criteria known in advance can help the vendor define a proposal that is more fitting to the needs of the contractor.

For negotiated procedures and for contracts in the private sector, the procedures mentioned above can be simplified.

Once the vendor is selected, a contract is stipulated among the parties. Contracts specify the work to be carried out and the conditions regulating timing and payments. These are usually specified through a technical annex, which describes the work and the project. Additional clauses determine the ownership, liabilities, and intellectual property rights. Laws governing the contract and the procedure for the resolution of disputes complete the required information.

6.4.2 Procurement Timing Activities

Procurement of services and products can be a lengthy matter. Needless to say, sufficient time and resources have to be allocated to ensure that the various activities are carried out by the book.

Table 6.1   Example of Selection Criteria for EU Research Projects

Criteria	Weight	Maximum Score
1. Relevance of the action		
1.1 How relevant is the proposal to the objectives and priorities of the call for proposals?	1	10
1.2 How relevant is the proposal to the particular needs and constraints of the target countries or regions?	1	10
1.3 How clearly defined and strategically chosen are those involved (final beneficiaries, target groups)? Have their needs been clearly defined and does the proposal address them appropriately?	1	5
1.4 Does the proposal contain specific added-value elements, such as environmental sustainability, promotion of gender equality and equal opportunities, good governance and human rights, or climate change?	1	5
2. Design of the action		
2.1 How coherent is the overall design of the action? In particular, does it reflect the analysis of the problems involved and take into account external factors and relevant stakeholders?	1	10
2.2 Is the action feasible and consistent in relation to the objectives and expected results?	1	10

In general, the schedule should consider

■ The preparation of the invitation to tender, during which attention must be paid to ensure that all the relevant requirements (technical, project, and support) are in place, since little (or nothing) can be done to change the terms of the contract, once the invitation is out.

■ Sufficient time for potential bidders to become aware of the bid and respond properly. Open tenders solicited by the public administration in Italy need to be published at least 50 days before the submission deadline. European project proposals have even longer deadlines.

■ Sufficient time to evaluate the proposals received. According to the procedures in place, this could include the time to select and appoint a commission. Once the commission is in place, it needs time to read and evaluate the proposals and write a report explaining the choices. In some cases, commissions might ask for clarifications from the bidders. In this case, additional time has to be allocated so that the bidders can respond properly.

■ Time to award the contract.

■ Time for the contractor to actually deliver the products or services agreed upon.

Table 6.2 Example of a Procurement Schedule

Activity	How	Calendar Time (Working Days)
Preparation of the invitation to tender	Involvement of the technical staff for the requirements and of the legal department for terms and conditions	5
Waiting for an offer from the vendor		15
Evaluation of the offers	Check with the technical staff that the requirements are met; check the additional conditions set by the vendor	2
Place the order	Involve the procurement office and send the request	1
Wait for hardware to be ready		20
	Total	**43**

For open tenders, this schedule results in months between the preparation of the bidding and the actual start of the work.

Procurement is best scheduled backward, starting from the date on which a specific good or service has to be obtained and moving backward as the time required by each activity is determined.

As a simple example, consider an activity to buy hardware. A possible schedule is shown in Table 6.2. Many other examples are available. See Mills and Reeve (2011) for another timescale.

6.5 An Example

Consider the Theater 3001 project we presented in Section 3.11.

To decide on a payment schedule, a simple approach is that of allocating costs proportionally to the effort required to achieve each project milestone.

Approximating the numbers a bit, we get

- M1 Specifications: €8500
- M2 Environment and system: €31,000
- M3 Experimentation: €1500.

To minimize the risks related to financial exposure, we have different possibilities:

1. We can choose a "time & materials" (or "retainer") contractual agreement, with payments fixed on a monthly basis. The schema ensures that we get paid for the work performed and, in the case of the retainer contract, for the work we will perform. However, these options might not be suitable for the client.

2. We can choose a "fixed cost" contractual agreement, requiring an advance payment to get started and other regular payments, based on the achievement of project milestones. This schema minimizes risks on both sides, as explained below.

A possible allocation of payments is shown in Table 6.3. We evaluate the schema considering financial exposure and fairness of the agreement between the client and the supplier.

Concerning the first point, we have a schema in which the client makes an initial investment that covers the expenses at the start of the project. The supplier then needs to cover the project costs with internal resources. The final payment is then used to balance any due. (Note, however, that the tariffs we use already include a profit; thus, the actual exposure of the supplier is lower than what the numbers show.)

It can also be observed that

■ The payment associated with M1, together with the advance payment, is about the value of the work to produce the deliverables associated with the milestone. It is thus fair both to the client and the supplier.

■ The payment associated with M2 is necessarily lower than the value of the deliverable, since we need to take from somewhere the funds to cover the initial payment.

■ The payment associated with M3 (end of project) is higher than the value of the work to achieve the milestone. This is to keep the commitment of the supplier in the project. Consider, for instance, the situation in which the payment associated with the last milestone is equal to or lower than the costs sustained by the supplier. Reasoning from a purely economical point of view, it would be indifferent or, worse, counterproductive for the supplier to continue work in the project.

For the reason highlighted above, the final payment usually has a higher incidence than the one shown in the table.

Table 6.3   The Payment Schema for the Theater 3001 Project

Event	Date	Amount	Euros	Cumulative
Kick-off	Jun 01	10%	€4100	€4100
M1	Jul 02	10%	€4100	€8200
M2	Sep 11	60%	€24,600	€32,800
End	Sep 30	20%	€8200	€41,000
		Total	€41,000	

6.6 Questions and Topics for Discussion

1. What are the main strategies to determine software price?
2. Consider the Theater 3001 project. Find the break-even point if we are given the opportunity to license the system at €3000 each. What would be the price we need to set if we intend to break even with 500 licenses?
3. What are the operational costs of the Theater 3001 system? Provide your estimation of the costs.
4. What are the aspects to consider when leasing a software?
5. Set a leasing price for the Theater 3001 system.
6. Are there components of the Theater 3001 project you could make open source without compromising opportunities for a business? What kind of additional benefits could you achieve with such an arrangement?

References

Black Duck Software, 2013. Ohloh home page. Available at http://www.ohloh.net. Last retrieved May 25, 2013.

Bruxam, P., H. Diefenbach, and T. Hess, 2013. *The Software Industry—Economic Principles, Strategies, Perspectives.* Springer-Verlag, Berlin, Heidelberg, Germany.

Burke, R., 2006. *Project Management, Planning and Control Techniques* (4th ed.). John Wiley & Sons, New York, NY, USA.

Davidson, N., 2012. *Don't Just Roll the Dice.* Efendi Minibooks, United Kingdom.

Feil, P., K.-H. Yook, and I.-W. Kim, 2004, Spring. Japanese target costing: A historical perspective. *International Journal of Strategic Cost Management*, 11, 10–19.

Free Software Foundation, 2007, June. GNU general public license. Available at http://www.gnu.org/licenses/gpl.html. Version 3, 29 June 2007. Last retrieved May 25, 2013.

GNU Software Foundation, 2013, March. Overview of the GNU system. Available at http://www.gnu.org/gnu/gnu-history.html. Last retrieved May 25, 2013.

Hunt, B., 2010. Tips on the structure and timing of payments for web site projects. Available at http://www.webdesignfromscratch.com/business/payment-timing-structure-tips/. Last retrieved July 8, 2013.

Kornblum, J., 1998, March. Netscape sets source code free. Available at http://news.cnet.com/2100-1001-209666.html. Last retrieved June 28, 2013.

Lewis, P. H., 1995, March. Netscape knows fame and aspires to fortune. Available at http://www.nytimes.com/1995/03/01/business/business-technology-netscape-knows-fame-and-aspires-to-fortune.html?pagewanted=all&src=pm. Last retrieved November 15, 2013.

Maylor, H., 2010. *Project Management* (4th ed.). Pearson, Harlow, England.

Mills & Reeve, 2011. Timescale tracker. Available at http://www.mrprocurement.co.uk/files/Uploads/Documents/timescale_tracker.pdf. Version 1.07. Last retrieved November 15, 2013.

MIT, 2013. The MIT license. A template is available at http://opensource.org/licenses/MIT. Last retrieved May 25, 2013.

Open Source Initiative, 2013. Open source initiative, license by name. Available at http://opensource.org/licenses/alphabetical. Last retrieved May 25, 2013.

Open Source Resource Center, 2012. Open source license data. Available at http://osrc.blackducksoftware.com/data/licenses/. Last retrieved May 25, 2013.

The Secretariat of the African, Caribbean and Pacific (ACP) Group of States, 2012. *ACP-EU Cooperation Programme in Science and Technology II—Guidelines for Applicants.* Available at http://www.acp-st.eu/content/acp-eu-cooperation-programme-science-and-technology-ii-st-ii-call-proposals-launched. Last retrieved November 15, 2013.

Sommerville, I., 2007. *Software Engineering* (8th ed.). Addison-Wesley, Redwood City, CA.

Stack Overflow, 2008. What payment structure do you use for small projects? Available at http://stackoverflow.com/questions/383975/what-payment-structure-do-you-use-for-small-projects. Last retrieved July 6, 2013.

US Government, 1998. 48 cfr 16.306—cost-plus-fixed-fee contracts—code of federal regulations. Available at http://www.gpo.gov/fdsys/granule/CFR-2010-title48-vol1/CFR-2010-title48%-vol1-sec16-306/content-detail.html. Last retrieved April 25, 2013.

Wysocki, R. K., 2011, October. *Effective Project Management: Traditional, Agile, Extreme* (6, illustrated ed.). John Wiley & Sons, New York, NY, USA.

Chapter 7

Managing Software Development Projects

7.1 Project Life Cycles

So far, we have looked at the activities to build software (Chapter 2) and at the activities to manage software development processes (Chapters 3 through 5). We paid less attention, however, to the way in which they integrate in a coherent process.

In this chapter, we look at the development processes that have been proposed to accommodate the needs of different types of software development. Some favor a more thorough definition of the problem and solution before moving to the implementation phase. Others embrace flexibility and start implementation with partial information. In some cases, processes also come with a set of best practices and prescriptions that explain how activities should be carried out. In all cases, these approaches influence the organization of work, the structure of teams, and also the typical documentation and paperwork that a project produces.

At a bare minimum, we can characterize processes along two main dimensions:

1. The *linearity of the process*: the order in which the development of more elementary components of the project is organized
2. The *formality of the process*: the amount of infrastructure a project requires.

Concerning linearity, we can distinguish **sequential**, **cyclical**, and **parallel** development. The first proceeds from specification to implementation, with *little opportunities for backtracking*. The second organizes development in different *rounds*, with each round delivering more or improved functionality. The third uses *concurrent* *development*: an initial activity organizes further development efforts, which are then carried out in independent and parallel tracks; a final activity integrates the contribution of the different tracks.

If we look at the formality of the process, authors distinguish among **traditional, agile**, and **extreme project** management.

The term **traditional project management** denotes highly structured frameworks, in which managers use the techniques described in Chapters 3 and 4 to plan and monitor projects. The underlying assumption is that *efficiency can be achieved with a top-down and planned organization of work.* Only with this approach, according to their advocates, it is possible to eliminate misunderstandings, errors, and rework, while at the same time promoting an efficient use of resources. To go back to our millefoglie example, traditional managers prefer a well-structured millefoglie, with each layer nicely laid out.

Agile project management, by contrast, focuses on efficiency and flexibility. For the supporters of agile methodologies, management is an infrastructure that adds unnecessary work and unnecessary rigidity to the process. According to their supporters, projects should exploit any opportunity to improve the quality of a product and the efficiency of its development. This cannot be achieved if the development process is highly structured and regulated. Agile thus favors *people over processes and interaction over formality.* Agile fans prefer a low-fat millefoglie.

Finally, high-risk and exploratory projects require even more flexibility than agile methodologies can provide. **Extreme project management** thus denotes a situation in which long-term planning is impossible: *high speed, high change,* and *high uncertainty* are the three conditions characterizing these projects. Extreme project managers do not know whether they will have a millefoglie for dessert.*

When starting a new software development project, managers are faced with the need to choose a management approach and a development process. There is no such thing as *the best process*. Factors such as the criticality of the application, uncertainty, and unpredictability of the project environment, organizations and people involved, and regulations and recommendations determine which is the most appropriate choice. Quoting McCracken and Jackson (1982), "To contend that a life cycle scheme, even with variations, can be applied to all system development is either to fly in the face of reality or to assume a life cycle so rudimentary as to be vacuous."

The next sections therefore provide some more information to take more informed decisions. The processes we present compose the elementary activities that we have presented in Chapter 2, organizing them in different ways in order to adapt to different project conditions. The focus will be on the organization of

---

* Notice that *extreme project management* is different from *extreme programming*, which we will see in Section 7.3.1.

the technical activities; the combination of a development process with a proper management framework will help ensure that all pieces fit together.

7.2 From Traditional to Agile

7.2.1 The Waterfall

The waterfall is traditionally the first process presented in books and courses, given its rationality and simplicity. We confirm the rule and start from the process defined by Royce in the 1970s.

Simplifying a bit, in the waterfall development activities proceed sequentially, from conceptualization of the problem to delivery of the final product. Each activity of the process takes as input the outputs produced by the previous activity of the chain, uses them to produce artifacts *closer* to the final product, and passes the outputs to the next activity in the chain (Royce, 1970).

A simplified version of the waterfall process is shown in Figure 7.1. (We changed the naming and number of activities, which are more articulated in the original definition.) The first activity is **requirements**, which outputs the **requirements documents**. This, in turn, is used to define the system architecture during the **design** phase. The phase produces a **system architecture**. This is the input for the next activity in the chain, namely, **implementation**, which produces the **system** to be tested. The last two phases in the process are **testing**, during which the system is checked for compliance with the requirements, and **deployment**, during which the system is installed in production.

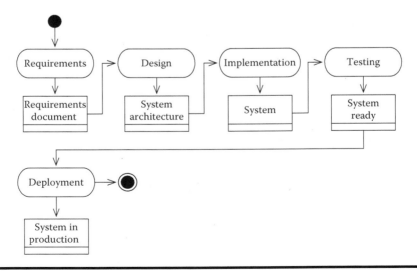

Figure 7.1   The waterfall.

The model can be easily extended to accommodate project management activities. In its simplest extension, the process starts with a **high-level planning** activity to define the project scope, schedule, risk, and budget. If algorithmic estimation techniques are used, after the *requirements* phase, a second detailed planning takes place. This generates the plan for the subsequent development activities of the waterfall. A **monitoring and control** activity runs in parallel with the development activities. A final **closing** activity properly terminates the project. This is shown in Figure 7.2.

In the ideal case, the waterfall is a **staged process** in which quality control on the outputs of an activity determine the transition to the next activity, with no possibility of backtracking. In practice, lack of information, misunderstandings, mistakes, and changed conditions cause some backtracking. For instance, during the coding phase, it might become necessary to revise the system architecture to fix a conceptual and unanticipated issue that is making implementation cumbersome.

The *rigidity* of the waterfall is, at the same time, its main advantage and weakness. In projects where the requirements are very clear or in which a controlled development environment is very beneficial, the waterfall process shows its advantages. However, in many other cases, the rigidity of the waterfall can hinder, rather than speed up, development.

Different variations of the waterfall have been proposed in the literature to overcome some of its limitations. For instance, McConnell (1996) mentions the **sashimi waterfall**, where activities are allowed to overlap, the **waterfall with subprojects**, in which the implementation of different components defined by the architecture

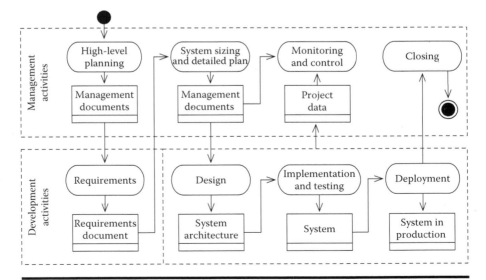

Figure 7.2 The waterfall with project management activities.

proceeds in parallel, and the **waterfall with risk reduction**, in which an initial risk analysis helps mitigate risks in the later phases of implementation.

The approaches just mentioned introduce some flexibility while retaining the waterfall's main characteristics. In many situations, however, even these changes are not sufficient and a more radical approach is necessary. Abstracting a bit, these models variate on the waterfall model by

- **Allowing for structural backtracking during the testing phase.** In the **V-cycle** model, testing activities provide systematic ways to consolidate the implementation or backtrack to the most appropriate development activity. This is explained in more detail in Section 7.2.2.
- **Allowing for an iterative and evolutionary development of the system.** All the phases are repeated various times to deliver increasingly refined versions of the system. This is explained in more detail in Section 7.2.4.
- **Blurring the boundaries between activities.** By further pushing the sashimi model, processes organize the development in stages in which different activities run in parallel with different levels of *intensity*. This is explained in more detail in Section 7.2.3.
- **Embracing flexibility and change.** By reducing management and paperwork in favor of flexibility and efficiency, software development becomes more efficient. This is explained in more detail in Section 7.3.

In the following paragraph, we present the different processes using a similarity approach, in which we slowly move away from the waterfall model, rather than a chronological approach, which would favor a historical presentation of the methods. One of the motivations is that older, in this context, does not mean obsolete. The waterfall is still applied in many development projects.

7.2.2 The V-Model

The V-Model is a process adopted by the German Federal Government that emphasizes the verification and validation of a system. As pointed out by IABG (2013), the model has undergone various revisions since its first definition in 1992, and it has been elaborated in different versions. Some of these versions focus on the development phases, while others propose a broader framework that includes technical, support, and managerial activities. We will focus on the technical activities only, pointing the reader to Testing (2013) and Christie (2008) for a discussion about some of the variations of the model.

As we have seen in Section 2.4.1, testing can be organized in different activities, according to their scope. The V-Model, in particular, distinguishes four types of testing:

1. **Unit testing**, which focuses on each component
2. **Integration testing**, which focuses on the integration of components

3. **System testing**, which evaluates the compliance of a system with its specified requirements
4. **Acceptance testing**, which is meant to evaluate that a system meets its customer's specification.

As we move from unit testing to acceptance testing, we increase the scope of the activity. The impact of bugs increases similarly. Bugs discovered during unit testing require local changes, while bugs discovered during acceptance testing require a more thorough analysis of the overall process. Consider the following two cases: a bug discovered during unit testing and a bug discovered during acceptance testing. The first is caused by an incorrect implementation of a module and it will be fixed by modifying the code of the module under test. A bug discovered during acceptance testing, however, has more far-reaching implications. The bug, in fact, could have originated during the system specification phase, when analysts incorrectly captured a customer requirement. The fix, in general, will require a revision of all choices taken after the error was made. This is the only way, in fact, to ensure that the correct fix is applied.

The V-Model accommodates such differences by having different testing activities causing backtracking at different depths in the process. The organization of core development activities foreseen by the V-Model is presented in Figure 7.3. The left side of Figure 7.3 shows the development/construction activities. The process proceeds from the specification of the requirements to coding in a way similar to the waterfall. The process differs when testing activities start, as shown on the

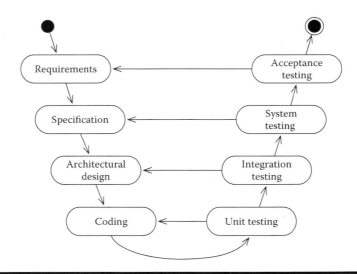

Figure 7.3   The V-cycle.

right side of Figure 7.3. More specifically, the V-Model organizes testing in the four activities we presented above. Bugs discovered in each testing phase will cause the process to restart from the first development activity that might have originated them. Thus, for instance, *unit testing* has two possible outcomes. If all tests pass, the process moves to the next phase, namely, *integration testing*. However, if some unit test fails, the process is restarted from the first development activity that might have caused the problem, namely, *coding*. Similar is the case for the other activities.

7.2.3 The Rational Unified Process

The **rational unified process** (RUP) is a framework designed by Rational Software, the company also behind the definition of the Unified Modeling Language.* RUP is a very articulated framework that aims at supporting a wide range of software development projects. Its application typically requires one to select which activities are relevant and to tailor the process to the needs at hand.

The specification of RUP is based on **best practices** and on **process specification**, which describes how to organize activities while taking advantage of tool automation.

There are six main practices behind RUP:

1. **Develop software iteratively**. The goal is to allow increasing understanding of the system to be developed, similar to the spiral model.
2. **Manage requirements**. The goal is to provide adequate support to communicate with the customer, to evaluate different alternatives, and to manage changes.
3. **Use component-based architectures**. The goal is to support an incremental approach to development by building robust components that can be integrated.
4. **Visually model software**. The goal is to simplify communication and to use a simple and unambiguous representation to build a shared vision.
5. **Verify software quality**. The goal is to ensure adequate quality of the final product.
6. **Control changes to the software**. The goal is to provide adequate change management practices that support iterative development.

See Sommerville (2007) and Rational Software (2011) for more details.

RUP recognizes that during software development, different activities run in parallel and overlap, rather than being neatly separated like in the waterfall. The process is thus presented according to two dimensions, one that takes into account time and **development phases** and the other that takes into account **development activities**.

---

* Rational Software is now a division of IBM.

RUP organizes **development activities** in nine workflows. Seven of the workflows correspond to those we have already seen in Chapter 3.

They are

- Business modeling
- Requirements
- Analysis and design
- Implementation
- Testing
- Configuration and change management
- Deployment.

RUP adds two additional workflows. A **project management** workflow includes all activities related to managing a system, while an **environment** workflow is concerned with making the proper tools available for development.

Workflows run throughout a project. However, as development progresses, concern and focus change and we can distinguish different phases. Thus, RUP organizes four **development phases**. These are

- **Inception**, during which the main ideas and operating requirements of a system are identified
- **Elaboration**, during which the requirements are used to define the system architecture
- **Construction**, during which the system is actually built
- **Transition**, during which the system is deployed and the next phase is planned for.

Each phase terminates with a well-defined milestone, during which the team verifies that key goals of the phase have been achieved. If necessary, each phase can be further organized into iterations to break the complexity of system development in more manageable chunks.

As mentioned earlier, all workflows are active during all phases of development, with different levels of *intensity*. Thus, for instance, the main effort during *inception* will be spent on *business modeling*. However, the team will also engage in some *requirements* elicitation. If necessary, some *analysis and design* will allow the team to analyze some of the issues that could emerge in later phases of development, thus minimizing the risks. Similar is the case for the other phases.

One of the advantages of RUP is that it comes with a step-by-step guide and a set of templates that can be used to kick-start a project. This simplifies a bit its application and the costs related to its adoption. On the other hand, as mentioned earlier, the process and templates are very elaborate (see Table 7.1 for some data). Its efficient and effective implementation therefore requires a customization step.

To overcome the problem, variations of the process have been proposed, among which are OpenUP. More information about RUP can be found in Kroll and Kruchten (2003), Kruchten (2004), and Rational Software (2011).

Table 7.1   Some Data about the RUP 2000 Model Definition

Discipline	Number of Deliverables
Business modeling	8
Requirements	7
Analysis and design	2
Test	2
Management	11
Configuration and change management	1
Deployment	3
Implementation	1
Environment	7
Total	**42**

7.2.4 The Spiral

The **spiral process** was first proposed by Boehm (1988) and the process was first used for the production of the TRW Software Productivity System, an integrated environment for software engineering systems.

The main motivation behind the spiral is to reconcile the rigidity of the waterfall with the uncertainties and flexibility required by software development projects. In its original formulation, in fact, the waterfall leaves little opportunities to analyze and assess risks. Even in its risk-driven variance, the process is still sequential, with no opportunities to take into considerations the risks identified and occurring during system development.

The spiral changes this approach by organizing development into a **risk-driven**, **iterative** process. Each iteration builds on the results achieved at the previous one. In the words of Boehm: "the model reflects the underlying concept that each cycle involves a progression that addresses the same sequence of steps, for each portion of the product and for each of its levels of elaboration, from an overall concept of operation document down to the coding of each individual program."

All iterations have the same structure, organized in four main activities:

1. **Determine objectives**, during which the team puts together the following information: the *objectives* to be achieved for the current portion of development, that is, the current loop of the spiral; the *constraints* that need to be satisfied (e.g., costs, time); the *potential alternatives* that could achieve the goals, while satisfying the constraints.
2. **Evaluate alternatives and risks**, during which the team *identifies and resolves the main risks*. During this phase, the alternatives identified at the previous step are evaluated to understand which solution fits the objectives and constraints better. The risk resolution phase includes a wide set of activities, such as prototyping, simulation, interviews, and modeling.

3. **Develop**, during which the team produces the outputs determined by the information gathered at the previous step. During the first cycles of the spiral, these outputs will consist of software concepts, specifications, and designs. Later stages will produce an implementation of the system.

4. **Plan the next iteration**, during which the team plans the next cycle of the spiral that is planned. Starting from the outputs of the other phases, a critical review of the results, and an analysis of the main objectives, the project manager and the team plan and prioritize the next activities.

7.2.5 Prototyping/Evolutionary

One big concern in software development is to bridge the communication gap between the customer and the development team, in order to facilitate the comprehension of the customer's needs, explain the main constraints posed by the existing technologies, and come out with a system that satisfies the customer's needs while respecting the cost and quality constraints. Any approach that facilitates such communication is therefore beneficial (McCracken and Jackson, 1982).

In the **prototyping** or **evolutionary** approach, the team builds one or more prototypes of the system, in order to verify various project assumptions about the system being built. The prototypes are incomplete versions of a system, demonstrating some of its functions. The simplest prototypes are **mockups**, which mimic the behavior of the system, using different technologies, and demonstrate to the customer how the system could work or behave.

Two types of system development are possible when using the prototype approach using **throwaway** prototypes or adopting an **evolutionary** model.

Throwaways are prototypes built to demonstrate a function or test a specific approach. For instance, a throwaway prototype could be defined to show how a user interface could behave or to verify whether certain nonfunctional constraints can be met, given the current requirements (e.g., performances). The prototype ceases to be useful when it has proven (or disproved) what it was built for.

Remark

Throwaway prototyping is a practice that can be easily embedded in many development processes. When it becomes necessary to verify a specific project assumption, the team starts the development of a throwaway prototype, in parallel to the other standard development activities. When the throwaway prototype has had its use, the prototyping activity terminates and the process proceeds as usual. Thus, for instance, a manager could extend the *requirements* phase of a waterfall process to include the construction of a prototype of the GUI. Short of the extra activity to build the prototype, the process will exactly follow the waterfall model.

Evolutionary prototypes, by contrast, evolve to the final product through successive refinements. This requires an iterative process. Each iteration ends with the production of a prototype, which is used as the basis for the next cycle. At the end of each cycle, the customer might be asked to validate the prototype, in order to steer development and take into account the customer's needs. As one can imagine, evolutionary development considerably limits the amount of time and effort dedicated to requirements and design, favoring coding instead.

For instance, McConnell (1996) highlights a process composed of the following four steps:

1. **Initial concept**, whose goal is to highlight the most evident characteristics of a system
2. **Design and implement the initial prototype**, whose goal is to sketch the system architecture and build an initial prototype
3. **Refine the prototype till acceptable**, whose goal is to progressively refine a system through different iterations
4. **Complete and release the prototype**, whose goal is to complete the last prototype so that it can be deployed

The evolutionary model is particularly suited for the development of new technologies or new ideas. Consider, for instance, a scenario in which a first cycle allows one to build a simplified prototype that explores a new concept in user interaction. The prototype is tested with some users and the information then used to develop the prototype into a fully functional system.

Some of the disadvantages include increased costs and delivery time.

The prototype model also has its difficulties, as can easily be imagined. As pointed out in Boehm (1988), it is difficult to plan system development. Moreover, premature (and wrong) choices made on early prototypes might make their evolution into the final product cumbersome and difficult. Finally, Boehm argues that it might be difficult to identify a good sequence of evolutionary prototypes to apply to a poorly structured and large legacy system, making the use of the evolutionary approach ineffective in such scenarios.

7.2.6 Cleanroom Software Engineering

Cleanroom software engineering is a development process based on formal methods and statistical testing, whose goal is to achieve zero-defect software (Linger, 1993). The process was tested on various systems in the 1990s, many of whom were safety-critical applications. Linger (1993) reports that the smallest system was an automated documentation system of about 1.8 KLOC, while the biggest was a control system for a NASA satellite of about 170 KLOC.

The zero-defect goal is achieved by a controlled, iterative process in which a pipeline of software increments accumulates to achieve the final product. The increments are developed and certified by small, independent teams, with teams of teams for large projects, a characteristic we also find in agile processes.

Formal verification techniques and statistical testing are used for the certi-fication.

Figure 7.4 illustrates the process. Starting from the customer requirements, a specification of the system behavior, formalized with a **functional specification** and a **usage specification**, defines the basis for further development. These two documents, the first of which is used for development and the second for testing, allow the team to define the system components and to plan the development and testing increments (**increments planning** in Figure 7.4). The implementation of each system increment is the responsibility of two independent teams. The *development team* develops the components, using formal methods (**formal design and**

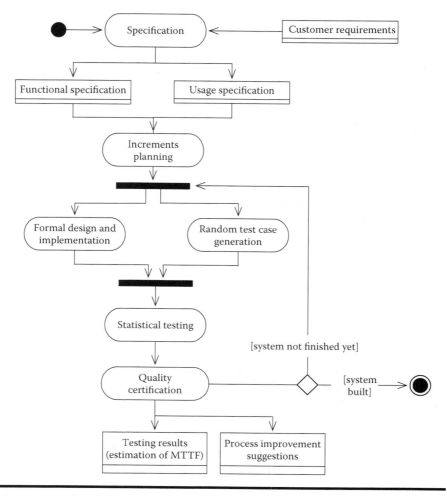

Figure 7.4   Cleanroom software engineering.

implementation), while the *testing team* is responsible for verifying the behavior of the components. This is achieved with statistical methods; the corresponding activities in the diagram are **random test case generation**, to generate test cases, and **statistical testing**, to perform the tests. A final **quality certification** activity produces an estimation of the *mean time to failure* (MTTF) and suggestions to improve results in the next increment.

An important remark is that the philosophy behind the process is **quick and clean**, rather than **quick and dirty**. As mentioned in Linger (1993), "Team correctness verification takes the place of unit testing and debugging, and software enters system testing directly, with no execution by the development team. All errors are accounted for from first execution on, with no private debugging permitted."

7.3 Agile Methodologies

The waterfall process and the other traditional software development processes structure the process to limit variability and changes. Each artifact and each step of the process consolidate and fix constraints, increasing one's confidence in the stability of artifacts that are easy to modify and, more important, that might not capture the actual needs. This approach draws from other engineering disciplines. Take, for instance, bridge construction. In the early phases, when the design of the bridge is blueprinted, the changes are relatively easy. As we move with development, however, making changes becomes increasingly costly and difficult, since we are constrained by the physical artifacts we have already built.

If the analogy promotes a vision of software that is as *solid as a bridge*, at the same time it fails to recognize its unique flexibility. Changes in software are not always costly. Thus, *imposing rigidity with a process where or when it is not needed* makes it impossible to exploit opportunities for building a better system, when these opportunities arise and are convenient to implement. In other words, the process should exploit, rather than limit, the unique characteristics of software and the opportunities it offers to make its development more efficient.

Agile methodologies start out of the frustration of practitioners with traditional techniques. The **Agile Manifesto**, written in 2001 during a gathering in the mountains of Utah, lists four main principles that differentiate agile development from traditional practices (Manifesto for agile software development, 2001; Highsmith and Fowler, 2001).

These are

- Individuals and interactions over processes and tools
- Working software over comprehensive documentation
- Customer collaboration over contract negotiation
- Responding to change over following a plan.

A set of software development methodologies and processes is based on the Manifesto's principles, and agile development has gained a lot of popularity in recent years. Today, the adoption of agile methodologies is comparable to that of traditional techniques. According to Geracie et al. (2012), who report on a survey conducted in 2012, when asked about the methods used to produce software, 18% of the respondents declared using agile or Kanban; another 18% declared using the waterfall model; and 53% declared using both.

7.3.1 Extreme Programming

Extreme Programming (XP) is an agile methodology designed by Kent Beck, Ward Cunningham, and others while working on the C3 project at Chrysler (Copeland, 2001; Wells, 2009). XP introduces various interesting concepts, which can improve the way in which software is developed, even when the method is not fully adopted.

XP starts from the consideration that change is an integral part of software development and that a sound software development process should embrace change rather than discourage it altogether. However, since resources are not infinite, appropriate practices and mechanisms must be in place to evaluate the importance and cost of changes so that choices are made, reasonable goals set, and work prioritized. Thus, XP ensures that the *cost of change is constant* throughout the development life of a product, rather than increasing as we move along the development process (Chromatic, 2003).

The XP process is characterized by the following three main elements:

1. **Values**, which define the inspirational principles that guide any XP project
2. **Practices**, which describe the techniques applied in XP projects
3. **Process**, which describes how activities are organized, what roles are identified, and what artifacts are to be produced.

The XP values are **open and honest communication, honest feedback, simplicity**, and **courage.**

The first value is **open and honest communication**. This is essential to reduce friction between the different stakeholders participating in a project and their different goals/interests. XP, in particular, has customers and developers speaking directly. So, rather than having a marketing department passing every customer's request to the developers as they come and irrespective of the complexity, XP favors an approach in which priorities are set and the work to be done discussed and chosen together by the customer and by the developers.

The second value is **honest feedback**, which is essential to build a shared view about the system and the project. For this reason, XP favors rapid feedback. The closer the feedback is to what is being commented on, in fact, the simpler it is to give it and to learn from it, as well as to adapt activities to changed conditions. As mentioned in Chromatic (2003), "rapid feedback reduces the investment of time and resources in ideas with little payoff. Failures are found as soon as possible, within days or weeks, rather than months or years."

The third value is **simplicity**, namely, keeping a system as simple as it can be, but not any simpler than that. The XP design philosophy is inspired to the **KISS** design principle, an acronym that stands for **keep it simple, Stupid**.

The fourth value is the **courage** to take difficult decisions, be they technical or managerial. If a system does not work, it has to be fixed, even if the work required might be significant and delay the actual delivery. If a project is late, it is better to tell the customer.

XP also prescribes a set of rules (Wells, 1999). Some of these rules are easier to implement than others and might also be the reason other agile processes, such as Scrum, have become more popular. Among the most interesting and controversial rules, we mention:

- Make small and frequent releases.
- Give the team an open workspace.
- Stand-up meetings are organized every day.
- People are moved around to facilitate communication.
- Prototypes are created to reduce risk related to planning.
- The customer is always available.
- Unit tests are written before the code.
- All code is pair programmed.
- Ownership of the code is collective.
- When a bug is found, tests are created.

Figure 7.5 shows a simplified version of the XP process. The process is based on an iterative development that favors small releases and continuous feedback, at different levels of granularity. Each iteration is a complete development cycle, which

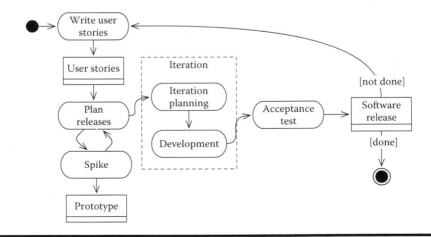

Figure 7.5 The XP process.

starts with an estimation and a selection of user requirements, written in the form of stories, and ends with a release.

We distinguish, in particular:

- **Write user stories**, which outputs the requirements of the system to be developed, in the form of user stories.
- **Plan releases**, which takes as input the *user stories* and outputs the overall project plan. Information, such as the number of **ideal hours*** required for each user story and the **team velocity** (number of ideal hours actually completed in a given time period), can be used to determine a rough plan for the project. An important aspect of the estimation is that, different from traditional techniques, it is performed by the developers.
- Development is structured in **iterations**, lasting between 1 and 3 weeks. The iteration starts with an **iteration planning** activity, during which the team selects the user stories to implement, according to priority, effort, and other constraints. **Development** then starts, using a test-driven approach, in which tests are written before the code is written, and pair programming. *Daily stand-up meetings, moving people around*, and promoting *collective ownership* of the code allow one to create a shared view on the system.

Iterations end with a release, that is, working software delivering some functions to the customer. The process is then iterated at the most appropriate level by adding user stories (if necessary), revising the release plan (if necessary), and starting the next iteration.

7.3.2 Dynamic System Development Method

The **Dynamic system development method** (DSDM) was first introduced by the DSDM Consortium, starting from the experience of RAD (rapid application development) and from three considerations: *people are key to project success, change is inevitable*, and *no software is perfect the first time it is released*. It is an agile methodology embracing the considerations of the Agile Manifesto, which would be published various years after DSDM.

The method has undergone various revisions; the current version was released in 2007 and is named **DSDM Atern**, after a bird, the "Arctic Tern."

Figure 7.6 shows the DSDM development process, which is iterative and organized in seven phases.

The **preproject** phase is where a project starts and all the activities necessary to set up a project are performed. The next two phases are **feasibility**, where the team investigates whether the goals are achievable with the given constraints, and

---

* An ideal hour is an hour fully dedicated to the development of a user story. No interruptions, no phone calls, no extra tasks—that is an ideal hour!

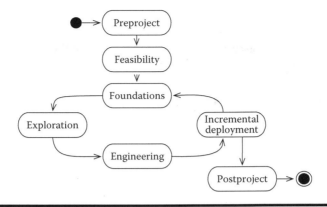

Figure 7.6   The DSDM process.

foundations, where the business value of the proposed project is analyzed, require-ments are prioritized using the MoSCoW approach, and the baseline architecture is sketched. The iterative process starts at the end of this activity.

Iterations are organized in three steps of fixed duration (time-boxed). The **explo-ration** step produces a prototype, which is used to refine requirements and priorities with the client, to identify nonfunctional requirements and to define an operational plan for the next activity.

The **engineering** step is where the nonfunctional requirements are added to the prototype and the prototype is made fit for delivery.

The **incremental deployment** step is where the results of the current increment are released.

Finally, a **postproject** phase hands over the final solution to the client and manages product maintenance.

The method is well documented and various resources are available on the Inter-net, including the official page of the DSDM consortium, which makes available, with certain restrictions, material and templates for practitioners and teachers alike (DSDM Consortium, 2013).

Another characteristic of the DSDM method is that it has been integrated with the PRINCE2® management framework, adding a sound management framework to the development practices proposed by the method. See, for instance, DSDM Consortium (2000, 2007).

7.3.3 Scrum

Scrum was first proposed in Takeuchi and Nonaka (1986) as a way to overcome the limitations of the traditional product development practices and achieve more speed and flexibility. The analogy is with the sport of rugby, where all players move together toward a goal, setting a rhythm and adapting quickly to variations in the external conditions.

The approach is based on six principles, which fit together like a jigsaw and are all essential in order to achieve results:

1. **Built-in instability**, achieved by giving teams broad goals and general strategic directions
2. **Self-organizing project teams**, achieved by allowing teams to self-organize roles, tasks, and work
3. **Overlapping development phases**, achieved by having different production phases overlap (similar to RUP), so that bottlenecks can be better dealt with
4. **Multilearning**, so that the team can learn both from internal and external sources and adapt quickly to changing conditions and environments
5. **Subtle control**, by providing the right steering to the project without interfering too much (e.g., selecting the right people for the job, creating an open environment, tolerating, and anticipating mistakes)
6. **Organizational transfer of learning**, by ensuring that the know-how acquired in a project is transferred and reused in other projects.

Jeff Sutherland and Ken Schwaber adapted the metaphor to software development in Sutherland (1995). Today, Scrum is probably the most popular agile methodology. According to VersionOne (2013), in fact, Scrum or Scrum variants account for 72% of agile projects.

The process is very simple and based on three roles (which we have already seen in Section 5.2.4), three main artifacts (the **product backlog**, the **Scrum board**, and a **potentially shippable product** (PSP)), and an iterative development process that proceeds in time-boxed sprints typically lasting between 2 and 4 weeks each.

Figure 7.7 shows the process. Similar to XP, the development in Scrum projects is driven by user stories (see Chapter 2). Simplifying a bit, user stories are the planning *chunks*, which define the work items of the project.*

The *product owner* labels user stories with a priority in which the *team* assigns each a *weight*, called **story points**. The priority represents the importance for the customer, while the weight measures the difficulty of implementing a user story. Different from traditional planning techniques, story points do not measure the effort, but rather they are an abstract measure of complexity. This measure is also team-dependent, since the same number might represent two different weights for two different teams. See Section 5.3.3.4 for a description of how teams assign story points to user stories.

---

* In practice, user stories are split into more elementary tasks, which are closer to actual implementation. This allows one to optimize work by identifying software elements that are common to different user stories; tasks can also be used for nonfunctional requirements, which are difficult to represent as user stories.

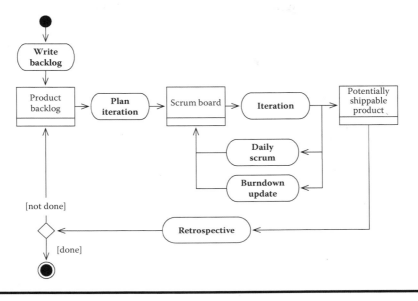

Figure 7.7   The Scrum process.

Iterations start with a planning phase, during which the team selects the user stories to implement according to priority and (story) points. The number of stories allocated to each sprint depends upon the **team velocity**, namely, the number of story points that the team can develop during a sprint. Note that since velocity is an essential planning measure and since its value depends on the actual time the team dedicates to a project, Scrum requires to use people full time on Scrum project.

The story allocated to a current sprint are collected in a **scrum board**, which is the basis for monitoring and control. The Scrum board is organized in columns. Each column corresponds to a specific status of a work item, such as, for instance, *to-do*, *doing*, *done*. A special area of the board might be dedicated to those user stories that are *blocked*, namely, have been allocated, but cannot be implemented in the current iteration. User stories are represented by post-it that are put on the Scrum board according to their status. Thus, during an iteration, they move from the left-hand side of the board to the right-hand side, as work proceeds.* Team members self-allocate work by choosing user stories and moving them on the board. The Scrum board thus also becomes a tool to quickly report on the project status. Figure 7.8 shows an example of a Scrum board, with different user stories (work items) in different states.

---

* When user stories are split in tasks, the whiteboard can also be organized in lines, with each line allocated to a specific user story and containing all the tasks necessary to implement the user story.

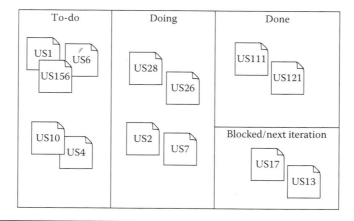

Figure 7.8   Scrum board.

The Scrum master monitors the overall progress updating the burndown chart and taking other quantitative measures. See Sections 3.9.5 and 3.9.6 for more details.

One important characteristic of sprints is that they are *shielded* from external influences. No change to the planned work can occur during a sprint, allowing the team to focus on the user stories selected at the beginning of the sprint.

During a sprint, daily stand-up meetings, called **scrum meetings**, are held. During these meetings, each team member answers three questions:

1. What have I done yesterday?
2. What will I do today?
3. What impediments do I have?

The daily meeting allows members to commit to the work to be done, while at the same time highlighting the main impediments which hinder work.

During the sprint, on a daily basis, the scrum master updates the burndown chart to monitor progress and measure the sprint velocity. See Section 3.9.5 for the details.

The sprint ends when the time has passed, independent of the stories actually implemented. The number of points actually implemented is used to determine the velocity achieved during the sprint. The stories allocated to the sprint, but not implemented, return to the product backlog.

At the end of a sprint, a PSP is released, that is, a product that the customer can use. The PSP is presented during a sprint review, during which the team demos what it has accomplished. While the method focuses on working software, it also allows for mockups and other products to be shipped. This makes the method also usable in complex projects, where a sprint might not be sufficient to start building software.

Finally, a **retrospective** about the sprint allows the team to analyze what has worked and what problems it has encountered during the sprint, so that the process can be improved in the next cycle.

7.3.4 Kanban

Lean manufacturing is a management practice mainly derived from the experience of the Toyota Production System, which starts from the consideration that everything that does not add value to the customer is *waste* and needs to be eliminated. Although the original definition had seven different sources of waste, three basic categories can be identified: **muda** (nonvalue-adding activities), **mura** (variations in production), and **muri** (overburden) (Ikonen et al., 2010).

Kanban is a lean-management practice that eliminates waste by using a just-in-time, pull-based production system. The system was first applied to the factory floor as a way to limit inventory levels. In the traditional process, production *pushes* products to the market *independent* of actual demand; if the production is higher than the actual demand, inventory builds up. Kanban reverts the process by creating a **pull system**, in which work is processed through being signaled, rather than being scheduled. Every time someone in the production chain has the need of a product upstream, he or she picks it, actually pulling an item from the chain and moving the demand upstream. The analogy is similar to that of supermarkets, where clients get what they need and shelves are filled based on the actual demand of customers.

Kanban means **signboard** in Japanese and the name derives from the fact that a signboard is used to monitor the pulling process. The signboard is organized in different areas, each corresponding to a different step of the production chain. Cards are used to represent different work items, with each card representing a different item being assembled in the production line. As work items are pulled into line, so do cards move on the billboard, allowing for a simple way to monitor progress and needs.

Kanban is becoming a popular technique for software development. According to Ikonen et al. (2010), in fact, various sources of waste can be identified in software development. Among them are *partially done work*, which ties up resources, *unnecessary paperwork* and *gold plating*, which consume resources without adding value, *task switching*, which consumes resources and delays delivery,* *waiting*, which keeps resources idle, and *defects*, which require extra work to be fixed.

The analogy between factory floor and software development is that software development can be thought of as a production *pipeline*, with feature requests entering on one end of the pipe and working software exiting on the other end (Peterson,

---

* If task *A* and task *B* require 5 man-days, if work is performed sequentially by one person, *A* will be delivered after 5 days and *B* after 10 days. However, if the person works on both items at the same time, *both* will be delivered in 10 days.

2009). The software pipeline is composed of different and distinct steps, as we have seen when presenting the waterfall model. The equivalent of inventory build-up are software features getting stuck during one development phase. Kanban thus tries to reduce the number of features being worked on in parallel. There are, in fact, various advantages in reducing the amount of work in progress, or "in process," using the terminology of Scotland (2010) including focusing and delivering early (earlier).

According to Peterson (2009), the implementation of a Kanban system for software production can proceed as follows:

- **Define the development process**, which allows one to identify where features come from and what steps they go through. For instance, it could be that each feature goes through the following steps: analysis, design, implementation, and testing.
- **Define the entry and exit points of the process**, which allows one to identify where you have control on the process
- Agree with your team **policies to pull items** and to set priorities. Having an explicit specification of the selection process is, in fact, the only way to discuss about it and improve it.
- **Get started** and **empirically adjust**. Empirical adjustment is based on creating effective feedback loops and creating an environment in which the team is willing to experiment and collaborates on improving the process.

One important aspect for the implementation of a Kanban system is that it requires a shift of mentality, since the method requires teams to improve their capacity to collaborate, for instance, to reduce buildup of work (Scotland, 2010).

Figure 7.9 depicts the process by showing a Kanban board. Four steps have been identified in the development process, "analysis," "design," "implementation," and "testing." Various feature requests, represented by cards in the board, are being worked on. For instance, three features are in the analysis phase, two in the design

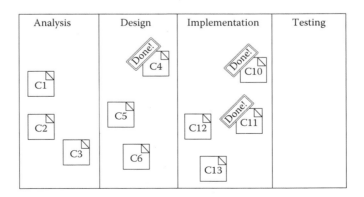

Figure 7.9   The Kanban board.

phase, and two in the implementation phase. Some features are done and ready to be pulled to the next step: see, in particular, C4, C10, and C11.

7.4 Open Source Development Practices

In Section 6.2.3, we introduced the concept of free software and discussed some revenue models. Here, we focus on the engineering aspects of the domain, highlighting the peculiarities and challenges. The analysis is interesting and useful also for projects that are not developed using an open source license.

7.4.1 Open Source Development Challenges

Open source software development is typically carried out by a geographically distributed community of volunteers under the steering of the owners of the project. Larger projects might also have companies behind, which tasks employees with the development or steering of the project.

The peculiar business model of the software being developed, together with the challenges posed by the team structure, requires one to pay particular attention to some steering, managerial, and technical activities.

Some challenges are related to maintaining a project *healthy*. This requires one to focus efforts on:

- **Community building and growth**, which include all the activities to have a large community of developers and users. The former, in fact, is necessary to develop and maintain the system. The latter is what makes a system useful and interesting to develop. Notice that some open source systems compete with commercial counterparts, backed by for-profit companies. For this reason, some projects have a specific *marketing* structure and *evangelists* to promote their software.
- **Financing and sustainability**. Even though open source software relies (mainly) on the work of volunteers, these projects incur various costs. We have seen some of the commercial models of open source software in Section 6.2.3.

Attention has also to be paid to development practices, since the methodologies we have seen so far do not cope very well with teams of volunteers. The impacts are at different levels and some of the concerns include

- **Project steering**. Adequate policies, means, and tools have to be defined for deciding on the evolution of a system. A system roadmap helps to keep a system coherent and functional, but at the same time, it might shift the interest of volunteers. A second aspect to consider is that many open source systems promote a *collective ownership* of the project, posing interesting questions on how the roadmap is formed in the first place.

- **Assignment of work**. Since contributions to open source systems are mainly based on the work of volunteers, tasks are often self-assigned. Completion time is more difficult (if not impossible) to control.
- **Maintain the system structure coherent**. Since contributions come from people with different background and experience, style, approach, and coding standards differ quite a bit. To keep the system maintainable, it becomes essential to enforce vision over a system's architecture, define a design philosophy, and enforce coding standards.
- **Quality control**. For the reasons mentioned above, effective quality control practices have to be in place to ensure that contributions do not introduce bugs.
- **User documentation**. Work in open source projects focuses on the *fun* parts, which is coding for many. As a result, finding volunteers for other important activities, such as writing user documentation, can be difficult.

7.4.2 An Open Source Development Process

Figure 7.10 shows a development process for open source systems. An open source software project rarely starts from scratch. More frequently, a project

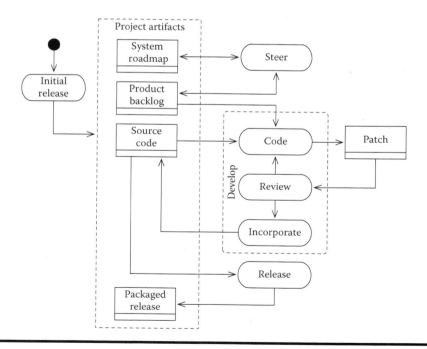

Figure 7.10　A development process for open source systems.

starts with an *initial release* performed by the person or team making a system available as open source. Together with the first release of a system, the team prepares the technical infrastructure to make the software artifacts available to the community.

The process then continues with a set of activities that are loosely interconnected:

- **Steer**, shown in the upper part of Figure 7.10, includes the activities to decide the roadmap of an open source system.
- **Develop**, shown in the middle portion of Figure 7.10 (and organized in three distinct activities), includes all software development activities to improve a system.
- **Release**, shown in the lower portion of Figure 7.10, includes the activities to release a new version of an open source system.

7.4.2.1 Open Source Project Steering

Like any other software product, open source projects benefit from the definition of a clear vision and evolution roadmap. Often, but not always, the roadmap tends to focus on the technical aspects of development, such as the architectural choices and approaches that have to be preferred.

According to the community that has been built around an open source project, different models can be used to define a roadmap. Two popular models include the **benevolent dictator model** and the **participatory model**.

In the **benevolent dictator** model, one person or a restricted team is in charge of taking final decisions. As pointed out in Fogel (2009), the benevolent dictators of successful projects work more as facilitators and moderators, integrating comments and observations of expert programmers participating in the community. This has two reasons. First, it is unlikely that one person has enough expertise to cover all technical areas of a project, and second, obsessive control is not an excellent way to build a community. The benevolent dictator is often the project initiator, because of the credibility gained in the community and the technical proficiency in managing the view of a project. Personal and communication skills are a plus, although not all project owners are famous for their politeness and diplomacy.

Completely different is the **participatory model**, in which decisions are taken by consensus and, when consensus is not reached, by voting. One issue to address in this kind of model is who participates in the discussion and who has the right to vote. Some models prefer to involve volunteers with more *seniority*, who have contributed significantly or steadily to a project. This is the model adopted for the development of Mozilla Thunderbird, as described in Mozilla Foundation (2013c). Others prefer to involve a larger base, which includes all people who ever contributed to the system. While the latter method is simpler to implement, as it has a measurable access criteria, it also has risks related to equally weighting the opinion of people with quite a lot of different experience on the system being developed.

Concerning the value of the roadmap as a project guidance, in this case, also two different models are in place. When there is a strong community of regular contributors, work and tasks are assigned similar to what happens in other software development projects. In this scenario, the roadmap is implemented and the system evolves as planned. In other situations, this is not feasible. In these cases, the roadmap can be considered as a list of features or desiderata, which are made public and available to contributors. Features land into the software when someone volunteers and takes charge to implement them.

7.4.2.2 Open Source Development

As mentioned earlier, one important aspect of any open source project is maintaining a coherent vision of a system. This is vital, since a loosely controlled evolution can lead to a system that is difficult or impossible to maintain.

For the reasons mentioned above, open source software relies on two practices:

1. The enforcement of **coding guidelines**, which describe good coding practices and standards and how to write code that is considered of high quality for the project at hand. Coding guidelines are documents that specify *naming conventions*, that is, how names are assigned to filenames, classes, variables, and constants; *minimum requirements for comments*, that is, how a specific method or class should be documented; *source code structuring*, for example, how the code should be indented or organized; other *syntactic rules*, like, for instance, what constructs to avoid; and other general guidance on how to write code. Several coding standards are available, some of which have been specifically devised for open source projects and some of which have been defined for specific programming language; see, for instance Free Software Foundation (2013), Batsov (2013), Oracle (1999), and Linux kernel coding style (2013e). Notice that coding standards devised for open source projects, such as Free Software Foundation (2013), are adopted and used in free and commercial development projects alike.
2. The use of a **version control** system ensures, on the one hand, that all contributors have the possibility of assessing system resources and, on the other, that changes and modifications are controlled and can be reversed, if necessary. Notice that while read access to the version control system is granted to anyone, writing and committing is granted to a controlled and restricted set of people.

Open source contributions are often in the form of incremental/evolutionary patches to an existing and consolidated code base. System evolution tends to be regulated by the following three-step process, called **patch contribution process** in Sethanandha et al. (2010):

■ **Code** is the process of creating a modification to an existing system. Coding is usually performed by a volunteer, either in response to a known problem or feature request in the **product backlog** or to follow up on a need or request originated by the volunteer. The coding process terminates with a **publish** and **discover** operation, to make the contribution available to the community. When a distributed versioning system is used, this operation takes the name of **fork** (the creation of a new branch in the code) and **pull request** (the request to include a particular contribution in the codebase of a system). Other methods used include distribution of patches to **mailing lists**.

■ **Review** is the process of verifying that a patch complies with the quality and coding standards defined by the project. This is performed or managed by volunteers with seniority, who are either tasked with quality control or who have the overall responsibility over a module or over the whole system. If the proposed patch meets the quality criteria, it is added to the code base; otherwise, more coding takes place till the minimum quality requirements are met.

■ **Incorporate** is the process of incorporating a patch into the codebase. An aspect during this step is to ensure that changes are well isolated. This is to ensure that they can be reversed, if need be and, more important, that it is possible to choose what changes are incorporated in the next release. See the next section for more details.

7.4.2.3 Open Source Releases

Releasing open source software requires one to address the following points:

■ Deciding/controlling what features make it into the next version
■ Deciding when to release.

To illustrate the issues, we will see the release process of the Firefox browser. According to the model, four different source code repositories (or branches) are made available to all contributors. Each repository is used to generate a version of the Firefox browser. The repositories are organized as a waterfall, with repositories that are *downstream* receiving changes from those *upstream*. In more detail:

1. The **mozilla-central** repository is the *topmost* repository and it is used to incorporate all changes and contributions of the community. It generates **nightly builds**, that is, versions of the browser incorporating the most recent changes. Nightly builds can be unstable (since the changes have undergone little quality control) and are used by a relatively small community. Crash reports are used to perform some quality control on the features contributed by the community.

2. The **mozilla-aurora** repository incorporates those changes of **mozilla-central** that are getting ready for production. The repository generates **alpha** builds, that is, versions of the browser that can be very unstable but are meant for a slightly larger user base.

3. The **mozilla-beta** includes all those features from **mozilla-aurora** that will land in the next release of the browser. The branch generates **beta** releases, which are meant for an even wider audience. The build and the repository are used to discover and fix any issue found in the browser, so that the browser can get ready for release.
4. Finally, the **mozilla-release** repository is used as a reference to keep track of the versions of Firefox that have been released.

For the sake of completeness, we remark that the Mozilla uses a fifth repository, called the **shadow repository**, for security fixes. The repository, however, is not public, to avoid publicizing ways in which a security bug could be exploited. The shadow repository merges into mozilla-central.

Development and fixes proceed in parallel on each repository, leading to a staggered development process. The approach has been chosen "to allow for continuous new feature development on mozilla-central, while the other channels are devoted to stabilizing features ready for a wider audience" (Mozilla Foundation, 2013a). The overall development cycle, from central to release, lasts about 16 weeks and is shown in Figure 7.11. Security, quality assurance, and other testing activities are conducted in parallel to development. The release process defines a specific procedure to decide whether to release the next version or not. The "go/no-go" decision is taken in a specific release activity. Compare activity 8 in the plan in Figure 7.11.

See Mozilla Foundation (2013a,b) for more details.

Mozilla has chosen an approach to software release in which the goals are fixed and duration varies according to achievement. That is, the release process is about 16 weeks, but it could last more or less, according to how quickly development and testing proceed. This is very similar to what happens in traditional software development.

A different approach is preferred by other projects. LibreOffice, for instance, adopts a **time-based release**, an approach according to which releases are predetermined and fixed in the calendar. Each release cycle for a significant release lasts 6 months, with minor releases given to the public more often. What features actually land on each release depend on the maturity of their implementation as release time

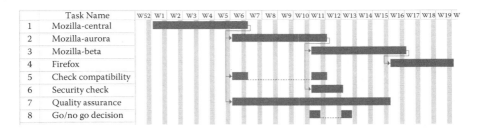

Figure 7.11 Firefox release process.

approaches: the schedule is fixed, but what functions are delivered is not. See Open Document Foundation (2013) for more details.

7.5 Questions and Topics for Discussion

1. What are the main advantages and disadvantages of traditional project management?
2. What are the main advantages and disadvantages of agile project management?
3. Could an agile process be used for the development of safety-critical systems? Which could be the point of attention? What are the opportunities?
4. Try and set up a Kanban board for the ticket tracking process described in Figure 2.5.
5. Set up a Kanban board for your to-do list and try to use it for a couple of weeks. Then discuss the advantages and issues you have encountered.
6. What are the similarities between Kanban and Scrum? What are the differences?

References

Batsov, B., 2013. Rails style guide. Available at BozhidarBatsov. Last retrieved May 25, 2013.

Boehm, B. W., 1988. A spiral model of software development and enhancement. *IEEE Computer 21*(5), 61–72.

Christie, J., 2008. The seductive and dangerous v-model. *Testing Experience*, (4):73–77. Available at http://www.scribd.com/doc/53329390/Testing-Experience-Issue-04-Dec-2008. Last retrieved November 22, 2013.

Chromatic, 2003. *Extreme Programming Pocket Guide*. O'Reilly, Sebastopol, CA.

Copeland, L., 2001. Extreme programming. Available at http://www.computerworld.com/s/article/66192/Extreme_Programming. Last retrieved November 22, 2013.

DSDM Consortium, 1997. Integrating DSDM® into an existing PRINCE2 environment. White paper, DSDM Consortium.

DSDM Consortium, 2000. Using DSDM® with PRINCE2. White paper, DSDM Consortium. Available at http://leadinganswers.typepad.com/leading_answers/files/DSDM_Prince2_WP_10.pdf. Last retrieved June 8, 2013.

DSDM Consortium, 2013. DSDM® consortium. Available at http://www.dsdm.org. Last retrieved June 26, 2013.

Fogel, K., 2009. *How to Run a Successful Free Software Project–Producing Open Source Software*. CreateSpace, Paramount, CA. Also available at http://producingoss.com/en/index.html.

Free Software Foundation, 2013, April. GNU coding standards. Available at http://www.gnu.org/prep/standards/. Last retrieved May 1, 2013.

Geracie, G., D. Heidt, and S. Starke, 2012. Product team performance. Technical report, Actuation Consulting.

Highsmith, J. and M. Fowler, 2001. The agile manifesto. *Software Development Magazine* 9(8), 29–30.

IABG, 2013. Das v-modell®. Available at http://v-modell.iabg.de/index.php. Last retrieved June 26, 2013.

Ikonen, M., P. Kettunen, N. Oza, and P. Abrahamsson, 2010. Exploring the sources of waste in Kanban software development projects. In *Proceedings of EUROMICRO Conference on Software Engineering and Advanced Applications*, pp. 376–381, Lille, France.

Kroll, P. and P. Kruchten, 2003. *The Rational Unified Process Made Easy: A Practitioner's Guide to the RUP*. The Addison-Wesley Object Technology Series. Addison-Wesley Publishing Company Incorporated, Boston, MA, USA.

Kruchten, P., 2004. *The Rational Unified Process: An Introduction*. The Addison-Wesley Object Technology Series. Addison-Wesley, Boston, MA, USA.

Linger, R. C., 1993. Cleanroom software engineering for zero-defect software. In *ICSE*, pp. 2–13.

Linux kernel coding style, 2013e. Available at https://www.kernel.org/doc/Documentation/CodingStyle. Last retrieved May 25, 2013.

Manifesto for agile software development, 2001. Available at http://agilemanifesto.org. Last retrieved May 19, 2013.

McConnell, S., 1996. *Rapid Development—Taming Wild Software Schedules*. O'Reilly, Sebastopol, CA, USA.

McCracken, D. D. and M. A. Jackson, 1982, April. Life cycle concept considered harmful. *SIGSOFT Software Engineering Notes* 7(2), 29–32.

Mozilla Foundation, 2013a. Mozilla firefox: Development process–draft. Available at http://mozilla.github.io/process-releases/draft/development_overview/. Last retrieved May 25, 2013.

Mozilla Foundation, 2013b. Mozilla firefox: Development specifics—draft version. Available at http://mozilla.github.io/process-releases/draft/development_specifics/. Last retrieved May 25, 2013.

Mozilla Foundation, 2013c. Thunderbird/new release and governance model. Available at https://wiki.mozilla.org/Thunderbird/New_Release_and_Governance_Model. Last retrieved June 28, 2013.

Open Document Foundation, 2013. Release plan. Available at https://wiki.documentfoundation.org/ReleasePlan. Last retrieved May 25, 2013.

Oracle, 1999. Code conventions for the java (TM) programming language. Available at http://www.oracle.com/technetwork/java/javase/documentation/codeconvtoc-136057.html. Last retrieved May 25, 2013.

Peterson, D., 2009. What is Kanban. Available at http://www.kanbanblog.com/explained/. Last retrieved June 7, 2013.

Rational Software, 2011. Rational unified process—Best practices for software development teams. White Paper TP026B, Rev 11/01, Rational Software. Available at http://www.ibm.com/developerworks/rational/library/content/03July/1000/1251/1251_bestpractices_TP026B.pdf. Last retrieved November 15, 2013.

Royce, W. W., 1970. Managing the development of large software systems. In *Proceedings of the Western Electronic Show and Convention (WESCON 1970)*, pp. 1–9. IEEE Computer Society. Reprinted in *Proceedings of the 9th International Conference on Software Engineering*, ACM Press, 1989, pp. 328–338, United States.

Scotland, K., 2010. Aspects of Kanban. *Software Development Magazine*. Available at http://www.methodsandtools.com/archive/archive.php?id=104. Last retrieved June 7, 2013.

Sethanandha, B., B. Massey, and W. Jones, 2010. Managing open source contributions for software project sustainability. In *Technology Management for Global Economic Growth (PICMET), 2010 Proceedings of PICMET '10*, pp. 1–9, Phuket, Thailand.

Sommerville, I., 2007. *Software Engineering* (8th ed.). Addison-Wesley, Redwood City, CA.

Sutherland, J., 1995, October. Business object design and implementation workshop. *SIGPLAN OOPS Messenger 6*(4), 170–175.

Takeuchi, H. and I. Nonaka, 1986. The new new product development game. *Harvard Business Review* (January–February).

Testing, C. 2013. The seductive and dangerous V-model. Available at http://www.clarotesting.com/page11.htm. Last retrieved November 22, 2013.

VersionOne, 2013. 7th annual state of agile development survey. Technical report, VersionOne. Last retrieved June 26, 2013.

Wells, D., 1999. The rules of extreme programming the rules of extreme programming. Available at http://www.extremeprogramming.org/rules.html. Last retrieved May 31, 2013.

Wells, D., 2009. Extreme programming. Available at http://www.extremeprogramming.org/donwells.html. Last retrieved November 22, 2013.

Chapter 8

Development and Management Standards

8.1 Microsoft Solutions Framework

Microsoft solutions framework (MSF) is a disciplined approach to software development, first introduced by Microsoft® in 1994, to overcome some of the limitations of existing development practices, such as the inability to adapt to changing requirements. The method emphasizes a deliberate application of proven techniques. In fact, it includes best practices applied in Microsoft®, observed in other organizations, and suggested by effective development processes.

The main motivation for MSF is to define a method that mixes agile and traditional techniques to get the best of the two approaches. In fact, according to the Visual Studio Team System (2004), agile relies too much on individual ability, while traditional techniques can be cumbersome and slow to adapt. The framework has evolved over time, accommodating the experience gotten from the field. See Microsoft (2013) for the latest definition of the framework.

The framework is based on the following concepts:

- **Foundational principles:** the core inspirational principles on which the framework is based.
- **Models:** the way in which the foundational principles are systematically applied to a project. We look, in particular, at the **team model**, which describes the team structure and interactions, and at the **process model**, which describes the organization of activities.
- **Disciplines:** namely, the *tools* that support the development process.

8.1.1 Foundational Principles

MSF is based on eight foundational principles, which establish the basic principles of the framework. They take inspiration from agile methodologies. They are simple and self-explaining and there is not much arguing about their usefulness in a software development project.

Four of them focus on team, team structure, and team organization. The first, in fact, suggests **foster open communication**; the second demands **empowering team members**, and the third requires **establishing clear accountability and shared responsibility**. The fourth principle states **learning from all experiences**.

The remaining four establish some basic properties about the project approach and the development process. The fourth and fifth principles suggest **working toward a shared vision** and **focusing on delivering business value**, so that focus can be kept during a project. The need for agility and flexibility is stated in the sixth principle, which recommends **staying agile and expecting change**. The seventh principle states the importance of **investing in quality**.

8.1.2 Team Model

MSF organizes software development by allocating activities and responsibilities to seven different roles, each corresponding to a different project concern. The roles are

- **Product management:** the role responsible for ensuring that the system being developed delivers value to the customer
- **Program management:** the role responsible for ensuring that the solution is delivered according to the project constraints
- **Architecture:** the role responsible for designing a solution that meets the requirements and constraints
- **Development:** the role responsible for building the solution according to the specification
- **User experience:** the role responsible for ensuring usability of the solution
- **Test:** the role responsible for quality assurance
- **Release/operations:** the role responsible for smooth transition from development to operations.

The coupling between roles and project concerns clearly allocates the responsibility of each major project concern to a specific set of people. Thus, for instance, people taking the *architecture role* in a project will be responsible for building a solution that meets the requirements and constraints, possibly negotiating and mediating with the team members with different roles.

Another distinguishing feature is that MSF favors small teams and a flat structure. The first simplifies interaction and maintains the process agile. The second empowers team members, simplifies building a shared vision, and eases the process of building a solution that meets all the required constraints and qualities.

8.1.3 Process Model

MSF supports an iterative development process, which takes inspiration from the waterfall model and the spiral model. It is shown in Figure 8.1.

The process is staged and based on five different activities. Each activity ends with a milestone, with specific acceptance criteria. Milestones are opportunities to verify the achievement of the goals of one phase, adjust scope, if needed, and decide the transition to the next phase. In the words of Lory et al. (2003), the "end of each phase represents a change in the pace and focus of the project." Similar to the agile disciplines, at the end of each cycle, a product is deployed and the process iterates with a broader scope.

The first activity is **envisioning** and the corresponding milestone is **vision/scope approved**. During this activity, the team, the customer, and the project sponsor define and agree on the scope of the project, on a preliminary plan, and on the project risks. At the end of the phase, all actors agree on the goals to be achieved and on the approach to achieve them.

Following the envisioning, the team can start the **planning** activity, with the corresponding milestone **project plans approved**. During this activity, the team defines the solution in detail, specifying *what* will be built, *how* it will be built, *who* will build it, and *when* it will be built. The starting point is the output of the previous step, and the main documents that are produced are

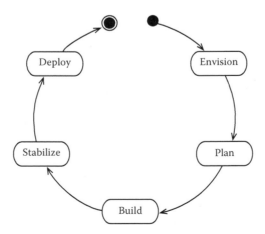

Figure 8.1 The MSF process model.

■ **Functional specification**, describing the functional and physical characteristics of the system to be built
■ **Master project plan** and **master project schedule**, describing the tasks performed by each role and their schedule.

The next two activities, **developing** and **stabilizing**, focus on building the system and readying it for deployment. The first activity, **developing**, builds a working system. Its milestone is **scope complete**. The second activity, **stabilizing**, performs testing on the system built, readying it for deployment. The milestone to transition to the next activity is **release readiness approved**.

The process ends with a **deployment** phase, during which the system is deployed and put in production.

8.1.4 Disciplines

During each iteration, three *tracks* run in parallel to the main development process, supporting its implementation. They are

■ Risk management
■ Readiness management
■ Project management.

Risk management is conducted following the approach and principles described in Section 4.2.

More interesting is the **readiness management** discipline, whose goal is to ensure that adequate *knowledge*, *skills*, and *abilities* (KSAs) are in place to successfully conduct a project. The discipline embeds a continuous learning environment in the development process and is organized in four activities.

An initial requirements definition activity allows one to identify the main characteristics of the project and, consequently, the main KSA requirements. Microsoft (2005) distinguishes among *high potential*, *strategic*, *key operational*, and *support* projects concerning, respectively, the development of new products, the experimentation of new technologies, and the upgrade and customization of existing products.

Following the definition of the requirements, an assessment phase conducted on the team through self-assessment or other types of evaluation allows one to identify the main needs and gaps.

These are filled in the next phases, making the team ready for the project activities.

Finally, concerning the **project management** discipline, one important and distinguishing ingredient of MSF is that there is no formal project manager. Various management activities in MSF projects, in fact, are allocated to the program management cluster, but the responsibility is distributed among the team. The organizational structure remains flat. This also applies to larger projects, for which MSF envisages the identification of a role with specific project management duties.

8.2 *PMBOK*® Guide

The **project management body of knowledge** (*PMBOK*® Guide) is one of the main references for project management. It is structured as a collection of practices and techniques that help ensure the sound management of a project. The framework is applicable to any kind of project, including software development projects. The body of knowledge is maintained by the Project Management Institute, an association of professionals in the area of project management (Project Management Institute, 2013).

PMBOK® Guide organizes management disciplines and activities in two dimensions. The first dimension defines the **knowledge area** to which a specific discipline applies. *PMBOK*® Guide, in particular, distinguishes 10 disciplines, which we describe in Section 8.2.1. The second dimension identifies the **project phase** during which a specific discipline can be applied. More information can be found in Section 8.2.2.

PMBOK® Guide is a comprehensive framework from which project managers need to select the activities that best suit the project needs.

8.2.1 Knowledge Areas

Knowledge areas identify the main management concerns in a project. These run throughout the life cycle of a project. *PMBOK*® Guide distinguishes 10 different areas that a manager should monitor in a project:

1. **Project integration management**, with the goal of harmonizing all management activities and ensuring that a project aligns with the performing organization's goals.
2. **Stakeholder management** with the goal of managing stakeholders. It is a new area, introduced in the fifth edition of the manual. Before that, *PMBOK*® Guide described activities related to managing stakeholders in the communications management area.
3. **Scope management**, with the goal of controlling the project scope.
4. **Time management**, with the goal of defining, managing, and controlling the project schedule and timing.
5. **Cost management**, describing how to manage and control the project budget and costs.
6. **Quality management**, describing how to manage quality in a project.
7. **Human resources management**, describing best practices to manage resources in a project.
8. **Communication management**, which focuses on managing communications.
9. **Risk management**, which focuses on identifying, assessing, and managing risks.
10. **Procurement management**, which focuses on the management procurement activities.

8.2.2 Process Groups

According to *PMBOK®* Guide, projects develop in five distinct activities:

1. **Initiating** includes all activities related to starting a project.
2. **Planning** includes all activities to plan and get organized with work.
3. **Executing** includes all activities necessary to implement and build what is specified in the project scope, according to the cost, time, and quality constraints.
4. **Controlling** includes all activities necessary to monitor a project. Running in parallel to the *executing* phase, this activity collects data about a project and compares them with the forecast defined in the planning phase.
5. **Closing** includes all activities necessary to close a project and hand over the project results.

8.2.3 Processes

Knowledge areas and process groups can be organized in a table, having the process groups as columns and the knowledge areas as rows. At the intersection of each knowledge area and process group, *PMBOK®* Guide identifies a set of activities that address a specific project concern in a specific project phase. These are summarized in Table 8.1. Thus, for instance, at the intersection of *time management* and *planning*, there is the *prepare schedule* activity, whose goal is that of coming out with a plan for the project.

Concerning the sequence in which the different activities can be executed, there is a *natural* ordering from left (process initiation) to right (project closing) and from top to bottom. Project activities, however, can also be organized according to a different ordering, if one prefers to do so.

8.2.4 PMBOK® Guide for Software Development

PMBOK® Guide collects a set of practices that are applicable to any project, including those related to software development. As a matter of fact, IEEE® and PMI® are drafting, at the time of the writing of this book, a specific guide to the application of *PMBOK®* Guide practices. Some considerations on the matter can be drawn independent of the report being developed.

PMBOK® Guide is a comprehensive framework. A full application of its practices is definitely best suited for traditional and very structured approaches to software development. This is the case, for instance, of the Waterfall model, RUP, and V-Model, although both RUP and the V-Model come with their own project management practices.

In a traditional scenario, in fact, various *PMBOK®* Guide knowledge areas and processes integrate rather well and, in some cases, overlap with the corresponding phases required by the traditional software development process. According to the

Table 8.1 *PMBOK*® Guide Activities

	Initiating	Planning	Executing	Controlling	Closing
Integration	Develop project charter Develop preliminary project scope	Develop project management plan		Monitor and control project work Integrated change control	Close project
Stakeholders	Identify stakeholders	Plan stakeholder management	Manage stakeholder engagement	Control stakeholder engagement	
Scope		Scope planning Scope definition Create WBS		Scope verification Scope control	
Time		Activity definition Activity sequencing Activity resource estimating Schedule development		Schedule control	
Cost		Cost estimating Cost building		Cost control	
Quality		Quality planning	Perform quality assurance	Perform quality control	
Human resources		Human resource planning Staff acquisition	Develop project team Manage project team		

continued

Table 8.1 (continued) ***PMBOK*® Guide Activities**

	Initiating	Planning	Executing	Controlling	Closing
Communications		Communication planning	Information distribution	Performance reporting	
Risks		Risk Management planning Risk identification Qualitative and/or quantitative risk analysis Risk response planning		Risk monitoring and control	
Procurement		Plan purchase and acquisitions Plan contracting	Request seller responses Select sellers Contract adminstration		Contract closure

project goals, in fact, the *requirements definition* phase of the waterfall responds or greatly overlaps with the *scope definition* activity of *PMBOK*® Gu. Similarly, most of the *quality assurance* activities of *PMBOK*® Guide correspond to the different testing activities of the waterfall model and the V-Model.

Not all activities of *PMBOK*® Guide are relevant for software development projects. Some activities, such as quantitative risk assessment, find niche applications in software development projects. Moreover, projects with a strong focus on software development might find the activities related to the *communications* and *procurement management* knowledge areas to be less important.

The application of *PMBOK*® Guide to agile development processes requires a lot more work. The best approach is one that picks only selected activities of those found in Table 8.1, according to the actual needs.

8.3 NASA Practices

NASA contributes significantly to the definition of good practices and standards for the management and development of (safety-critical) systems. Today, it defines and enforces the application of standards to contractors in the most diverse engineering disciplines. In the following sections, we focus on three important publications. The first is relative to the engineering practices of complex systems; the second describes the requirements that currently apply to the software development process; the third shows an example of a software development process, taken from NASA guidelines and documents released in the 1990s, but still relevant and applicable. All documents provide insightful information on the organization of projects.

8.3.1 NASA System Engineering Practices

NASA's system engineering practices are collected in NASA (2007), where **systems engineering** is defined as a "methodical, disciplined approach for the design, realization, technical management, operations, and retirement of a system. A *system* is a construct or collection of different elements that together produce results not obtainable by the elements alone."

The manual, clear and very readable, describes how to organize the development of a complex system. There are two main characterizing aspects in the organization of a project.

The first is what is called the **system engineering engine**, which breaks the complexity of system development using a product work breakdown structure. In this way, in fact, each node of the WBS defines a set of technical and managerial goals to lower levels, while at the same time ensuring that the technical and managerial constraints imposed by the upper nodes of the WBS are met.

The second feature is that system engineering is a linear and staged process organized in seven main phases (NASA, 2012). The first three end with a concept, which if validated allows a project to move to the actual construction phase. They are

- **Prephase A: concept study**, during which possible solutions are investigated
- **Phase A: concept and technology development**, where the project is defined
- **Phase B: preliminary design and technology**, during which the preliminary design is established.

A successful exit from *Phase B* moves the project to the actual construction and operation, which is organized in the following four phases:

- **Phase C: final design and fabrication**, where the system is designed and components built
- **Phase D: system assembly, integration and test, launch**, during which the components are integrated
- **Phase E: operations and sustainment**, where the system is operated and maintained
- **Phase F: closeout**, during which a system is properly disposed of.

The transition from one phase to the next is regulated by **key decision points**, or KDPs. There is at least one decision point per phase, but the actual number of KDPs per phase depends on the type of system being developed. This is illustrated in Figure 8.2. As can be seen from the figure, the first three phases are dedicated to the formulation of a solution, in the form of a design. After Phase B, a *formal approval* moves the project to system production and, after Phase D, to operations. The cycle terminates with the disposal of the system.

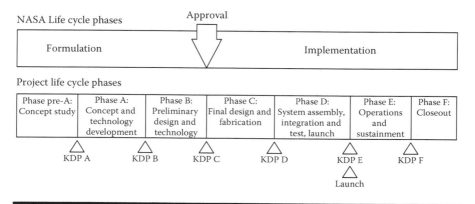

Figure 8.2 The NASA life cycle.

8.3.2 NASA Software Management Process Requirements

NASA has an articulated set of policies and standards related to software development. We will look at NASA (2009). The starting point is that NASA distinguishes eight different classes of software, which differ for their effect, should they fail.

The classes are identified by a letter. The first class identifies the most critical software. Thus, for instance, **class A** software is safety-critical software used in manned missions, while **class H** is general-purpose desktop software.

Clearly, different requirements apply to the development of different classes of software. Thus, rather than suggesting a specific process, NASA (2009) does not include any recommendation about the best software life cycle model; rather, it lists the requirements that a development process for a specific class of software should have. In this way, a manager is free to choose the process that fits better the system at hand, as long as it meets the requirements specified in the document.

The requirements of the admissible development processes are organized in the following areas:

- **Software management requirements**, which regulate many aspects of software development projects, such as interfaces with other organizations, estimation of costs, and verification and validation of minimum requirements
- **Software engineering life cycle requirements**, which define the minimum set of activities that have to be performed in any software development project
- **Supporting software life cycle requirements**, which identify the support processes that need to accompany development
- **Software documentation requirements**, which list the minimum set of documents and minimum set of information they need to contain.

Concerning *software management requirements*, a minimum of five different software plans have to be defined independent of the software class. These cover, respectively, **overall management**, with the *software development or management plan*; **quality**, with the *software test plan* and the *software assurance plan*; **configuration management**, with the *software configuration management plan*; and **operations**, with the *software maintenance plan*. In addition, safety-critical software requires the definition of a *software safety plan*.

As one might expect from a document by NASA, various other requirements of NASA (2009) cover safety-critical and mission-critical software, spelling the minimum functional requirements, support activities, and minimum requirements for contractors. For instance, different classes of software are bound to different maturity levels of subcontractors. Class A software requires a CMMI® level 3 certification (see Section 8.5).

As mentioned earlier, no specific constraint is imposed on a development process. However, at a minimum, any project must include the following activities:

- **Requirements definition**, which collects user and customer requirements and for which traceability and change management practices must be in place.

- **Software design**, which defines the architecture of a system; the standard requires to maintain a bidirectional traceability between design and requirements.
- **Implementation**, which produces code that must be unit tested and checked using static checkers. Bidirectional traceability with the design and explicit software versioning policies ensures that the software can be traced to each element of the architecture (and, by transitivity, to a set of requirements) and is properly versioned.
- **Testing**, which verifies the software functionality. Class A to C software (safety- and mission-critical software) requires some form of formal verification to be performed.
- **Software operations**, **maintenance**, and **retirement**, which require the definition of appropriate plans for the operational and retirement phases of a software system.

Six supporting activities complete the requirements of a sound development process. They are

1. **Software configuration management**
2. **Risk management**
3. **Software peer reviews/inspections**
4. **Software measurement**
5. **Best practices**
6. **Training**.

Of these, the first four are more directly related to the development, while the last two are more focused on exploiting and improving NASA organizational assets.

8.3.3 NASA Software Development Practices

NASA (1990) and NASA (1992) describe a disciplined approach for the development of software systems. It is an implementation of the requirements described in the previous section.

The development process is based on a *sashimi waterfall* (compare Section 7.2.1), which is organized in phases and activities.

The phases are

- **Requirements definition** and **requirements analysis**, which define and organizes the requirements
- **Preliminary design phase**, and **detailed design phase**, which define the system architecture with different levels of consolidation and certainty
- **Implementation**, which builds the system

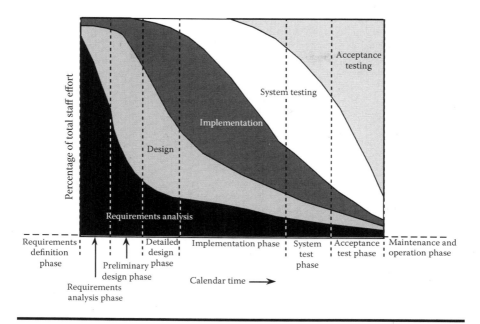

Figure 8.3 Relative weight of different activities in the NASA development process.

■ **System test** and **acceptance test phase**, which perform the system and acceptance tests, respectively.

The document also recognizes five different types of activities, which are necessary to build a software system. They are **requirements analysis**, **design**, **implementation**, **system testing**, and **acceptance testing**.

Similar to RUP, different activities are performed concurrently during system development. For instance, during the *requirements analysis* phase, most of the effort is dedicated to the *requirements analysis* activity, but some *design* and, possibly, some *implementation* activities will also take place. This is shown in Figure 8.3, taken from NASA (1992), where the relative weight of each activity is shown for each development phase.

Also of particular interest are the practices suggested for metrics collection. Table 8.2, adapted from NASA (1992), in particular, shows the timing and the type of data that should be collected during a project. In more detail, the guidelines suggest collecting metrics concerning *estimated size* (measured in SLOC), *actual effort spent* (man-hours), *project status* (SLOC written, test completed), and *change and error traffic* (requirements growth, errors, and changes). These data, in fact, allow one to monitor the main aspects of a development project, as discussed in Chapters 3 and 4.

Table 8.2   Metrics Collection Program

	Measure	Source	Frequency	Major Application
Estimates	Estimates of: Total SLOC (new, modified, reused) Total effort Major dates	Managers	Monthly	Project stability Planning aid
Resources	Staff hours (total and by activity)	Developers	Weekly	Project stability Replanning indicator Effectiveness/impact of the development process being applied
Status	Requirements (growth TBDs, changes, Q&As)	Managers	Biweekly	Project progress
	Units designed, coded, tested SLOC (cumulative)	Developers Automated	Biweekly Weekly	Adherence to defined process Stability and quality of requirements
Errors changes	Tests (complete, passed) Errors (by category)	Developers Developers	Biweekly By event	Effectiveness/impact of the development processes
Final closeout	Changes (by category) Changes (to source) Actuals at completion: Effort Size (SLOC, units) Source characteristics Major dates	Developers Automated Managers	By event Weekly 1 time, at completion	Adherence to defined process Build predictive models Plan/manage new projects

8.4 PRINCE2®

PRINCE2® (Project in a Controlled Environment, version 2) is a *de facto* standard for projects conducted with the UK government. It started as an evolution of the PROMPTII methodology, defined in the 1970s by Simpact Systems (Offices of Government Commerce, 2009).

The initial consideration is that PRINCE2® recognizes that project management is seldom linear and straightforward. In a project, therefore, four management levels interact, exercise influence and control, and need to exchange inputs and information.

They are

- **Corporate or program management**. The highest level of the hierarchy, corporate and program management, influences projects by setting the business context for a project.
- **Project direction**. Immediately below the previous level, project direction ensures strategic steering to the project mediating and interpreting in the project context requests and constraints coming from the upper level. Strategic steering is performed by senior management and is based on **management by exception** strategy. Project direction approves a plan and then delegates its execution to the project manager; senior management intervenes only if some significant deviation from the plan occurs.
- **Project management**. Responsible for conducting a project, the project manager focuses on the daily planning and management of activities.
- **Product delivery**. The last management level, **product delivery** focuses on the delivery of planned products, that is, project deliverables.

The definition of PRINCE2® is based on a **process model**, which defines the management activities to carry out, and on a set of **components**, which support the management activities. Eight is the magic number. There are eight main activities in the PRINCE2® process model and eight different components. We analyze them in more detail in the next sections.

8.4.1 PRINCE2® Process Model

PRINCE2® adopts a staged approach to project development. We can distinguish, in particular, an **initial phase**, a **development phase**, and a **closing phase**:

- The **initial phase** is composed of **starting** and **initiating**, which have the goals of setting up a project and getting the project started.
- The **development phase** is organized in stages (or iterations), which can run sequentially or in parallel, according to the project's logic. Each stage is composed of three different groups of activities: **managing product delivery**, **controlling a stage**, and **managing stage boundaries**, which have the goals

of preparing activities of a specific iteration, controlling how work develops in the iteration, and closing the iteration.

■ The **closing phase** is composed by **closing a project**, which manages all project closing activities.

The main development cycle is governed by two processes that run throughout a project. The first, **directing a project**, includes all activities meant to give strategic guidance to a project. The second, **planning**, includes daily and routine management activities.

Let us see in more detail the goals and content of each process.

8.4.1.1 Starting a Project

Different from many frameworks, PRINCE2® explicitly allocates time for the preparation of a project management structure. Thus, the goal of **starting a project** is to define a project's objectives and allocate sufficient time and resources to properly plan the project.

The process successfully ends when the *project manager*, the *project team*, and the *project board* are identified and appointed, the *project benefits* are assessed and considered worth pursuing, a *project approach* to the delivery of products is chosen, and the next step (project initiation) is planned.

8.4.1.2 Initiating a Project

Given the information of the previous step, during **project initiation**, the *actual plans* for the project are defined.

This includes planning the schedule, risks, quality, and project outputs. During this phase, the technical infrastructure is also set up. This includes a *document repository* and *location for logs*, such as, for instance, risk logs.

The process successfully ends when the project plans are defined and the project is authorized.

8.4.1.3 Directing a Project

Directing a project mainly involves the project board and it has the goal of providing strategic steering to a project.

Based on the information obtained from the project manager and the other processes, the project board authorizes project phase transitions, the application of exception plans, and confirms project closure.

If a project requires it, this process also provides ad hoc steering.

8.4.1.4 Controlling a Stage

Work in PRINCE2® projects proceeds in stages, with each stage corresponding to a project cycle, a work-package element, or other project element with a clear scope and output.

Controlling a stage properly starts a stage. The work required includes *authorizing the work in a stage, allocating the necessary resources*, and *monitoring the stage execution*, so that the expected product is actually built.

The main goals are to ensure that the quality, cost, and time constraints are satisfied, so that the planned benefits are achieved.

8.4.1.5 Managing Product Delivery

The main activities in **managing product delivery** are the *authorization of the work in a stage* and *reporting to the project manager* about the progress and the main parameters (quality, cost, time). When a product is completed, the process ends with the team manager getting the *approval for the work performed*.

The process allows for a clear separation of duties and responsibilities between the **project manager**, who is responsible for controlling a stage, and the **team manager**, who is responsible for carrying out the work envisaged in a stage. This is similar to the distinction between a project manager and a work package leader, which we have seen in Section 5.2.1.

In large projects, this process also allows one to clarify the allocation of duties and responsibilities between the contractor and the suppliers, similar to what was explained in Chapter 3 when we considered the Contract Work Breakdown Structure (CWBS); see page 56.

8.4.1.6 Managing Stage Boundaries

The **managing stage boundaries** process performs all the activities necessary to close a stage, including the *collection of performance data* and *planning for the next stage, verifying that no significant changes have occurred* in the project environment and in the expected benefits, and *preparing a report for the project board*.

8.4.1.7 Closing a Project

Closing includes all those activities necessary to verify project outputs, collect project data, assess benefits, and report on performances.

This is similar to what we have already discussed in Section 3.10.

8.4.1.8 Planning

Planning is the set of activities that allows one to build a project plan. Most of the activities required to build a plan have already been illustrated in Chapter 3.

Some of the distinguishing features are that PRINCE2® planning requires a **project narrative** to be developed and the definition of **exception plans**.

A **project narrative** is a textual description of a plan, explaining its structure and providing insights on the motivations driving one to specific project choices. The project narrative makes the project assumptions clear, simplifying comprehension and helping in the approval process.

An **exception plan** is a plan that is applied to put the project back on track, should an exceptional situation occur. PRINCE2® recognizes that plans are not perfect and that replanning is necessary. Thus, if, during project execution, someone recognizes the occurrence of an exceptional situation, the management board might authorize the definition and the application of an **exception plan**, which applies to activities up to the end of the current stage and which are meant to put the project back on track. The exception plan updates or replaces the nominal plan.

A final aspect to highlight is the British aplomb with which the guide recommends performing estimations in a project. At p. 174 of Offices of Government Commerce (2009), in fact, we find: "Estimating cannot guarantee accuracy, but it is better than not estimating at all."

8.4.2 PRINCE2® Components

Eight components support the implementation of the processes we have just described. They are concerns and best practices spanning the different processes and phases of a project.

PRINCE2®, in particular, defines the following components:

- Business case
- Organization
- Plans
- Controls
- Management of risk
- Quality in a project environment
- Configuration management
- Change control.

Of these, the practices suggested for the management of risks, quality, and configuration management are very similar to what we have already seen in Chapters 3 and 4. In the rest of this section, therefore, we focus on the remaining components, highlighting some characterizing aspects proposed by the methodology.

8.4.2.1 Business Case

Business case is the reason for a project to exist. The higher level of the management structure authorizes a project based on a business justification and a project continues as long as it has a business case.

A business case is fully specified by providing the following information:

- A **reason**, which explains why the project outcome is needed.
- The **options**, which outline the alternatives to the project output.
- The **benefits** provided by the project outputs.
- The **risks**, which could seriously affect the outputs.
- The **cost and timescale** and **investment appraisal**, which evaluate a solution based not only on the development costs but also considering the operational, maintenance, and support costs. As specified in Offices of Government

Commerce (2009), "the baseline for investment appraisal is the 'do nothing' option, i.e., what will the picture of costs and benefits be if the project is not undertaken?"

8.4.2.2 Organization

PRINCE2® proposes a **reference organizational structure** for a project, which identifies and clearly allocates roles and responsibilities.

In synthesis, the structure proposed by the methodology is a hierarchical structure, organized around the four layers identified above: thus, we can identify a *project board* that provides strategic guidance, a *project manager*, who is responsible for the management of a project, and *team managers*, responsible for organizing work in stages.

One noteworthy aspect is that the project board needs to include representatives, which can ensure that the three different interests of a project are represented, namely, the **business** (the product meets a business need), the **user** (the product satisfies a user need), and the **supplier** (the product is built according to the supplier's capabilities and skills).

A second important aspect that is highlighted by Offices of Government Commerce (2009) is that the project board is not a democracy, but rather, a key decision maker. This is to avoid the **management by committee** syndrome, in which project decisions reflect a mediation of different interests and people, rather than focusing on the most appropriate action to have the project succeed.

8.4.2.3 Plans

Plans are the basis for any project. According to PRINCE2®, a good plan identifies the products to be produced; the activities, resources, time, and dependencies necessary to produce the products; a schedule of the activities, coherent with the dependencies among activities; and agreed tolerances. The identification of assumptions and prerequisites allow the project manager to understand the opportunities and constraints and build a plan that is coherent with this information.

In PRINCE2®, plans are organized at different levels of granularity, ranging from the **program plan**, the highest level, to the **team plan**, which defines how to achieve a specific deliverable. An **exception plan** allows one to manage nonnominal situations. The plans are interconnected, with higher-level plans setting constraints and framing boundaries of more detailed plans.

8.4.2.4 Control

Control is about verifying that the project is proceeding according to plans and verifying that the planned products are produced according to quality, cost, and time.

A first good practice we find in this component is that PRINCE2® acknowledges variations in planning, by *incorporating tolerances in the plan*. Thus, rather than having plans with fixed data, project managers in PRINCE2® reason with ranges of values.

The definition of tolerances in a project proceeds from the top of the hierarchy to the bottom, with higher levels defining what deviations are acceptable. Control allows the monitoring of actual results and creates a flow of *deviations* from the nominal plan from the lower levels of the management structure to the upper levels.

A second interesting aspect is the suggestion to use a **daily project log**. The manual suggests that the project manager should make *writing the daily log* a regular routine. Entries in the log can be organized by product and highlight any significant event, such as the status of work, outstanding issues, and products that will be due soon.

8.4.2.5 Change Control

PRINCE2® recognizes that change is structural in a project and that a sound change control system is essential to any project. Change management is based on a **project issue log**, that is, a way to systematically capture changes. Project issues include

- Changes in requirements, independent of their (apparent) impact. Even changes that seem minor, in fact, might have major consequences.
- Changes in the project environment, including, but not limited to, changes in regulations, suppliers, team members, and policies.
- New risks that occurred or were identified during project execution; risk that occurred.
- Problems or errors occurring on work being carried out.
- Queries about any aspect of the project.

Similar to what is described in Section 4.1, issues can either be a *request for changes* or *nonconformance reports* (**off-specifications**, using PRINCE2® terminology) and they need to be captured, assessed, and decided upon, documenting all the steps along the way.

PRINCE2® is flexible in defining what decision process should be applied for change management. This, in fact, depends on various project characteristics. Not surprisingly, the guide states that it is important to define processes and responsibilities in the initial phases of the project.

8.5 Capability Maturity Model Integration

Capability maturity model integration (CMMI®) is a certification program developed by the Software Engineering Institute, which is meant to measure the ability, or *maturity*, of an organization to develop and manage projects. The program starts from the consideration that there are three main components in an organization: the first is *people*, the second is *tools and equipment*, and the third is *procedures*.

These components are held together by **processes**. Thus, measuring and improving an organization's processes helps to improve the capabilities and performances of an organization. CMMI®, in particular, focuses on three domains: *product and service development, service establishment and management*, and *product and service acquisition*.

CMMI® measures the maturity in levels. Each level defines a set of organizational capabilities and builds on the previous one by adding some new capabilities. CMMI® identifies five different **levels**:

1. **Initial**. This is the starting level, where no process is defined or, when it defined, it is not controlled. As mentioned in CMMI® Product Team (2010), "Success in these organizations depends on the competence and heroics of the people in the organization and not on the use of proven processes." Any organization is at least at level one.
2. **Repeatable**. This is the level of organizations that have a *managed* process. Projects are planned and managed by skilled people, who apply practices and standards and ensure an adequate control. The actual practices in place, however, are project-specific.
3. **Defined**. This is the level of organizations that have *defined* standards for managing projects. These standards are proactively applied and are used organization-wide.
4. **Quantitatively managed**. This is the level of organizations that are able to measure process performances.
5. **Optimizing**. This is the level of organizations that can make sense of the quantitative data they measure and that can use the data to improve their process.

The positioning of an organization at a specific level is determined by establishing and applying a set of good practices in different process areas.

A **process area** is a set of practices that are important for successfully managing a project. For instance, *CMMI® for product and service development* defines 22 process areas. Among them, we find those defined in the previous chapters of this book and some specific ones, such as, for instance, *causal analysis and resolution* and *decision analysis and resolution*. Some areas are relevant only for higher maturity levels.

In more detail, the methodology defines a number of **generic** and **specific** goals. Generic goals apply to multiple process areas, while specific goals are particular to an area. For instance, one generic goal at level 2 is that responsibility is assigned for "performing the process, developing the work products, and providing the services of the products." Although the methodology defines *practices* that help achieve each specific goal, the model is flexible with respect to the way in which an organization satisfies it. The only important aspect is that the goals are met. Table 8.3 lists the CMMI® process areas for product and service development and summarizes the number of practices suggested by the methodology to achieve the goals of a specific

Table 8.3 CMMI® Practices

Area	Level 1 Level	Level 2 Practices	Level 3 Practices	Level 4 Practices	Level 5 Practices	Practices
Generic practices	1–3	1		2		
Configuration management	2		10			
Measurement and analysis	2		7			
Project monitoring and control	2		8			
Project planning	2		10			
Process and product quality assurance	2		14			
Requirements management	2		4			
Supplier agreement management	2		5			
Decision analysis and resolution	3			6		
Integrated project management	3			10		
Organizational process definition	3			7		
Organizational process focus	3			9		
Organizational training	3			7		
Product integration	3			9		
Requirement development	3			10		
Risk management	3			7		
Technical solution	3			8		
Validation	3			5		
Verification	3			8		
Organizational process performance	4				5	
Quantitative project management	4				7	
Causal analysis and resolution	5					5
Organizational performance management	5					10

area. They are only a very indirect measure of the difficulty of achieving a level, since different practices might be of different complexity.

In an ideal process, an organization implements an increasing number of practices to move up the certification ladder. CMMI® envisages two approaches to certification, **staged** and **continuous**. They differ in scope and method. In the **staged** approach, an organization achieves *maturity levels* by satisfying all the goals defined at a specific level. In the **continuous** approach, organizations achieve *capabilities* in specific process areas. A capability is achieved when all the goals of a specific process area are met. Thus, the continuous model allows for a more gradual or selective introduction of the practices. As a matter of fact, it defines a **level 0**, in which an organization has achieved the goals of one or more key process areas. The continuous model can be applied only up to level 3, since the higher levels of CMMI® require all practices to be achieved together.

See CMMI® Product Team (2010) for more information.

8.6 Questions and Topics for Discussion

1. Discuss the main differences and similarities between PRINCE2® and *PMBOK®* Guide.
2. Discuss the similarities and differences between the NASA development process presented in Section 8.3.3 and RUP.

References

CMMI® Product Team, 2010. CMMI® for development, version 1.3. Technical Report CMU/SEI-2010-TR-033, ESC-TR-2010-033, Software Engineering Institute.

Lory, G., D. Campbell, A. Robin, G. Simmons, and P. Rytkonen, 2003, June. Microsoft Solutions Framework white paper. Technical Report, Microsoft. More information and downloadable copy available at http://www.microsoft.com/msf. Last retrieved June 1, 2013.

Microsoft, 2005. Migrating Oracle on UNIX to SQL server on Windows. Technet, Microsoft.

Microsoft, 2013. Microsoft Solutions Framework (MSF) overview. Available at http://msdn.microsoft.com/en-us/library/jj161047.aspx. Last retrieved June 1, 2013.

NASA, 1990. Manager's handbook for software development. Software Engineering Laboratory Series SEL-84-101, NASA Goddard Flight Center.

NASA, 1992. Recommended approach to software development. Software Engineering Laboratory Series SEL-81-305, Revision 3, NASA.

NASA, 2007, December. Systems engineering handbook. Technical Report NASA/SP-2007-6105 Rev1, NASA.

NASA, 2009. NASA software engineering requirements. NASA Procedural Requirements NPR 7150.2A, NASA. Available at http://nodis3.gsfc.nasa.gov/. Last retrieved June 1, 2013.

NASA, 2012. NASA space flight program and project management requirements w/changes 1-10. NASA Procedural Requirements NPR 7120.5E, NASA. Last retrieved June 3, 2013.

Offices of Government Commerce, 2009. *Managing Successful Projects with PRINCE2* (2009 ed.). The Stationery Office, London, UK.

Project Management Institute, 2013. Project Management Institute home page. Available at http://www.pmi.org. Last retrieved June 1, 2013.

Visual Studio Team System, 2004, May. Visual studio 2005 team system: Microsoft Solutions Framework. Available at http://msdn.microsoft.com/en-us/library/aa302179.aspx.

Chapter 9

Tools
Projects

l in used a number of tools to support
n fact, simplifies quite a bit of various
with stakeholders and getting organized

he common requirements of a project
ive to implement such functions using
structure from scratch has a cost, even
ources to select, configure, and install
n, and aspects related to their quali-
the contributing factors. The general
s a starting point for the identifica-
ns, perhaps simplifying the selection

mponent related to making sense of
st of the tools presented in this chap-
cases, they do both. They, however,
sound management. The best Gantt
lanning. Similarly, the best document
am does not use it to store change

9.1 Project Information Flow

Figure 9.1 shows the main pieces of information that a project generates. The figure is organized in two parts. The top part shows the stakeholders, while the lower part shows the information produced and exchanged in a project.

The first column shows the roles in the project. We distinguish, in particular, the *(external) stakeholders*, the *project manager*, and the *team*. As the reader can imagine, the diagram depicts the situation typical of a medium/small project managed using traditional techniques. Larger projects involve more roles (e.g., a work package leader) and, consequently, structure the information in more layers.

The lower part of Figure 9.1 shows the information typically produced in a project. Each leaf of paper shows some kind of information exchanged in a project. The arrows show how the information flows.

We start from the second column, that of the project manager. The *project manager* manages information about the project scope, schedule, and costs, together with other important aspects of a project, such as analyses about project status (*EVA* in the diagram), quality, and risks. Finally, a *project log* maintains the history of the project.*

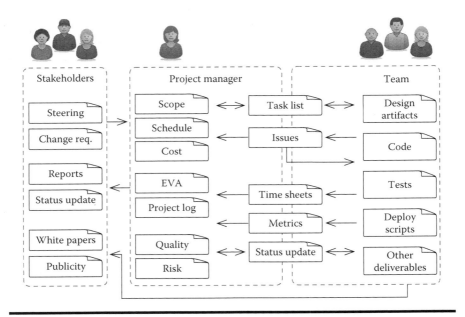

Figure 9.1   Information flow in a project.

---

* Notice that in larger projects, this information is structured hierarchically or split into various levels, as we have already seen.

We continue with the last column, that of the *team*. Design artifacts and code define the system being built; test cases and deploy scripts support the validation and the release. Other deliverables complete the set of information produced by the team; their number and nature depend on the goals agreed on in the project.

The project manager and the team exchange information to coordinate their work. A list of *tasks* determines the actual work items to be performed. It starts from the project plan, which is updated by the team and the project manager as new work items are individuated. As development proceeds, a number of *issues* arise. They are stored and used by the project team to improve the code quality. At the same time, they can be used to compute some quality metrics, as we have seen in Chapter 4.

The team regularly sends project data, such as *time sheets* and *metrics*, shown in the third column to the project manager. *Status updates* about the project align the project manager and team about the current status of the project. To go into more detail, the data help determine the current project status along its main dimensions, for example, time, costs, quality, and risks. This is also the basis for replanning, if necessary. Compare Section 3.9.

The first column of Figure 9.1 presents all the other project stakeholders, without distinguishing their different roles. In general, information between the stakeholders and the project manager includes *steering* (in whatever form it comes, from emails to written documents) and *change requests*. The project manager keeps the stakeholders informed about the project status with regular *status updates* and *reports*. More generic information, such as *white papers* and *publicity*, helps engage other stakeholders.

An effective **project technical infrastructure** supports the production, storage, and exchange of the information that is produced and consumed in a project. There are two main choices in setting up an infrastructure.

The first is between integrated tools or a set of independent tools. Integrated tools reduce issues related to data duplication and provide a single access point to all project data. However, they might introduce constraints that make their use impossible in a project. It might also be difficult to find a tool that accommodates all the data collection needs of a project.

The second choice is between using a commercial service or installing the tools in-house. Commercial services provide environments that are ready to use and come with additional advantages, such as high availability and data backup and recovery. Since most of the commercial services for projects are web-based today, they also provide a simple approach to sharing data with other stakeholders. Privacy and protection of data, however, might be a cause for concern. Costs are another matter of concern.

The rest of this chapter lists the requirements of a technical infrastructure organizing its description in four sections. We start by describing the *basic infrastructure*, namely, the tools necessary in any project, no matter how informal or simple the project is. The basic infrastructure focuses on the tools to share and makes information available to other stakeholders. We then extend the basic infrastructure by adding tools that improve traceability and configuration management, which we call the *basic + infrastructure*. We continue by presenting some approaches to collaborative document writing and conclude the chapter by looking at some tools specifically built for managing projects. This is what we call the *management infrastructure*.

Software production uses a wide array of tools to support development activities, such as integrated development environments, debuggers, and modeling tools, to name a few. These are outside the scope of this chapter. Suffice it to say here that some projects might also need to select the most appropriate development tools.

9.2 Basic Infrastructure

At a bare minimum, a project needs tools to *manage communications* and to *collect and store the project assets*, namely, the project deliverables and other information produced in the project.

Taking for granted email and an office suite (e.g., MS Office or LibreOffice), a slightly more efficient infrastructure achieves the following goals:

1. **Tracing communications**, so that we can keep a log of what information was sent to whom
2. **Providing a unique point of access to project documents**, so that all project stakeholders will have access to the same information
3. **Simplifying bookkeeping of data**, for example, allowing project stakeholders to update their contact point
4. **Implementing some form of access control**, if required, so that different stakeholders will have different privileges on the project documents.

Some of the tools that can be used for this purpose include

- **Mailing lists**, which simplify communication by defining email addresses that reach groups of people. In many systems, people can update their own data, like, for example, the email address they use to receive email. More important, in many cases, mailing lists keep historical data about all communications. Some open source solutions include Sympa and GNU Mailman. Many big companies, such as Yahoo! and Google, offer mailing list services for free.
- **Chat and messaging** allow project teams to have real-time conversations in virtual "rooms." As pointed out in Foster (2013), the definition of chat rooms such as a "water cooler" simplifies communications by creating informal environments where people feel freer to talk. This helps improve the flow of communication and helps bind the team together. Various open source solutions are available. Also, in this case, free services are made available by big providers.
- **Document repositories** provide a virtual directory to store all project documents. The directory can be available on the cloud and possibly include some mechanisms to keep the historical records of documents. The most famous

service is probably Dropbox, but Google, Amazon, and other companies offer theirs. One of the potential issues with these kind of systems is that they do not support configuration management practices very well. For this purpose, a versioning tool is more appropriate. Sparkleshare, for instance, is an open source alternative to Dropbox, which is based and integrates with *git*, a distributed versioning system. Sparkleshare stores documents on a server and uses a notification mechanism that pushes all changes directly to the computers of the users that have been granted access; a local copy of the document is thus always available. Also see the next section.

■ **Collaborative software** or **groupwares** are web-based systems that offer a space on the web for a project. Groupwares are feature-rich, offering modules for storing documents, planning, sharing to-do lists, and managing contacts and calendars. Some popular choices oriented to software development include Redmine and Trac. Many other solutions are available, among which are Wiki engines (e.g., MediaWiki, MoinMoin, PMWiki, Gollum), which allow one to upload documents and write webpages using a special markup language.

9.3 Basic + Infrastructure

Establishing some basic configuration management practices is a good idea in any project, even those that do not have it as a specific requirement. This, in fact, allows one to control changes to documents and, more important, to unambiguously associate a given version of a software system to the corresponding documentation.

Version control systems implement mechanisms to keep track of all changes ever made to project assets. We have already seen that this is usually achieved by storing all changes in a **repository** and that two different paradigms exist: centralized and distributed. See Section 4.1.3.2 for more details.

Configuration control tools implement various functions on top of a versioning system to cover different aspects of the development process, including the management of dependencies among components (see TechWell Contributor (2013) for a comparison of version and configuration control systems).

For versioning systems, various open source solutions exist, among which some very popular choices include *git*, *mercurial*, and *svn*. The first two are distributed versioning systems, while the third is based on a centralized paradigm. Some services on the Internet provide ready-made solutions. Among them we mention GitHub and Bitbucket, probably the two most famous names.

The systematic use of a versioning system for managing documents helps achieve various goals. The first is that it is possible to trace the evolution of a document over time. The second is that we can revert a file to a previous version, if necessary. The third is that we can manage parallel contributions to the same document, if the file is text-based—unfortunately, this does not apply to most of the formats used for management documents; see the next section for another solution. The fourth is to tag files with specific labels. This is useful when the tag marks a specific project milestone or an important project event.

9.4 Collaborative Document Writing

On many occasions, it becomes necessary to work on the same document in parallel. Unfortunately, the formats used by the main office suites do not work very well with version control systems and the process of manually incorporating changes from different reviewers is one of those tedious activities many managers sooner or later will have to deal with.

Some approaches can help make the process a bit less painful. The first solution is using the internal revision control system implemented by many office suites. This makes it possible to trace changes and merge different versions of a document. Keeping a document history, however, is more difficult than with version control systems, such as git. A similar consideration can be made for the *meta-information* that is usually attached to a document revision, such as author, date, and motivation: revision control systems of office suites typically provide little support for this data.

The second solution is using a wiki or another tool, such as Google Document, which allows the simultaneous editing of documents on the web. The advantages are similar to those in the previous case, with some additional support to parallel editing and history tracking. The main weakness is that these tools "separate" the documents from the other artifacts of a project (unless all documents are stored using the same service, something difficult to achieve) and make it more difficult to enforce basic configuration management practices.

The third solution is using a text-based format for the document. Some possible choices include markup language such as HTML, Textile or Markdown, and LaTeX. This allows one to easily integrate documents with the other artifacts of a project, most notably source code. However, their format might be difficult to manage for some stakeholders. A possible approach is using a tool such as MS Word and imposing HTML and the output format. However, the approach solves the problem only for textual documents and reports; spreadsheets and other types (e.g., Gantt's charts) still need to be treated as described in the previous section.

9.5 Management Infrastructure

Many management documents are text-based or spreadsheets. This is the case for the *scope* document, *budget*, *time sheets*, *earned value analysis*, and various other project plans, including *risk* and *quality*.

Specific tools can be used for Gantt's charting. Some open source choices include

■ **ProjectLibre:** an open source solution derived from **OpenProj**. Multiplatform, it comes with a rich set of scheduling and analysis features. It has some functions that are rarely found in other tools, such as those to plot earned value. Actively developed at the time of writing (June 2013), it has some usability glitches and some odd behaviors. Do not expect much documentation.

■ **GanttProject:** another Gantt charting tool written in Java. It provides basic scheduling features and does a fair job. Scheduling is only duration-driven.

■ **TaskJuggler:** a text-based scheduling tool. The input is a text-based specification of a plan and the output is a text-based specification of a schedule, in which different activities are allocated to time-respecting hard and soft constraints. It is a nice option if one is trying to understand what scheduling options there are for a specific plan. Drafting a plan without a GUI is demanding.

Several tools are available to manage a list of tasks and a list of issues, thanks also to the increasing popularity of agile tools. Historically, **bug and issue tracking tools** have been developed first; they can also be used as a task list, since the distinction between an issue and a task is subtle from the point of view of the data needed to represent them. Good solutions include **Bugzilla** and **Mantis**. **Redmine** and **Trac** also provide their own issue and bug-tracking lists.

If we broaden our search to tools to support backlogs and agile development, we come across a huge amount of services and tools for personal and team productivity. **Fulcrum** is an open source choice based on Kanban. **Kunagi** is an open source solution that implements the Scrum process.

Finally, some tools allow for an integrated management of project information. We mention two open source solutions:

1. **Achievo**, which provides functions to plan projects, manage resources, and control costs. The tool, implemented as a web application, allows a manager to sketch a high-level plan organized in phases, each having a set of to-dos. Achievo allows one to allocate resources and assign a budget to each project/phase. The plan can then be monitored in its execution. A project dashboard, available to all project members, allows one to get a list of tasks and other information about a project. Team members can also submit their own time sheets.

2. **Project-open** is another web application available in open source. Project-open is based on a rich set of modules and covers various project and enterprise resource management needs. Sixteen different modules are available and organized in three areas: project management, collaboration, and finance. It is thus possible to deploy a solution that covers increasingly complex functions, starting from planning and ending with financial reports and indicators.

A final word can be spent about maintaining a project log. On top of simple solutions, such as a text file, the use of slightly more specialized tools, such as a blog, can provide a bit more structure to the data and more opportunities to share it with the project team.

References

Foster, W., 2013, June. 21 months in: How to manage a remote team. Available at https://zapier.com/blog/how-manage-remote-team/. Last retrieved July 2, 2013.

TechWell Contributor, 2013. Version control vs. configuration management. A template is available at http://www.cmcrossroads.com/article/version-control-vs-configuration-management. Last retrieved June 9, 2013.

Index